SIDE by SIDE

Plus

BOOK 2

Life Skills, Standards, & Test Prep

PEARSON
Longman

Steven J. Molinsky • **Bill Bliss**

Illustrated by Richard E. Hill

Dedicated to Tina Carver with gratitude for her inspiration and contribution to the development of the original *Side by Side* program.

Steven J. Molinsky
Bill Bliss

Side by Side Plus, Book 2

Pearson Education, 10 Bank Street, White Plains, NY 10606

Editorial director: *Pam Fishman*
Vice president, director of design and production: *Rhea Banker*
Director of electronic production: *Aliza Greenblatt*
Director of manufacturing: *Patrice Fraccio*
Senior manufacturing manager: *Edith Pullman*
Director of marketing: *Oliva Fernandez*
Production editor: *Diane Cipollone*
Senior digital layout specialists: *Wendy Wolf; Warren Fischbach; Lisa Ghiozzi*
Text design: *Wanda España, Wee Design Group; Wendy Wolf*
Cover design: *Wanda España, Wee Design Group; Warren Fischbach*
Realia creation: *Wendy Wolf; Warren Fischbach*
Image archivist: *Paula Williams*
Illustrations: *Richard E. Hill*
Principal photographer: *Paul I. Tañedo*
Contributing authors: *Laura English, Elizabeth Handley, Meredith Westfall*
Manager, visual research: *Beth Brenzel*
Image permission coordinator: *Angelique Sharps*
Photo researcher: *Teri Stratford*

Additional photos: p.10c Spencer Grant/Photo Researchers, Inc.; p.18a (*center, right*) Valerie Schultz/Merrill Education; p.27 (*left*) Fotolia.com, (*right*) Rudy Von Briel/PhotoEdit; p.28 (*top*) Cosmo Condina/Stone, (*bottom*) Eric Larrayadieu/Getty Images, (*center*) Don Smetzer/Stone; p.38c Ariel Skelley/Blend Images/Getty Images; p.48a (*top row, first*) David Mager, (*top row, second*) Lenovo Group Limited, (*top row, third*) Macdaddy/Dreamstime, (*top row, fourth*) Z.Legacy.Images Resource Centers/Epson American, Inc., (*second row, first*) Paul Wilkinson, (*second row, second*) David Mager, (*second row, third*) Don Farrall/Getty Images; p.48b (*left*) Johann Helgason/iStockphoto, (*right*) Shutterstock; p.58a (*top row, third*) William Milner/Shutterstock, (*top row, fourth*) Hrudinin Vasyl/Shutterstock; p.59 (*top*) Courtesy Guinness World Records, Ltd., (*center, left*) Inacio Teixeira/AP/Wide World Photos, (*center, right*) Hugh Sitton/Stone, (*bottom, left*) Chad Ehlers/Stone; p.60 (*top*) Ray Stott/The Image Works, (*center*) Margot Granitsas/The Image Works, (*bottom*) Popperfoto/Archive Photos; p.70b (*first*) Harris Shiffman/Shutterstock, (*second*) Harris Shiffman/Shutterstock, (*fifth*) Stephen Finn/Shutterstock; p.70c Ryan McVay/Getty Images; p.81 SuperStock, Inc.; p.82 (*top, left*) ©Steve Raymer/CORBIS, (*top, right*) ©Martin Rogers/CORBIS, (*center, left*) Adrian Arbib/Alamy, (*right, center*) AP Images/MEIGNEUX/SIPA, (*bottom, left*) Capital Features/The Image Works, (*bottom, right*) Ranald Mackechnie/Stone; p.102a (*1st row, right*) Michael Brown/Getty Images; p.103 (*center*) Tom McCarthy/PhotoEdit, (*left*) Corbis Flirt/Alamy, (*right*) Jose Pelaez/The Stock Market; p.104 (*top*) Notimex/Newscom, (*center*) Stephanie Maze/Corbis, (*bottom*) Bob Daemmrich/The Image Works; p.137 Robert Brenner/PhotoEdit, p.138 (*top*) Jeff Greenberg/International Stock Photography Ltd., (*center*) Bill Bachmann/PhotoEdit, (*bottom*) Fritz Hoffmann/The Image Works.

Library of Congress Cataloging-in-Publication Data

Molinsky, Steven J.
  Side by side plus: life skills, standards & test prep / Steven J.
Molinsky, Bill Bliss; illustrated by Richard E. Hill.— 3rd ed.
    v. cm.
  ISBN-13: 978-0-13-240255-2 (student book)
  1. English language—Conversation and phrase books. 2. English
language—Textbooks for foreign speakers. I. Bliss, Bill. II. Molinsky,
Steven J. Side by side. III. Title.
  PE1131.M584 2008
  428.3'4—dc22

                    2007026849

Pearson Longman on the Web
PearsonLongman.com offers online resources for teachers and students.
Access our Companion Websites, our online catalog, and our local offices around the world.
Visit us at longman.com.

ISBN 978-0-13-240255-2; 0-13-240255-6

Printed in the United States of America
11 12 13 14 15 16 – V082 – 17 16 15 14 13

CONTENTS

Red type indicates new standards-based lessons.

Red type indicates new standards-based lessons.

Dear Friends,

Welcome to *Side by Side Plus*—a special edition for adult learners that offers an integrated standards-based and grammar-based approach to language learning!

Flexible Language Proficiency *Plus* Life Skills

The core mission of *Side by Side Plus* is to build students' general language proficiency so they can use English flexibly to meet their varied needs, life circumstances, and goals. We strongly believe that language teachers need to preserve their role as true teachers of language even as we fill our lesson plans with required life-skill content and prepare students for standardized tests. Our program helps you accomplish this through a research-based grammatical sequence and communicative approach in which basic language lessons in each unit lead to standards-based lessons focused on students' life-skill roles in the community, family, school, and at work.

Keys to Promoting Student Persistence and Success

STUDENT-CENTERED LEARNING   The core methodology of *Side by Side Plus* is the guided conversation—a brief, structured dialog that students practice in pairs and then use as a framework to create new conversations. Through this practice, students work together to develop their language skills "side by side." They are not dependent on the teacher for all instruction, and they know how to learn from each other. This student-centered methodology and the text's easy-to-use format enable students to study outside of class with any speaking partner—a family member, a friend or neighbor, a tutor, or a co-worker, even if that person is also an English language learner. If students need to attend class intermittently or "stop out" for a while, they have the skills and text material to continue learning on their own.

MEANINGFUL INSTRUCTION RELEVANT TO STUDENTS' LIVES   Throughout the instructional program, civics topics and tasks connect students to their community, personalization questions apply lesson content to students' life situations, and critical-thinking activities build a community of learners who problem-solve together and share solutions.

EXTENDING LEARNING OUTSIDE THE CLASSROOM   The magazine-style Gazette sections in *Side by Side Plus* provide motivating material for students to use at home. Feature articles, vocabulary enrichment, and other activities reinforce classroom instruction through high-interest material that

students are motivated to use outside of class. A bonus Audio CD offers entertaining radio program-style recordings of key Gazette activities. (See the inside back cover for a description of other media materials and software designed to extend learning through self-study.)

SUFFICIENT PRACTICE + FREQUENT ASSESSMENT = SUCCESS   Students need to experience success as language learners. While other programs "cover" many learning objectives, *Side by Side Plus* offers students carefully-sequenced intensive practice that promotes mastery and the successful application of language skills to daily life. Students can observe their achievement milestones through the program's frequent assessments, including check-up tests and skills checklists in the text and achievement tests in the accompanying workbook.

THE "FUN FACTOR"   We believe that language instruction is most powerful when it is joyful. There is magic in the power of humor, fun, games, and music to encourage students to take risks with their emerging language, to "play" with it, and to allow their personalities to shine through as their language skills increase. We incorporate these elements into our program to motivate students to persist in their language learning not only because they need it, but also because they enjoy it.

MULTILEVEL INSTRUCTION   *Side by Side Plus* provides exceptional resources to support multilevel instruction. The Teacher's Guide includes step-by-step instructions for preparing below-level and at-level students for each lesson and hundreds of multilevel activities for all students, including those above-level. The accompanying Multilevel Activity & Achievement Test Book and CD-ROM offer an array of reproducible multilevel worksheets and activities.

We hope your students enjoy using *Side by Side Plus*. We are confident that these resources will help them persist and succeed through a language learning experience that is effective . . . relevant to their lives . . . and fun!

Steven J. Molinsky
Bill Bliss

Guide to Life Skills, Standards, & Test Prep Features

Side by Side has helped over 25 million students worldwide persist and succeed as language learners. Now, in this special edition for adult learners in standards-based programs, *Side by Side Plus* builds students' general language proficiency *and* helps them apply these skills for success meeting the needs of daily life and work.

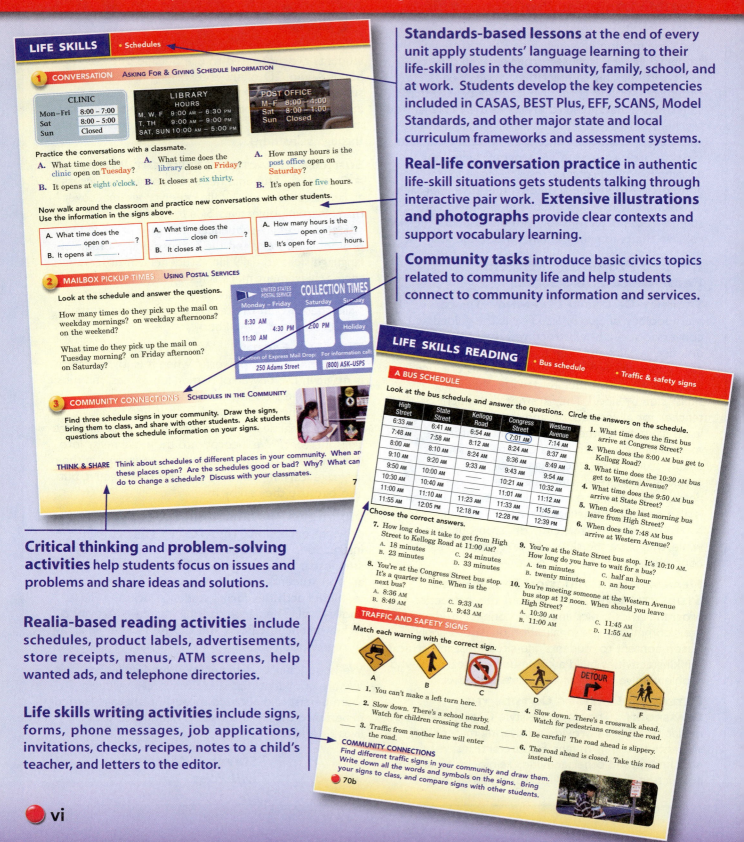

Standards-based lessons at the end of every unit apply students' language learning to their life-skill roles in the community, family, school, and at work. Students develop the key competencies included in CASAS, BEST Plus, EFF, SCANS, Model Standards, and other major state and local curriculum frameworks and assessment systems.

Real-life conversation practice in authentic life-skill situations gets students talking through interactive pair work. **Extensive illustrations and photographs** provide clear contexts and support vocabulary learning.

Community tasks introduce basic civics topics related to community life and help students connect to community information and services.

Critical thinking and **problem-solving activities** help students focus on issues and problems and share ideas and solutions.

Realia-based reading activities include schedules, product labels, advertisements, store receipts, menus, ATM screens, help wanted ads, and telephone directories.

Life skills writing activities include signs, forms, phone messages, job applications, invitations, checks, recipes, notes to a child's teacher, and letters to the editor.

Safe Driving

More than 3.5 million people get hurt in car accidents in the United States each year. Here are some things you can do so that you and your passengers are safe.

Always wear a seat belt. Also, make sure that all the passengers in your car wear their seat belts. Children under the age of five should ride in child safety seats that you attach to the back seat of the car. The center back seat is the safest.

Many accidents happen when cars are in bad condition. Take good care of your car. Check the brakes every week to be sure that you can stop the car when you need to. Keep the windshield clean so you can see the road ahead. Be sure the windshield wipers work in the rain.

Be a careful driver. Pay attention to traffic signs, road conditions, and other drivers. Look before you make a turn or change lanes on the highway. Don't "tailgate"—don't stay too close to the car in front of you. The driver might stop without warning. Be especially careful when the weather is bad. Slow down and use your headlights in the rain, snow, and fog. Pay attention to the speed limit. When

the speed limit is sixty miles an hour, that's the fastest you should drive. On the other hand, don't be a slow driver. Slow drivers can cause accidents.

You can't pay attention to the road when you're tired or busy doing too many things. Don't eat, drink, or talk on your cell phone while you're driving. Don't take any medicine that can make you sleepy before you drive. The label on such medicine usually has the warning "May cause drowsiness." Remember, other drivers are not always as careful as you are. Be prepared for their mistakes. If you are in an accident, the police will ask to see your papers. Always have your license, car registration, and insurance card with you to show to the police.

1. The best place for a child safety seat is ____.
   A. in the front seat
   B. in the back seat next to the door
   C. in the center back seat
   D. next to the driver

2. According to this article, drivers should ____.
   A. use headlights when it's foggy
   B. always drive sixty miles per hour
   C. ride in safety seats
   D. make mistakes

3. According to this article, drivers should NOT ____.
   A. be prepared for other drivers' mistakes
   B. look before changing lanes
   C. use their windshield wipers in the rain
   D. use a cell phone while they're driving

4. A driver who *tailgates* ____.
   A. is a slow driver
   B. drives too close to the car ahead
   C. stops without warning
   D. is a careful driver

5. We can infer that *the windshield* in paragraph 3 ____.
   A. stops the car
   B. cleans the car
   C. is in the back of the car
   D. is in the front of the car

6. *May cause drowsiness* means the medicine ____.
   A. is old
   B. is bad for you
   C. might make you tired
   D. might make you nervous

Narrative reading passages offer practice with simple newspaper and magazine articles on topics such as safe driving practices, cross-cultural expectations, the education system, and nutrition. Reading tips highlight key concepts and skills such as differentiating facts and inferences and recognizing signal words.

Reading comprehension exercises in multiple-choice formats help students prepare for the reading section of standardized tests.

Check-up tests allow a quick assessment of student achievement and help prepare students for the kinds of test items found on standardized tests.

More complete **Achievement Tests** for each unit, including listening test items, are available as reproducible masters and printable disk files in the Teacher's Guide with Multilevel Activity & Achievement Test Book and CD-ROM. They are also available in the companion Activity & Test Prep Workbook.

Vocabulary checklists and **language skill checklists** help students review words they have learned, keep track of the skills they are developing, and identify vocabulary and skills they need to continue to work on. These lists promote student persistence as students assess their own skills and check off all the ways they are succeeding as language learners.

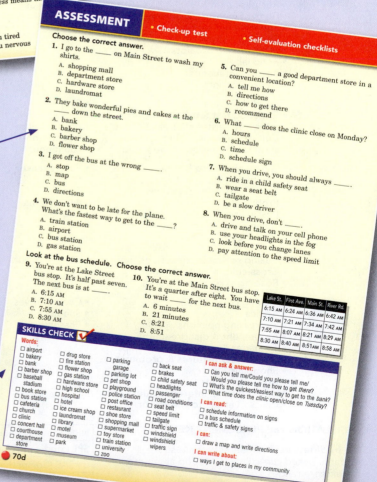

Choose the correct answer.

1. I go to the ____ on Main Street to wash my shirts.
   A. shopping mall
   B. department store
   C. hardware store
   D. laundromat

2. They bake wonderful pies and cakes at the ____ down the street.
   A. bank
   B. bakery
   C. barber shop
   D. flower shop

3. I got off the bus at the wrong ____.
   A. stop
   B. map
   C. bus
   D. directions

4. We don't want to be late for the plane. What's the fastest way to get to the ____?
   A. train station
   B. airport
   C. bus station
   D. gas station

5. Can you ____ a good department store in a convenient location?
   A. tell me how
   B. directions
   C. how to get there
   D. recommend

6. What ____ does the clinic close on Monday?
   A. hours
   B. schedule
   C. time
   D. schedule sign

7. When you drive, you should always ____.
   A. ride in a child safety seat
   B. wear a seat belt
   C. tailgate
   D. be a slow driver

8. When you drive, don't ____.
   A. drive and talk on your cell phone
   B. use your headlights in the fog
   C. look before you change lanes
   D. pay attention to the speed limit

Look at the bus schedule. Choose the correct answer.

9. You're at the Lake Street bus stop. It's half past seven. The next bus is at ____.
   A. 6:15 AM
   B. 7:10 AM
   C. 7:55 AM
   D. 8:30 AM

10. You're at the Main Street bus stop. It's a quarter after eight. You have to wait ____ for the next bus.
    A. 6 minutes
    B. 21 minutes
    C. 8:21
    D. 8:51

Lake St.	First Ave.	Main St.	River Rd.
6:15 AM	6:24 AM	6:36 AM	6:42 AM
7:10 AM	7:21 AM	7:34 AM	7:42 AM
7:55 AM	8:07 AM	8:21 AM	8:29 AM
8:30 AM	8:40 AM	8:51 AM	8:58 AM

SKILLS CHECK ✓

Words:
- ☐ airport
- ☐ bakery
- ☐ bank
- ☐ barber shop
- ☐ baseball stadium
- ☐ book store
- ☐ bus station
- ☐ cafeteria
- ☐ church
- ☐ clinic
- ☐ concert hall
- ☐ courthouse
- ☐ department store
- ☐ drug store
- ☐ fire station
- ☐ flower shop
- ☐ gas station
- ☐ hardware store
- ☐ high school
- ☐ hospital
- ☐ hotel
- ☐ ice cream shop
- ☐ laundromat
- ☐ library
- ☐ motel
- ☐ museum
- ☐ park
- ☐ parking garage
- ☐ parking lot
- ☐ pet shop
- ☐ playground
- ☐ police station
- ☐ post office
- ☐ restaurant
- ☐ shoe store
- ☐ shopping mall
- ☐ supermarket
- ☐ toy store
- ☐ train station
- ☐ university
- ☐ zoo
- ☐ back seat
- ☐ brakes
- ☐ child safety seat
- ☐ headlights
- ☐ passenger
- ☐ road conditions
- ☐ seat belt
- ☐ speed limit
- ☐ tailgate
- ☐ traffic signs
- ☐ windshield
- ☐ windshield wipers

I can ask & answer:
- ☐ Can you tell me/Could you please tell me/ Would you please tell me how to get *there*?
- ☐ What's the quickest/easiest way to get to the *bank*?
- ☐ What time does the *clinic* open/close on *Tuesday*?

I can read:
- ☐ schedule information on signs
- ☐ a bus schedule
- ☐ traffic & safety signs

I can:
- ☐ draw a map and write directions

I can write about:
- ☐ ways I get to places in my community

70d

Scope and Sequence

Unit	Topics, Vocabulary, & Math	Grammar	Functional Communication	Listening & Pronunciation	Writing
1	• Describing present, past, & future actions • Birthdays & gifts • Telling about friendships • Days of the week • Months of the year • Seasons • The calendar & dates • Reading a date using ordinal numbers • School registration • The American education system	• Tense review: Simple Present, Present Continuous, Simple Past, Future: Going to • Like to • Time expressions • Indirect object pronouns	• Talking about likes & dislikes • Describing future plans & intentions	• Listening for correct tense in information questions • Pronouncing contrastive stress	• Writing about your last birthday • Writing about a friendship • Filling out a personal information form • Filling out a school registration form
2	• Food • Buying food • Being a guest at mealtime • Describing food preferences • School personnel & locations • Reading a school floor plan • Reading skill: Facts & inferences • Following written instructions • Technology: Setting up a computer	• Count/Non-count nouns	• Asking the location of items • Making a suggestion • Complimenting about food	• Listening for key words to determine subject matter of conversations • Pronouncing reduced *for*	• Making a list of foods in the kitchen and their location • Writing about favorite foods • Writing about school • Writing information in a chart
3	• Buying food • Describing food • Eating in a restaurant • Recipes • Units of measure & abbreviations • Supermarket sections • Reading a store directory • Supermarket receipts • Food labels • Restaurant menus • Dollar amounts in numerals	• Partitives • Count/Non-count nouns • Imperatives	• Asking for information • Asking for and making recommendations about food • Giving and following instructions	• Listening for key words to determine subject matter of conversations • Pronouncing *of* before consonants & vowels	• Making a shopping list • Writing a recipe • Writing about a special meal • Writing about a supermarket
Gazette	• Food shopping • Ordering fast food • Interpreting statistics about food • Culture concept: Where people shop for food around the world	• Simple past tense • Present tense • Count/Non-count nouns	• Describing people's customs & consumer behavior	• Listening to & interpreting announcements in a supermarket correctly	• Writing an e-mail or instant message to tell about the meals you eat
4	• Telling about the future • Identifying life events • Health problems & injuries • Probability • Possibility • Talking about favorite season • Warnings • Calling in sick • Calling school to report absence • Cross-cultural expectations • Reading skill: Signal words	• Future tense: Will • Time expressions • Might	• Asking & telling about future events • Asking for and making predictions • Asking for repetition • Expressing fears • Providing reassurance • Social interaction: Offers & invitations	• Listening to & responding appropriately to a speaker in a telephone conversation • Pronouncing *going to*	• Writing a note to a child's teacher to explain an absence • Writing about your future • Writing about plans for the weekend • Writing invitations
5	• Making comparisons • Advice • Expressing opinions • Agreement & disagreement • Teenager & parent relationships • Community features & problems • Shopping • Advertisements • Reading skill: Inference questions • Civics: Letters to the editor	• Comparatives • Should • Possessive pronouns	• Asking for & giving advice • Agreeing & disagreeing • Comparing things, places, & people • Exchanging opinions • Compliments	• Listening to determine the subject matter of a conversation • Pronouncing yes/no questions with *or*	• Writing about a comparison of two places • Writing a letter to the editor of a newspaper

CORRELATION and PLACEMENT KEY

Side by Side Plus 2 correlates with these standards-based curriculum levels and assessment system score ranges.

For correlation keys to other major state and local curriculum frameworks, please visit:
www.pearsonlongman.com/sidebysideplus

NRS (National Reporting System) Educational Functioning Level	High Beginning
SPL (Student Performance Level)	3
CASAS (Comprehensive Adult Student Assessment System)	191–200
BEST Plus (Basic English Skills Test)	418–438
BEST Oral Interview	29–41
BEST Literacy	36–46

Life Skills, Civics, & Test Preparation	EFF	SCANS/Employment Competencies	CASAS	LAUSD	Florida*
• Asking & answering personal information questions • Providing information about family members • Calendars, dates, & ordinal numbers • Writing months, days, & dates • Writing ordinal numbers • Registering for school • Reading a community center activity calendar • Identifying types of schools • The American education system	• Interact in a way that is friendly • Identify family relationships • Identify supportive friendships • Work together	• Sociability • Allocate time • Participate as a member of a team • Understand an organizational system (the education system)	0.1.2, 0.1.6, 0.2.1, 0.2.2, 0.2.4, 2.3.2, 2.5.5	1, 2, 3, 4, 5, 6, 7a, 11e, 13, 25	3.05.01, 3.08.03, 3.08.04, 3.14.01, 3.14.02, 3.14.04, 3.16.02
• School personnel & locations • Classroom instructions • School registration • Reading a class schedule • The education system • Learning skills: Chronological order, Steps in a process • Reading a diagram • Technology: Setting up a computer	• Manage resources: Identify those resources you have; Determine where they are • Understand, interpret, and work with symbolic information • Use technology	• Identify resources • See things in the mind's eye (Interpret a diagram) • Understand an organizational system (a school; the education system) • Work with technology	0.1.2, 0.1.4, 0.1.5, 2.5.5, 4.5.1, 4.5.2	9a, 10c, 12, 13, 14, 15, 59, 60, 61	3.04.01, 3.07.05, 3.14.02, 3.14.03, 3.16.06
• Food containers & quantities • Food weights & measures: Abbreviations • Asking about availability & location of items in a store • Food advertisements • Food packaging & label information • Reading a supermarket receipt • Reading a menu & computing costs • Ordering a meal • Learning skill: Categorizing food	• Manage resources • Understand, interpret, & work with numbers • Work together • Gather, analyze, & use information	• Identify resources • Allocate money • Serve clients/customers • Participate as a member of a team • Acquire & evaluate information	0.1.2, 0.1.3, 1.1.4, 1.1.7, 1.2.1, 1.2.2, 1.3.8, 1.3.9, 1.6.1, 2.6.4, 3.5.1, 6.6.4, 8.1.4	27, 30, 31, 32, 34, 35, 36	3.07.05, 3.08.05, 3.11.01, 3.11.03, 3.12.03, 3.16.06
• Interpreting a reading about customs & consumer behavior • Interpreting statistical facts • Ordering fast food • Interpreting store announcements	• Analyze information • Identify community needs & resources • Respect others & value diversity	• Acquire & evaluate information • Identify resources • Work with cultural diversity	0.1.2, 1.1.7, 1.3.8	34, 36	3.07.05, 3.15.12, 3.16.02, 3.16.06
• Small talk at work & at school • Invitations & offers • Asking for clarification • Interpreting a narrative reading about cross-cultural expectations	• Interact in a way that is friendly • Seek input from others • Identify problems • Provide for family members' needs • Create a vision & goals for the future • Respect others & value diversity	• Sociability • Identify goal-relevant activities • Identify workplace safety problems & state warnings • Self-management • Responsibility • Work with cultural diversity	0.1.2, 0.1.4, 0.1.6, 0.2.4, 2.5.5, 4.4.1	7, 9, 11, 16a, 55a	3.02.01, 3.02.02, 3.02.03, 3.03.02, 3.05.02, 3.05.03, 3.05.04, 3.07.03, 3.15.12, 3.16.02
• Small talk at work & at school • Thank-you notes • Expressing opinions • Teenager & parent relationships • Community features & problems • Comparing store products • Interpreting advertisements • Letters to the editor	• Seek input from others • Guide & support others • Identify supportive family relationships • Meet family needs & responsibilities • Advocate & influence • Gather, analyze, & use information • Work together	• Sociability • Decision making • Understand a social system (community) • Acquire & evaluate information • Participate as a member of a team	0.1.2, 0.1.4, 0.2.4, 1.2.1, 1.2.2	7, 10, 32	3.02.03, 3.03.02, 3.05.01, 3.05.02, 3.05.03, 3.05.04, 3.11.03, 3.14.01, 3.16.03

EFF: Equipped for the Future (Content standards, Common activities, & Key activities for Citizen/Community Member, Worker, & Parent/Family role maps; EFF Communication and Reflection/Evaluation skills are covered in every unit)

SCANS: Secretary's Commission on Achieving Necessary Skills (U.S. Department of Labor)

CASAS: Comprehensive Adult Student Assessment System

LAUSD: Los Angeles Unified School District (ESL Beginning High content standards)

Florida: Adult ESOL High Beginning Standardized Syllabi

(*Florida benchmarks 3.15.01, 3.15.02, 3.15,03, 3.15.04, 3.15.05, 3.15.11, 3.15.13, 3.16.01, 3.16.02, 3.16.05, 3.16.06, 3.16.07, 3.16.09, 3.17.01, 3.17.02, and 3.17.03 are covered in every unit.)

Scope and Sequence

Unit	Topics, Vocabulary, & Math	Grammar	Functional Communication	Listening & Pronunciation	Writing
6	• Describing people, places, & things • Shopping in a department store • Expressing opinions • Store directories • Returning & exchanging items • Using an ATM • Checks • Store return policies • Identifying different types of stores and comparing prices, quality of products, convenience, & service	• Superlatives	• Expressing an opinion • Offering assistance	• Listening to determine a speaker's attitude or opinion • Pronouncing linking words with duplicated consonants	• Writing about the most important person in your life • Writing checks to pay bills
Gazette	• Interpreting numerical and descriptive facts about world records and geographic features • Culture concept: Recreation & entertainment around the world	• Superlatives • Adjectives with negative prefixes	• Interpreting factual statements • Describing	• Listening to and interpreting radio advertisements correctly	• Writing an e-mail or instant message to tell about a favorite vacation place
7	• Getting around town • Places in the community • Public transportation • Following a map or diagram indicating directions to a destination • Schedules of building hours • Bus schedules • Traffic & safety signs • Safe driving practices	• Imperatives • Directions	• Giving & following instructions • Asking for repetition • Asking for & giving recommendations	• Listening for specific information in directions • Listening to make deductions about the location of conversations • Pronouncing *could you* & *would you*	• Drawing a map & writing directions to your home • Writing about how to get to different places in the community • Drawing schedule signs found in the community • Drawing traffic signs found in the community
8	• Describing people's actions • Occupations • Describing plans & intentions • Consequences of actions • Job interview • Stating skills & work experience • Asking for permission at work • Help wanted ads • Reading a paycheck & pay stub • Employee accident report	• Adverbs • Comparative of adverbs • Agent nouns • If-clauses	• Expressing an opinion • Expressing agreement • Asking for & giving feedback about job performance • Asking about & giving information about future plans • Giving & receiving advice	• Listening to determine the correct consequences of actions • Pronouncing contrastive stress	• Writing about something you want to do and the consequences of doing it • Filling out a job application form • Filling out an employee accident report form
Gazette	• Tips for a successful job interview • Occupations • Culture concept: Men's & women's jobs in different countries	• Adverbs • Agent nouns	• Interpreting advice • Describing self	• Listening to & interpreting announcements at a workplace correctly	• Writing an e-mail or instant message to tell about your skills & activities
9	• Describing ongoing past activities • Describing an accident • Reporting a home emergency • Emergency preparedness • First-aid instructions • Warning labels on household products • Safety procedures: Earthquakes & hurricanes	• Past continuous tense • Reflexive pronouns • While-clauses	• Asking about & giving information about past events • Expressing concern about someone • Expressing sympathy • Reacting to bad news • Describing a sequence of events	• Listening to make deductions about the context of conversations • Pronouncing *did* & *was*	• Writing about preference for doing things alone or with other people

Life Skills, Civics, Test Preparation, Curriculum Standards and Frameworks

Life Skills, Civics, & Test Preparation	EFF	SCANS/Employment Competencies	CASAS	LAUSD	Florida*
• Expressing pride in a child's personal qualities • Shopping requests & locating items • Comparing store prices, products, convenience, & service • Learning skills: Steps in a process; Categorizing types of products • Understanding ATM instructions • Interpreting a check • Problems with purchases • Returning & exchanging items • Store sales	• Interact in a way that is friendly • Identify a strong sense of family • Advocate & influence • Identify community resources • Use technology to accomplish goals • Work together • Gather, analyze, & use information • Use technology	• Sociability • Integrity/Honesty • Serve clients/customers • Identify resources • Participate as a member of a team • Acquire & evaluate information • Work with technology	0.1.3, 0.1.4, 1.3.3, 1.3.9, 1.6.3, 1.8.1, 1.8.2, 8.1.4	10a, 28, 29, 30, 33, 59	3.08.05, 3.08.06, 3.11.02, 3.11.03, 3.16.03
• Interpreting statistical facts • Interpreting radio advertisements	• Analyze & use information • Understand, interpret, & work with numbers • Respect others & value diversity	• Acquire & evaluate information • Work with cultural diversity	0.1.3, 1.3.9	30	3.15.12, 3.16.03
• Interpreting schedules • Locating places on a map • Compass directions • Reading a bus schedule • Traffic & safety signs & symbols • Police commands & traffic signs • Postal services • Simple written directions • Drawing a map • Safe driving practices	• Identify community resources • Seek & receive assistance • Give direction • Understand, interpret, & work with numbers & symbolic information • Gather, analyze, & use information • Reflect & evaluate • Provide for family members' safety & physical needs	• Identify resources • Communicate information • See things in the mind's eye (Interpret a simple route map; Draw a simple route map; Interpret symbols on signs) • Acquire & evaluate information • Problem solving	0.1.2, 1.1.4, 1.9.1, 2.2.1, 2.2.2, 2.4.2, 2.4.4, 2.5.4, 2.6.1, 2.6.2, 6.6.4	8a, 22, 23, 24, 31, 41, 42	3.02.02, 3.08.02, 3.09.02, 3.09.03, 3.09.04, 3.09.05, 3.09.06, 3.12.01, 3.12.02, 3.15.08
• Help wanted ads (with abbreviations) • Job interview questions about skills & work history • Describing a work schedule • Calling in sick & late • Requesting a schedule change • Employee accident reports • Reading a paycheck & pay stub • Nonverbal behavior at the job interview • Identifying ways to improve performance at work & at school	• Cooperate with others • Work together • Seek input from others • Guide & support others • Work within the big picture • Create goals • Reflect & evaluate • Gather, analyze, & use information • Work together	• Participate as a member of a team • Self-management: Monitor progress • Responsibility • Decision making • Self-esteem • Identify human resources (occupations; work skills) • Problem solving • Acquire & evaluate information • Participate as a member of a team	0.1.3, 0.2.1, 0.2.2, 4.1.2, 4.1.3, 4.1.5, 4.1.6, 4.1.7, 4.2.1, 4.3.4, 4.4.1, 4.4.3, 4.6.5	8, 51, 52, 53, 54, 55, 56, 57	3.01.01, 3.01.02, 3.01.03, 3.01.05, 3.01.06, 3.02.01, 3.02.02, 3.02.03, 3.02.04, 3.05.01, 3.16.08
• Identifying appropriate job interview behaviors, including dress, promptness, eye contact, speaking style, honesty, & confidence • Identifying occupations • Interpreting announcements over a workplace P.A. system	• Analyze & use information • Develop & express sense of self • Interact in a way that is friendly & courteous • Respect others & value diversity	• Acquire & evaluate information • Self-esteem • Integrity/Honesty • Sociability • Work with cultural diversity	0.2.1, 4.1.5, 4.1.6, 4.1.7	53, 54	3.01.01, 3.01.02, 3.01.06, 3.02.02, 3.02.03, 3.03.02, 3.05.02, 3.05.03, 3.05.04, 3.15.12, 3.16.08
• Calling 911 • First-aid instructions • Describing a suspect's physical characteristics to the police • Warning labels on household products • Interpreting emergency procedures on safety posters • Learning skills: Categorizing words, Word sets	• Interact in a way that is friendly • Identify problems • Develop & express sense of self • Identify resources • Provide for family members' safety & physical needs • Work together • Reflect & evaluate	• Sociability • Self-esteem • Communicate information • Participate as a member of a team • Problem solving	0.1.2, 0.1.4, 0.2.2, 0.2.4, 2.1.2, 3.4.1, 3.4.2, 3.4.3, 7.2.3	3, 6, 7a, 7b, 10b, 20, 48, 49, 50, 64	3.05.01, 3.06.01, 3.10.01, 3.10.02, 3.13.01, 3.14.01, 3.15.07, 3.16.02

Scope and Sequence

Unit	Topics, Vocabulary, & Math	Grammar	Functional Communication	Listening & Pronunciation	Writing
10	• Expressing past & future ability • Expressing past & future obligation • Giving an excuse • Renting an apartment • Housing ads • Reading a floor plan • Requesting maintenance & repairs • Building rules & regulations	• Could • Be able to • Have got to • Too + adjective	• Asking and telling about ability to do things • Expressing obligation • Describing physical states & emotions	• Listening for correct situation or context • Pronouncing *have to* & *have got to*	• Writing about a time you were frustrated, disappointed, or upset • Writing about an apartment or home • Drawing a floor plan • Writing a housing ad
Gazette	• Families & time • Interpreting a table with number facts • Home appliances • Culture concept: Child-care around the world	• Tense review • Have to / Have got to	• Describing daily life & customs	• Listening to messages on a telephone answering machine	• Writing an e-mail or instant message to tell about activities and occurrences during the week
11	• Medical examinations • Medical advice • Health • Foods • Nutrition • Home remedies • Making a doctor appointment • Calling in sick • Reporting absence from school • Medicine labels • Medicine safety tips • Nutrition & recipes	• Past tense review • Count/Non-count noun review • Must • Mustn't vs. Don't have to • Must vs. Should	• Asking for & giving advice • Describing a future sequence of events • Describing a past sequence of events • Expressing concern	• Listening for key words to determine subject matter of conversations • Pronouncing *must* & *mustn't*	• Making a list of healthy and unhealthy foods • Writing about rules in life • Writing a note to a teacher to explain a child's absence • Writing about favorite healthy foods • Writing a recipe • Filling out a medical history form
12	• Describing future activities • Expressing time & duration • Making plans by telephone • Handling wrong-number calls • Leaving & taking phone messages • Telephone directory: White pages, government pages, & yellow pages • Using a telephone response system	• Future continuous tense • Time expressions	• Asking and telling about future plans & activities • Calling people on the telephone • Borrowing & returning items	• Listening to messages on a telephone answering machine • Pronouncing contractions with *will*	• Writing about a family holiday celebration • Writing telephone messages
13	• Offering help • Indicating ownership • Household problems • Using the telephone to request household maintenance and repairs • Reading a rental agreement • Tenants' rights • Car trouble • Friends	• Some/Any • Pronoun review • Verb tense review	• Offering help • Asking & telling about past events • Asking for & giving advice • Describing problems	• Listening for correct pronouns in conversations • Listening to make deductions about the subject of conversations • Pronouncing deleted *h*	• Writing about relying on friends for help • Writing about a very good friend • Filling out an apartment maintenance/repair request form
Gazette	• Communities—urban, suburban, & rural • Interpreting a bar graph with population data in millions • Household repair people • Culture concept: Where friends gather in different countries around the world	• Present tense review • Future tense review	• Describing community life • Describing future events	• Listening to telephone conversations & answering machine messages to make deductions about the subject of conversations	• Writing an e-mail or instant message to tell about a future family celebration

LIFE SKILLS, CIVICS, TEST PREPARATION, CURRICULUM STANDARDS AND FRAMEWORKS

Life Skills, Civics, & Test Preparation	EFF	SCANS/Employment Competencies	CASAS	LAUSD	Florida*
• Housing ads (with abbreviations) • Inquiring about rentals • Describing maintenance & repairs needed in a rental unit • Interpreting a floor plan/diagram • Interpreting an apartment building regulations notice	• Interact in a way that is tactful • Identify supportive friendships • Reflect & evaluate • Work together • Gather, analyze, & use information • Exercise rights & responsibilities	• Sociability • Self-esteem • Participate as a member of a team • Acquire & evaluate information • See things in the mind's eye (Interpret and draw diagrams)	0.1.2, 0.1.4, 1.4.2, 1.4.7, 7.4.1	7b, 9b, 10a, 37, 38, 39, 62	3.11.04, 3.15.08, 3.16.03
• Interpreting a narrative reading about daily life & customs • Interpreting statistical facts in a table • Interpreting telephone messages on an answering machine	• Analyze information • Identify supportive family relationships • Meet family needs & responsibilities • Understand, interpret, & work with numbers • Respect others & value diversity • Use technology & other tools to accomplish goals	• Acquire & evaluate information • Work with cultural diversity • Work with technology (telephone answering device)	0.1.2, 0.2.4, 2.1.7, 7.4.1	7a, 18, 62	3.06.02, 3.14.03, 3.15.08, 3.15.12, 3.16.02
• Identifying parts of the face & body • Common symptoms • Calling to report an absence • Making a doctor appointment • Procedures during a medical exam • Common prescription & non-prescription medicines • Interpreting medicine label dosages & instructions • A note to the teacher explaining a child's absence • Learning skill: Categorizing foods & nutrients	• Seek guidance & support from others • Guide & support others • Meet family needs & responsibilities • Work together	• Acquire & evaluate information • Self-management • Understand a social system • Participate as a member of a team	0.1.2, 2.5.5, 3.1.1, 3.1.2, 3.2.1, 3.3.1, 3.3.2, 3.3.3, 4.4.1	16, 43, 44, 45, 46, 47, 55	3.07.01, 3.07.03, 3.07.04, 3.07.05, 3.14.04, 3.16.02, 3.16.06
• Life cycle—stages & events • Holidays • Beginning & ending a telephone conversation • Using the telephone directory: White pages, government pages, & yellow pages • Phone messages • Recorded telephone information • Fahrenheit & Celsius temperatures	• Interact in a way that is friendly & courteous • Manage resources: Allocate time • Create a vision for the future • Identify a strong sense of family • Gather information • Identify community resources • Use technology	• Identify goal-relevant activities • Allocate time • Self-esteem • Acquire & evaluate information • Identify resources • Work with technology (recorded telephone announcements; telephone response system)	0.1.4, 0.2.4, 1.1.5, 2.1.1, 2.1.7, 2.1.8, 2.3.2, 7.4.5	7a, 9, 17, 18, 19, 21, 25, 26, 58	3.05.01, 3.06.02, 3.06.03, 3.06.05, 3.12.04, 3.13.01, 3.14.01, 3.16.02
• Household repair problems • Securing household repair services • Interpreting a lease • Tenants' rights & responsibilities • Reading a TV schedule • Recorded telephone instructions • Making a schedule	• Identify problems • Interact in a way that is tactful • Identify supportive friendships • Identify problems • Seek & receive assistance • Reflect & evaluate • Exercise rights & responsibilities	• Participate as a member of a team • Understand a social system (an apartment building & neighbors) • Identify resources • Work with technology (recorded telephone instructions) • Problem solving	1.4.7, 2.1.7, 2.1.8, 2.6.1, 2.6.2	17, 18, 22, 39, 63	3.05.01, 3.06.02, 3.06.05, 3.08.03, 3.11.04, 3.14.01, 3.15.08, 3.16.02
• Interpreting a narrative reading about types of communities • Interpreting statistical facts in a bar graph • Identifying home repair needs & home repair services	• Analyze & use information • Identify community needs & resources • Understand, interpret, & work with numbers & symbolic information • Respect others & value diversity • Use technology & other tools to accomplish goals	• Acquire & evaluate information • Understand a social system (communities) • See things in the mind's eye (Interpret a bar graph) • Work with cultural diversity	0.1.2, 0.2.4, 1.4.7, 7.4.1	7a, 39, 62	3.05.01, 3.15.08, 3.15.12, 3.16.02

Review of Tenses:
Simple Present
Present Continuous
Simple Past
Future: Going to

Like to
Time Expressions
Indirect Object Pronouns

1

- **Describing Present, Past, and Future Actions**
- **Birthdays and Gifts**
- **Telling About Friendships**
- **School Registration**
- **The Calendar and Dates**
- **Filling Out a Registration Form**
- **The American Education System**

VOCABULARY PREVIEW

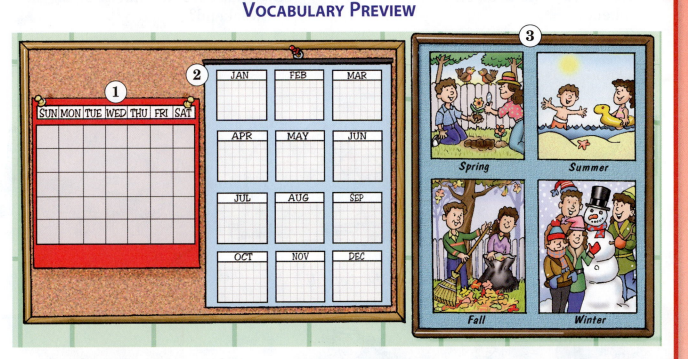

Spring *Summer* *Fall* *Winter*

1. **Days of the Week**
   Sunday
   Monday
   Tuesday
   Wednesday
   Thursday
   Friday
   Saturday

2. **Months of the Year**
   January   July
   February   August
   March   September
   April   October
   May   November
   June   December

3. **Seasons**
   spring
   summer
   fall / autumn
   winter

What Do You Like to Do on the Weekend?

I We You They	like to
	eat.
He She It	likes to

A. What do you like to do on the weekend?

B. I like to read.

A. What does Ron like to do on the weekend?

B. He likes to go to the mall.

1. *Mr. and Mrs. Johnson?*
watch TV

2. *Tom?*
play basketball

3. *Sally?*
go to the beach

4. *you and your friends?*
chat online

5. *your grandmother?*
go hiking

6. *you?*

cook	play	swim	write
cooks	plays	swims	writes
cooked	played	swam	wrote
cooking	playing	swimming	writing

Robert likes to cook.
He cooks every day.
He cooked yesterday.
He's cooking right now.
He's going to cook tomorrow.
As you can see, Robert REALLY likes to cook.

Irene likes to play the piano.
She plays the piano every day.
She played the piano yesterday.
She's playing the piano right now.
She's going to play the piano tomorrow.
As you can see, Irene REALLY likes to play
the piano.

Jimmy and Patty like to swim.*
They swim every day.
They swam yesterday.
They're swimming right now.
They're going to swim tomorrow.
As you can see, Jimmy and Patty REALLY
like to swim.

Jonathan likes to write.
He writes every day.
He wrote yesterday.
He's writing right now.
He's going to write tomorrow.
As you can see, Jonathan REALLY likes to
write.

Using these questions, talk about the people above with students in your class.

What does _____ like to do?
What does he/she do every day?
What did he/she do yesterday?
What's he/she doing right now?
What's he/she going to do tomorrow?

What do _____ like to do?
What do they do every day?
What did they do yesterday?
What are they doing right now?
What are they going to do tomorrow?

Then use these questions to talk about other people you know.

* swim – swam

3

Are You Going to Cook Spaghetti This Week?

A. Are you going to cook spaghetti this week?

B. No, I'm not. I cooked spaghetti LAST week, and
I don't like to cook spaghetti very often.

1. Are you going to watch videos today?

2. Are you going to drive downtown this weekend?

3. Is Mrs. Miller going to plant flowers this spring?

4. Is your father going to make pancakes this morning?

5. Are Mr. and Mrs. Jenkins going to the mall* this Saturday?

6. Are you and your friends going skiing this December?

7. Are you going to write letters tonight?

8. Is Dave going to clean his room this week?

9. Are you and your family going to WonderWorld this year?

10.

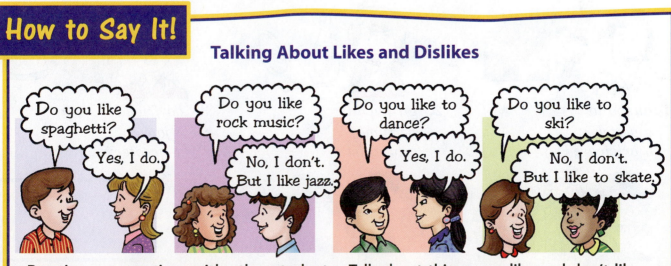

How to Say It!

Talking About Likes and Dislikes

Do you like spaghetti?

Yes, I do.

Do you like rock music?

No, I don't. But I like jazz.

Do you like to dance?

Yes, I do.

Do you like to ski?

No, I don't. But I like to skate.

Practice conversations with other students. Talk about things you like and don't like. Talk about things you like to do and don't like to do.

* going to the mall = going to go to the mall

What Are You Going to Give Your Wife?

I'm going to give { my husband / my wife } a present.   I'm going to give { him / her } a present.

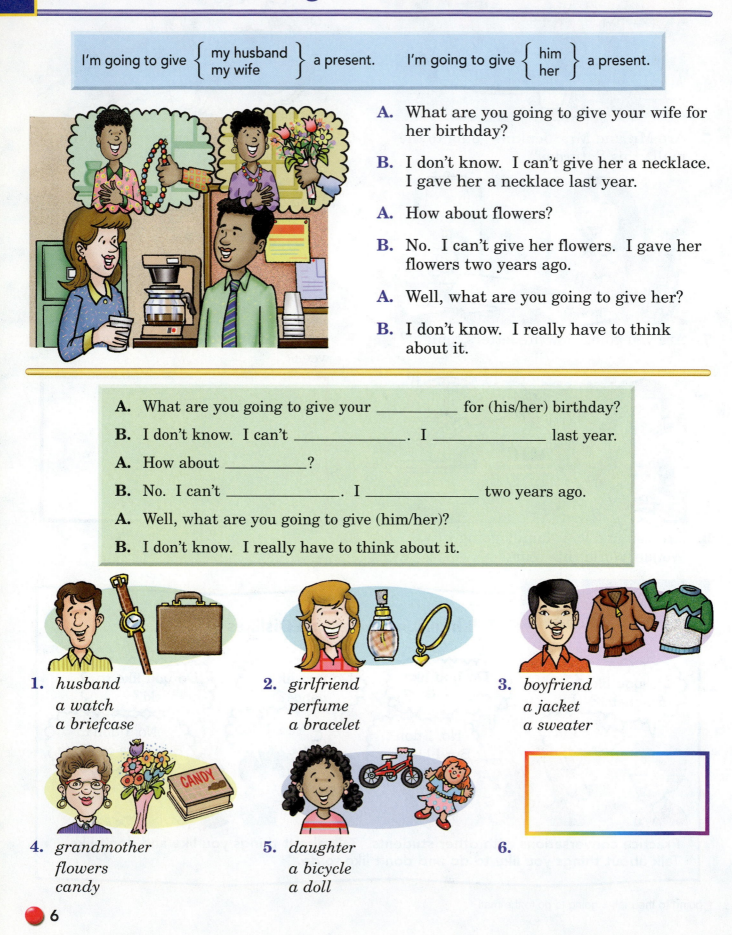

A. What are you going to give your wife for her birthday?

B. I don't know. I can't give her a necklace. I gave her a necklace last year.

A. How about flowers?

B. No. I can't give her flowers. I gave her flowers two years ago.

A. Well, what are you going to give her?

B. I don't know. I really have to think about it.

A. What are you going to give your _____ for (his/her) birthday?

B. I don't know. I can't _____. I _____ last year.

A. How about _____?

B. No. I can't _____. I _____ two years ago.

A. Well, what are you going to give (him/her)?

B. I don't know. I really have to think about it.

1. *husband*
   a watch
   a briefcase

2. *girlfriend*
   perfume
   a bracelet

3. *boyfriend*
   a jacket
   a sweater

4. *grandmother*
   flowers
   candy

5. *daughter*
   a bicycle
   a doll

6.

What Did Your Parents Give You?

I	me
he	him
she	her
we	us
you	you
they	them

A. What did your parents give you for your birthday?

B. They gave me a CD player.

1. What did you give your parents for their anniversary?

a painting

2. What did Mr. Lee's grandchildren give him for his birthday?

a computer

3. What did your children give you and your wife for your anniversary?

a plant

4. I forget. What did you give me for my last birthday?

a purple blouse with pink polka dots

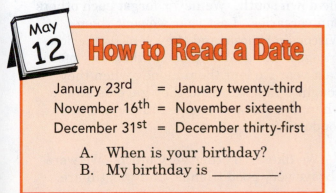

How to Read a Date

May 12

January 23rd	=	January twenty-third
November 16th	=	November sixteenth
December 31st	=	December thirty-first

A. When is your birthday?
B. My birthday is _____.

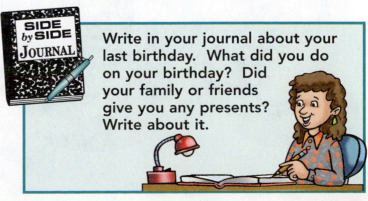

SIDE by SIDE JOURNAL

Write in your journal about your last birthday. What did you do on your birthday? Did your family or friends give you any presents? Write about it.

VERY GOOD FRIENDS: EAST AND WEST

Eric and Susan are very good friends. They grew up together, they went to high school together, and they went to college together. Now Eric lives in California, and Susan lives in New Jersey. Even though they live far apart, they're still very good friends.

They write to each other very often. He writes her letters about life on the West Coast, and she writes him letters about life on the East Coast. They never forget each other's birthday. Last year he sent* her some CDs, and she sent him a wallet. Eric and Susan help each other very often. Last year he lent* her money when she was in the hospital, and she gave him advice when he lost* his job.

Eric and Susan like each other very much. They were always very good friends, and they still are.

VERY GOOD FRIENDS: NORTH AND SOUTH

Carlos and Maria are our very good friends. For many years we went to church together, we took vacations together, and our children played together. Now Carlos and Maria live in Florida, and we still live here in Wisconsin. Even though we live far apart, we're still very good friends.

We communicate with each other very often on the Internet. We send them messages about life up north, and they send us messages about life down south. We never forget each others' anniversaries. Last year we sent them Wisconsin cheese, and they sent us Florida oranges. We also help each other very often. Last year we lent them money when they bought a new van, and they gave us advice when we sold* our house and moved into a condominium.

We like each other very much. We were always very good friends, and we still are.

* send – sent   lose – lost
lend – lent   sell – sold

8

✔ READING *CHECK-UP*

TRUE OR FALSE?

1. Eric and Susan are in high school.
2. Eric lives on the West Coast.
3. Susan sent Eric some CDs last year.
4. Susan was sick last year.
5. They were friends when they were children.

6. Carlos and Maria don't live in Wisconsin now.
7. Florida is in the north.
8. Carlos and Maria send messages on the Internet.
9. Carlos and Maria moved into a condominium last year.

LISTENING

Listen and choose the correct answer.

1. a. I like to play tennis.
   b. I'm going to play tennis.
2. a. I went to the beach.
   b. I go to the beach.
3. a. Yesterday morning.
   b. Tomorrow afternoon.
4. a. I gave them a plant.
   b. I'm going to give them a plant.

5. a. We went to the mall.
   b. We're going to the mall.
6. a. They sent messages last week.
   b. They send messages every week.
7. a. He gave her flowers.
   b. She gave him flowers.
8. a. Last weekend.
   b. Tomorrow morning.

IN YOUR OWN WORDS

FOR WRITING AND DISCUSSION

A VERY GOOD FRIEND

Do you have a very good friend who lives far away? Tell about your friendship.

How do you know each other?
How do you communicate with each other?
  (Do you call? write? send e-mail messages?)
What do you talk about or write about?
Do you send each other presents?
Do you help each other? How?

PRONUNCIATION *Contrastive Stress*

Listen. Then say it.

I'm not going to clean my room this week.
I cleaned my room LAST week.

I'm not going to make pancakes this morning.
I made pancakes YESTERDAY morning.

Say it. Then listen.

I'm not going to watch videos tonight.
I watched videos LAST night.

I'm not going to write letters this evening.
I wrote letters YESTERDAY evening.

SIMPLE PRESENT TENSE

I We You They	cook.
He She It	cooks.

LIKE TO

I We You They	like to / don't like to	cook.
He She It	likes to / doesn't like to	

PRESENT CONTINUOUS TENSE

(I am)	I'm	
(He is)	He's	
(She is)	She's	
(It is)	It's	cooking.
(We are)	We're	
(You are)	You're	
(They are)	They're	

SIMPLE PAST TENSE

I He She It We You They	cooked.

FUTURE: GOING TO

I'm He's She's It's We're You're They're	going to cook.

Am	I	
Is	he she it	going to cook?
Are	we you they	

	I	am.
Yes,	he she it	is.
	we you they	are.

	I'm	not.
No,	he she it	isn't.
	we you they	aren't.

INDIRECT OBJECT PRONOUNS

He gave	me him her it us you them	a present.

PAST TIME EXPRESSIONS

yesterday
yesterday morning / afternoon / evening
last night
last week / weekend / month / year
last Sunday / Monday /. . ./ Saturday
last January / February /. . ./ December
last spring / summer / fall (autumn) / winter

IRREGULAR VERBS

drive – drove
give – gave
go – went
lend – lent
lose – lost
sell – sold
send – sent
swim – swam
write – wrote

Complete each sentence with the correct form of the verb.

drive	give	go	watch	write

1. My parents are _____ TV in the living room. They _____ TV every evening.
2. I _____ my car downtown yesterday. I don't like to _____ downtown very often.
3. Monica likes to _____ letters. Last night she _____ a letter to her grandfather.
4. I'm not going to _____ my brother a tie for his birthday. I _____ him a tie last year.
5. My wife and I _____ swimming very often. We _____ swimming last weekend.

Match the questions and answers.

____ **6.** What did your brother give you for your birthday?
____ **7.** What did you give your brother for his birthday?
____ **8.** What did your grandmother give your sister?
____ **9.** What did your grandfather give your brother?
____ **10.** What did you give your parents?
____ **11.** What did your parents give you for your birthday?

a. She gave her a necklace.
b. They gave me a CD player.
c. I gave them a painting.
d. He gave me a watch.
e. He gave him a shirt.
f. I gave him a briefcase.

1 CONVERSATION GIVING PERSONAL INFORMATION

Look at the form. Practice the conversation with a classmate.

School Registration Form

NAME Abdi   Hassan
      First   Last

ADDRESS 257 2nd Avenue   12B
         Number   Street   Apartment

         New York   NY   10003
         City   State Zip Code

AGE 6   DATE OF BIRTH   10   06   01
                                Month   Day   Year

*We write:
October 6, 2001
10/06/01
| 1 0 | 0 6 | 0 1 |
Month Day   Year
We say:
October sixth,
two thousand one

A. May I help you?

B. Yes, please. I want to register my son for school.

A. Okay. What's his last name?

B. _____.

A. And his first name?

B. _____.

A. How old is he?

B. _____.

A. What's his date of birth?

B. _____.*

A. And what's your address?

B. _____.

2 TEAMWORK REGISTERING FOR SCHOOL

Work with a classmate. This parent is registering her daughter for school.
Fill out the form and practice the conversation. (Use any information you wish.)

School Registration Form

NAME _____   _____
      First   Last

ADDRESS _____
         Number   Street   Apartment

         _____   _____ _____
         City   State Zip Code

AGE _____   DATE OF BIRTH   ____ ____ ____
                                Month Day   Year

A. May I help you?

B. Yes, please. I want to register my daughter for school.

A. Okay. What's her last name?

B. _____.

A. And her first name?

B. _____.

A. How old is she?

B. _____.

A. What's her date of birth?

B. _____.

A. And what's your address?

B. _____.

Read about the activities at the Canton Community Center. When are they?
Circle the dates on the calendar below.

JANUARY

S	M	T	W	Th	F	S
			1	2	3	4
5	6	7	8	9	10	11
12	13	14	15	16	17	18
19	20	21	22	23	24	25
26	27	28	29	30	31	

FEBRUARY

S	M	T	W	Th	F	S
						1
2	3	4	5	6	7	8
9	10	11	12	13	14	15
16	17	18	19	20	21	22
23	24	25	26	27	28	

MARCH

S	M	T	W	Th	F	S
						1
2	3	4	5	6	7	8
9	10	11	12	13	14	15
16	17	18	19	20	21	22
23	24	25	26	27	28	29
30	31					

APRIL

S	M	T	W	Th	F	S
		1	2	3	4	5
6	7	8	9	10	11	12
13	14	15	16	17	18	19
20	21	22	23	24	25	26
27	28	29	30			

MAY

S	M	T	W	Th	F	S
				1	2	3
4	5	6	7	8	9	10
11	12	13	14	15	16	17
18	19	20	21	22	23	24
25	26	27	28	29	30	31

JUNE

S	M	T	W	Th	F	S
1	2	3	4	5	6	7
8	9	10	11	12	13	14
15	16	17	18	19	20	21
22	23	24	25	26	27	28
29	30					

Activities at Your Community Center – January to June

1. There are movies on the first Sunday of every month.

2. The Center is celebrating Martin Luther King, Jr. Day on the third Monday in January.

3. There are jazz concerts on the second Friday of every month.

4. There's a pancake breakfast on April twentieth.

5. Arnold McCall is reading from his new book, *When I Was Young*, on May thirtieth.

6. There's a dance for young people on February twenty-second.

7. There are swimming classes every Thursday in June.

8. Marta Fernandez is giving a piano concert on April thirteenth.

9. There's a rock concert on January twenty-fifth.

10. High school students can get help with their homework on the fourth Tuesday of every month.

11. You can go hiking in the White Mountains on May eighteenth and June fifteenth.

12. Chef Marconi is giving cooking classes on the second and fourth Wednesdays in June.

13. There's a ski trip to Mount Snow on January twenty-first.

14. Boys and girls can play basketball on the first and third Saturday of every month.

15. You can go skating every Wednesday from February fifth to March nineteenth.

16. There's a trip to Sandy Beach on June twenty-eighth.

17. There are exercise classes every Thursday from April twenty-fourth to May twenty-ninth.

Read the article and answer the questions.

The American Education System

There are many different kinds of schools in the United States. Most children go to public schools that are free, but there are also private schools that students pay to attend. Free public education begins with kindergarten (the first year of elementary school) and finishes with the twelfth grade (the last year of high school).

Many parents send their young children to day-care centers and pre-schools before kindergarten. They pay for their children to attend these schools. In most states, children do not have to attend kindergarten, but they must start elementary school in the first grade when they're six years old. They have to attend school for ten years or more. Each state has its own law about when students can leave school.

Most elementary schools have five grades plus kindergarten. After elementary school, children usually go to middle school for sixth, seventh, and eighth grade. Most students enter high school in the ninth grade and graduate after four years.

Many people continue their education after high school at a technical or vocational school, a two-year community college, a four-year college, or a university. Technical and vocational schools teach students the skills they need for a job. Community colleges also have vocational programs that prepare students for work.

Four-year colleges can be very expensive. Many students spend their first two years of college at a community college. After that, they can apply to study for two more years at a four-year college and then graduate. Some colleges are part of large universities. These universities also have graduate schools where students continue to study after they graduate from college. Students who want to be doctors, for example, go to college for four years and then study at a medical school in a university.

1. Kindergarten is the first year of _____.
   A. pre-school
   B. day care
   C. elementary school
   D. middle school

2. Students usually go to middle school for _____.
   A. four years
   B. three years
   C. two years
   D. one year

3. Students have to pay to go to _____.
   A. kindergarten
   B. high school
   C. middle school
   D. private school

4. Children usually have to go to school when they're _____.
   A. three years old
   B. four years old
   C. five years old
   D. six years old

5. The tenth grade is usually the _____ year of high school.
   A. second
   B. third
   C. first
   D. fourth

6. A medical school is part of a _____.
   A. community college
   B. four-year college
   C. university
   D. vocational school

10c

Choose the correct answer.

1. Brian is very athletic. Every weekend he likes to _____.
   A. chat online
   B. go hiking
   C. watch videos
   D. cook

2. My brother likes clothes. I'm going to give him a _____ for his birthday.
   A. briefcase
   B. CD player
   C. sweater
   D. plant

3. My parents _____ their house and bought a condominium.
   A. sent
   B. gave
   C. moved
   D. sold

4. I like to listen to music on my _____.
   A. CD player
   B. wallet
   C. watch
   D. painting

5. Every day I _____ with my friends over the Internet.
   A. call
   B. grow up
   C. send
   D. communicate

6. When I have a problem, my parents always give me good _____.
   A. advice
   B. message
   C. friends
   D. letters

7. I live on the West Coast, and you live on the East Coast. We live _____ each other.
   A. near
   B. far apart from
   C. between
   D. next to

8. I want to _____ my children for school.
   A. registration
   B. form
   C. registration form
   D. register

9. My seven-year-old daughter goes to a very good _____.
   A. middle school
   B. vocational school
   C. elementary school
   D. high school

10. My birthday is _____.
    A. the first Thursday of every month
    B. November 16th
    C. April 10, 1991
    D. from May ninth to May twelfth

SKILLS CHECK ✔

Words:
- ☐ chat online
- ☐ clean
- ☐ cook
- ☐ drive
- ☐ go *hiking*
- ☐ go to *the mall*
- ☐ make *pancakes*
- ☐ plant
- ☐ play *basketball*
- ☐ play the *piano*
- ☐ read
- ☐ swim
- ☐ watch TV
- ☐ write

Days of the week:
- ☐ Sunday
- ☐ Monday
- ☐ Tuesday
- ☐ Wednesday
- ☐ Thursday
- ☐ Friday
- ☐ Saturday

Months of the year:
- ☐ January
- ☐ February
- ☐ March
- ☐ April
- ☐ May
- ☐ June
- ☐ July
- ☐ August
- ☐ September
- ☐ October
- ☐ November
- ☐ December

Types of schools:
- ☐ day-care center
- ☐ pre-school
- ☐ elementary school
- ☐ middle school
- ☐ high school
- ☐ technical school
- ☐ vocational school
- ☐ community college
- ☐ college
- ☐ university
- ☐ graduate school
- ☐ medical school

I can ask & answer:
- ☐ What do you do every day?
- ☐ What are you doing right now?
- ☐ What are you going to do tomorrow?
- ☐ What did you do yesterday?
- ☐ What do you like to do?
- ☐ Do you like *rock music*?
- ☐ Do you like to *ski*?

I can:
- ☐ read dates & use a calendar
- ☐ fill out a registration form

I can write about:
- ☐ my last birthday
- ☐ a close friendship

Count/Non-Count Nouns

- **Food**
- **Buying Food**
- **Being a Guest at Mealtime**
- **Describing Food Preferences**
- **School Personnel and Locations**

- **Reading a School Floor Plan**
- **Reading Skill: Fact and Inference Questions**
- **Following Written Instructions**
- **Technology: Setting Up a Computer**

VOCABULARY PREVIEW

1. apples	7. chicken	13. lettuce	19. pears
2. bananas	8. eggs	14. mayonnaise	20. pepper
3. bread	9. fish	15. meat	21. potatoes
4. cake	10. grapes	16. mustard	22. salt
5. carrots	11. ketchup	17. onions	23. soy sauce
6. cheese	12. lemons	18. oranges	24. tomatoes

Practice conversations with other students. Talk about the foods in this kitchen.

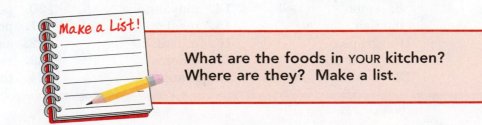

Make a List!

What are the foods in YOUR kitchen?
Where are they? Make a list.

Let's Make Sandwiches for Lunch!

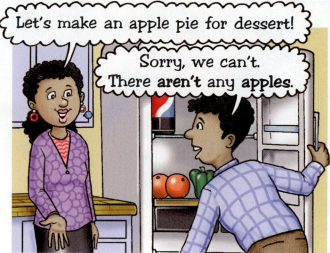

1. Let's make pizza for lunch!
   cheese

2. Let's make some fresh lemonade!
   lemons

3. Let's make a salad for dinner!
   lettuce

4. Let's make an omelet for breakfast!
   eggs

5. Let's bake a cake for dessert!
   flour

6. Let's make some fresh orange juice for breakfast!
   oranges

7. Let's have french fries with our hamburgers!
   potatoes

8. Let's have meatballs with our spaghetti!
   meat

9.

How Much Milk Do You Want?

how much? too much	how many? too many
a little	a few

A. How much milk do you want?

B. Not too much. Just a little.

A. Okay. Here you are.

B. Thanks.

A. How many cookies do you want?

B. Not too many. Just a few.

A. Okay. Here you are.

B. Thanks.

1. *rice*

2. *french fries*

3. *ice cream*

4. *coffee*

5. *meatballs*

6.

14

Some of your friends are having dinner at your home. How do they like the food? Ask them.

A. How do you like the _____?

B. I think (it's / they're) delicious.

A. I'm glad you like (it / them). Would you care for some more?

B. Yes, please. But not (too much / too many). Just (a little / a few).
My doctor says that (too much / too many) _____ (is / are) bad for my health.

chocolate cake

cookies

ice cream

How to Say It!

Complimenting About Food

A. This *chicken* is delicious!*
B. I'm glad you like it.

A. These *potatoes* are delicious!*
B. I'm glad you like them.

* delicious / very good / excellent / wonderful / fantastic

Practice conversations with other students.

READING

TWO BAGS OF GROCERIES

Henry is at the supermarket, and he's really upset. He just bought some groceries, and he can't believe he just spent* sixty dollars! He bought only a few oranges, a few apples, a little milk, a little ice cream, and a few eggs.

He also bought just a little coffee, a few onions, a few bananas, a little rice, a little cheese, and a few lemons. He didn't buy very much fish, he didn't buy very many grapes, and he didn't buy very much meat.

Henry just spent sixty dollars, but he's walking out of the supermarket with only two bags of groceries. No wonder he's upset!

* spend – spent

✔ READING *CHECK-UP*

Q & A

Using these models, make questions and answers based on the story.

A. How many *oranges* did he buy?
B. He bought only a few *oranges*.

A. How much *milk* did he buy?
B. He bought only a little *milk*.

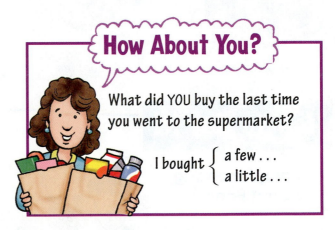

How About You?

What did YOU buy the last time you went to the supermarket?

I bought { a few . . .
a little . . .

LISTENING

Listen and choose what the people are talking about.

1. a. cake   b. carrots
2. a. fish   b. potatoes
3. a. cookies   b. milk
4. a. cheese   b. meatballs

5. a. eggs   b. butter
6. a. rice   b. french fries
7. a. oranges   b. salad
8. a. lemonade   b. lemons

🔴 16

DELICIOUS!

Lucy likes french fries. In fact, she eats them all the time. Her friends often tell her that she eats too many french fries, but Lucy doesn't think so. She thinks they're delicious.

Fred likes ice cream. In fact, he eats it all the time. His doctor often tells him that he eats too much ice cream, but Fred doesn't think so. He thinks it's delicious.

TASTES TERRIBLE!

Daniel doesn't like vegetables. In fact, he never eats them. His parents often tell him that vegetables are good for him, but Daniel doesn't care. He thinks they taste terrible.

Alice doesn't like yogurt. In fact, she never eats it. Her children often tell her that yogurt is good for her, but Alice doesn't care. She thinks it tastes terrible.

ON YOUR OWN

Tell about foods you like.

What foods do you think are delicious?
How often do you eat them?
Are they good for you, or are they bad for you?

Tell about foods you don't like.

What foods do you think taste terrible?
How often do you eat them?
Are they good for you, or are they bad for you?

Listen. Then say it.

Let's make a salad *for* dinner!

Let's make eggs *for* breakfast!

Would you care *for* some more cake?

It's bad *for* my health.

Say it. Then listen.

Let's make pizza *for* lunch!

Let's have ice cream *for* dessert!

Would you care *for* some more cookies?

They're bad *for* my health.

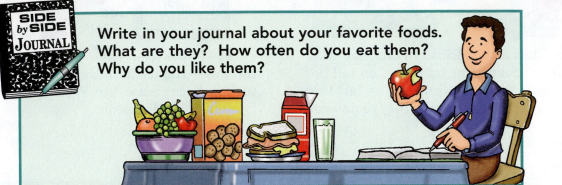

SIDE by SIDE JOURNAL

Write in your journal about your favorite foods. What are they? How often do you eat them? Why do you like them?

GRAMMAR FOCUS

COUNT / NON-COUNT NOUNS

There isn't any	bread. lettuce. flour.

There aren't any	apples. eggs. lemons.

How much	milk cheese ice cream	do you want?
How many	cookies french fries meatballs	

Not too	much. many.

Just	a little. a few.

Choose the correct word.

1. We can't make a cake now.
   There (**isn't**   aren't) any flour.

2. There (**isn't**   aren't) any mayonnaise
   in the refrigerator.

3. We can't make an omelet.
   There (isn't   **aren't**) any eggs.

4. I don't want too (**much**   many) ice cream.
   Just a (**little**   few).

5. How (**much**   many) cake do you want?

6. I don't want too (much   **many**) cookies.
   Just a (little   **few**).

7. I bought just a (**little**   few) meat today.

8. My doctor often tells me that I eat too
   (**much**   many) desserts.

9. I bought a (little   **few**) carrots and a
   (**little**   few) cheese at the store.

10. How (**much**   many) rice did you buy?

11. I ate too (much   **many**) french fries!

1 CONVERSATION ASKING & GIVING LOCATION OF SCHOOL PERSONNEL

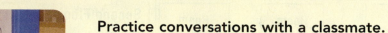

Practice conversations with a classmate.

A. Where's the _____?

B. He's/She's in the _____.

1. school nurse
nurse's office

2. librarian
library

3. guidance counselor
guidance office

4. cafeteria worker
cafeteria

5. security officer
hall

6. school secretary
school office

7. principal
principal's office

8. music teacher
auditorium

9. P.E. teacher
gym

2 SCHOOL CONNECTIONS PEOPLE & LOCATIONS IN YOUR SCHOOL

Fill in the chart with information about some people who work in your school.

NAME	JOB	LOCATION AT SCHOOL

Look at the floor plan of Madison Middle School and answer the questions.

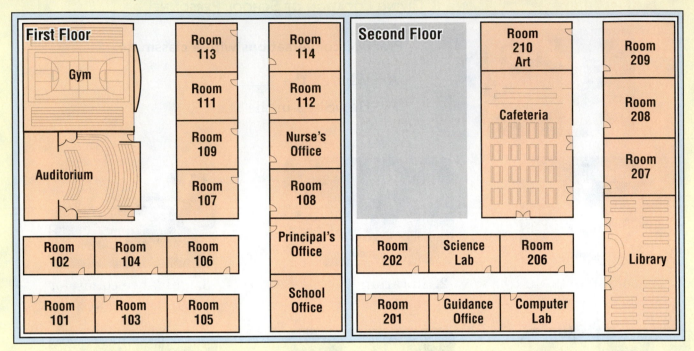

1. The school office is ____.
   A. next to Room 102
   B. across from the gym
   C. on the second floor
   D. next to the principal's office

2. There are ____ offices in Madison Middle School.
   A. two
   B. three
   C. four
   D. five

3. The nurse's office and ____ are on different floors.
   A. the library
   B. the principal's office
   C. Room 107
   D. the school office

4. Students go to the first floor when ____.
   A. it's time for lunch
   B. they feel sick
   C. they want to use a computer
   D. they're looking for books to read

5. Room 208 is probably noisy at noon because ____.
   A. it's next to the library
   B. it's on the second floor
   C. it's across from the cafeteria
   D. it's near the computer lab

6. The librarian and the ____ work on different floors.
   A. guidance counselor
   B. science teacher
   C. lunchroom monitor
   D. P.E. teacher

Reading Tip   Facts and Inferences

Fact questions ask for information you can find in a reading. Question 1 is a fact question. The floor plan shows you that the school office is next to the principal's office.

To answer **inference questions**, you have to think about information in a reading and put it together with other things you know about the subject. Question 4 is an inference question. To answer it, you have to know what students do in different rooms of a school. That information is not on the floor plan.

What are the other inference questions on this page? What information do you need to know to answer them?

Read the instructions for setting up a new computer and answer the questions.

- Place the CPU and the monitor on a table or desk.
- There are several ports (openings) for cables on the back of your CPU. The port for the power cable is in the center, near the top. Connect the power cable to the port. Plug the other end of the power cable into an outlet with a surge protector.
- Connect the monitor cable to the port below the power cable port. Connect the other end of the cable to your monitor.
- There are three USB ports below the monitor port. Connect the cable on your keyboard to a USB port.
- Connect the mouse cable to a port on your keyboard.
- To use the Internet, you need an Ethernet cable and a modem. Connect the cable to an Ethernet port on the back of your CPU. There are two Ethernet ports at the bottom of the CPU below the USB ports. Connect the other end of the Ethernet cable to your modem.
- Turn on your computer and monitor. Use the power button on the front of your CPU.
- To finish setting up your computer, follow the instructions on the screen.
- To add a printer to your computer, connect the printer cable to a USB port on the back of your CPU. Then follow the instructions that come with your printer.

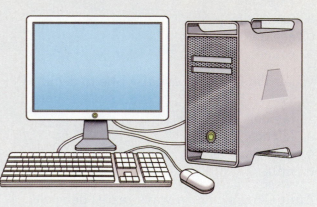

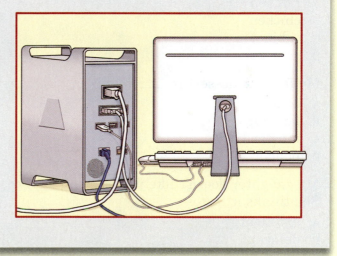

1. Plug your _____ into an outlet with a surge protector.
   - A. mouse cable
   - B. keyboard cable
   - C. power cable
   - D. Ethernet cable

2. The monitor port is on the back of the _____.
   - A. keyboard
   - B. CPU
   - C. printer
   - D. modem

3. There are three _____ on the back of the CPU.
   - A. USB ports
   - B. power cable ports
   - C. Ethernet ports
   - D. monitor ports

4. Connect the cable on your mouse to _____.
   - A. a cable on your keyboard
   - B. a port on your keyboard
   - C. a port on your CPU
   - D. an Ethernet cable

5. To use the Internet, you need _____.
   - A. a printer
   - B. a mouse
   - C. a surge protector
   - D. a modem and an Ethernet cable

6. You can use the same ports for the printer and the _____ cables.
   - A. Ethernet
   - B. monitor
   - C. keyboard
   - D. power

18c

Choose the correct answer.

1. Do you want to bake some _____ today?
   A. salad
   B. ice cream
   C. cookies
   D. coffee

2. When I'm thirsty, I usually like to drink _____.
   A. lemons
   B. lettuce
   C. mayonnaise
   D. milk

3. Aunt Clara's _____ always tastes delicious.
   A. kitchen
   B. chicken
   C. cabinet
   D. counter

4. My favorite dessert is _____.
   A. cake
   B. ketchup
   C. mustard
   D. pepper

5. My daughter doesn't like yogurt. She thinks it tastes _____.
   A. excellent
   B. delicious
   C. terrible
   D. fantastic

6. Mr. and Mrs. Mendoza _____ seventy-five dollars at the supermarket.
   A. spent
   B. lent
   C. bought
   D. sold

7. The _____ is usually in our school's halls all day.
   A. P.E. teacher
   B. guidance counselor
   C. cafeteria worker
   D. security officer

8. The school secretary works in the _____.
   A. computer lab
   B. school office
   C. guidance office
   D. gym

9. When students at our school feel sick, they go to the _____.
   A. auditorium
   B. cafeteria
   C. nurse's office
   D. guidance office

10. There are three _____ on the back of the CPU.
    A. printers
    B. ports
    C. monitors
    D. keyboards

SKILLS CHECK ✔

Words:

☐ apple pie	☐ french fries	☐ onions	☐ spaghetti
☐ apples	☐ grapes	☐ orange	☐ sugar
☐ bananas	☐ hamburgers	juice	☐ tea
☐ bread	☐ ice cream	☐ oranges	☐ tomatoes
☐ butter	☐ ketchup	☐ pears	☐ vegetables
☐ cake	☐ lemonade	☐ pepper	☐ yogurt
☐ carrots	☐ lemons	☐ pizza	
☐ cheese	☐ lettuce	☐ potatoes	☐ cafeteria worker
☐ chicken	☐ mayonnaise	☐ rice	☐ guidance
☐ coffee	☐ meat	☐ salad	counselor
☐ cookies	☐ meatballs	☐ salt	☐ librarian
☐ eggs	☐ milk	☐ sandwich	☐ music teacher
☐ fish	☐ mustard	☐ soda	☐ P.E. teacher
☐ flour	☐ omelet	☐ soy sauce	☐ principal

☐ school nurse
☐ school secretary
☐ security officer

☐ auditorium
☐ cafeteria
☐ computer lab
☐ guidance office
☐ gym
☐ hall
☐ library
☐ nurse's office
☐ principal's office
☐ school office

I can ask & answer:
☐ Where are the *cookies*?
☐ Where's the *cheese*?
☐ How much *milk* do you want?
☐ How many *cookies* do you want?

I can compliment about food:
☐ This *chicken* is/These *potatoes* are delicious!

I can write about:
☐ my favorite foods

I can:
☐ interpret a floor plan diagram
☐ follow instructions for setting up a computer

3

Partitives
Count/Non-Count Nouns
Imperatives

- **Buying Food**
- **Describing Food**
- **Eating in a Restaurant**
- **Recipes**
- **Supermarket Sections**
- **Reading a Store Directory**
- **Supermarket Receipts**
- **Food Labels**
- **Restaurant Menus**

VOCABULARY PREVIEW

1. a **can** of soup
2. a **jar** of jam
3. a **bottle** of ketchup
4. a **box** of cereal
5. a **bag** of flour
6. a **loaf** of white bread
7. two **loaves** of whole wheat bread
8. a **bunch** of bananas
9. a **head** of lettuce
10. a **dozen** eggs
11. a **pint** of ice cream
12. a **quart** of orange juice
13. a **gallon** of milk
14. a **pound** of meat
15. a **half pound** / **half a pound** } of cheese

Do We Need Anything from the Supermarket?

My Shopping List

a can of soup
a jar of jam
a bottle of ketchup
a box of cereal
a bag of flour
a loaf of white bread
2 loaves of whole wheat bread
a bunch of bananas
2 bunches of carrots

a head of lettuce
a dozen eggs

a pt.* of ice cream
a qt.* of orange juice
a gal.* of milk
a lb.* of meat
1/2 lb.* of cheese

* pt. = pint
  qt. = quart
  gal. = gallon
  lb. = pound

A. Do we need anything from the supermarket?

B. Yes. We need a loaf of bread.

A. A loaf of bread?

B. Yes.

A. Anything else?

B. No. Just a loaf of bread.

1.   2.   3.   4.   5.

6.   7.   8.   9.   10.

Make a Shopping List!

What do you need from the supermarket?
Make a shopping list.

How Much Does a Head of Lettuce Cost?

1¢	$.01	one cent		$1.00	one dollar
25¢	$.25	twenty-five cents		$10.00	ten dollars

A. How much does **a head of lettuce** cost?

B. **A dollar ninety-five.*** ($1.95)

A. A DOLLAR NINETY-FIVE?! That's a lot of money!

B. You're right. **Lettuce** is very expensive this week.

* $1.95 = { a dollar ninety-five
one dollar and ninety-five cents

A. How much does **a pound of apples** cost?

B. **Two eighty-nine.*** ($2.89)

A. TWO EIGHTY-NINE?! That's a lot of money!

B. You're right. **Apples** are very expensive this week.

* $2.89 = { two eighty-nine
two dollars and eighty-nine cents

1.

2.

3.

4.

5.

6.

7.

8.

READING

NOTHING TO EAT FOR DINNER

Joan got home late from work today, and she was very hungry. When she opened the refrigerator, she was upset. There was nothing to eat for dinner. Joan sat down and made a shopping list. She needed a head of lettuce, a bunch of carrots, a quart of milk, a dozen eggs, two pounds of tomatoes, half a pound of chicken, and a loaf of bread.

Joan rushed out of the house and drove to the supermarket. When she got there, she was very disappointed. There wasn't any lettuce. There weren't any carrots. There wasn't any milk. There weren't any eggs. There weren't any tomatoes. There wasn't any chicken, and there wasn't any bread.

Joan was tired and upset. In fact, she was so tired and upset that she lost her appetite, drove home, didn't have dinner, and went to bed.

✔ READING *CHECK-UP*

Q & A

Joan is at the supermarket. Using these models, create dialogs based on the story.

A. Excuse me. I'm looking for *a head of lettuce*.
B. Sorry. There isn't any more *lettuce*.
A. There isn't?
B. No, there isn't. Sorry.

A. Excuse me. I'm looking for *a bunch of carrots*.
B. Sorry. There aren't any more *carrots*.
A. There aren't?
B. No, there aren't. Sorry.

LISTENING

Listen and choose what the people are talking about.

1. a. chicken   b. milk
2. a. oranges   b. flour
3. a. cookies   b. bread
4. a. potatoes   b. lettuce

5. a. eggs   b. meat
6. a. cereal   b. bananas
7. a. cake   b. soup
8. a. onions   b. soda

What Would You Like?

A. What would you like **for dessert**?

B. I can't decide. What do you recommend?

A. I recommend our **chocolate ice cream**. Everybody says **it's** delicious.*

B. Okay. Please give me **a dish of chocolate ice cream**.

A. What would you like **for breakfast**?

B. I can't decide. What do you recommend?

A. I recommend our **scrambled eggs**. Everybody says **they're** out of this world.*

B. Okay. Please give me **an order of scrambled eggs**.

* delicious / very good / excellent / wonderful / fantastic / magnificent / out of this world

1. for lunch?
   a bowl of

2. for breakfast?
   an order of

3. for dessert?
   a piece of

4. to drink?
   a glass of

5. for dessert?
   a bowl of

6. to drink?
   a cup of

7. for dessert?
   a dish of

8.

How to Say It!

Making a Recommendation About Food

A. What do you recommend for *breakfast*?*

B. I { recommend / suggest } the *pancakes*.

* breakfast / lunch / dinner / dessert

Practice conversations with other students. Ask for and make recommendations.

23

Stanley's Favorite Recipes

Are you going to have a party soon? Do you want to cook something special? Stanley the chef recommends this recipe for VEGETABLE STEW. Everybody says it's fantastic!

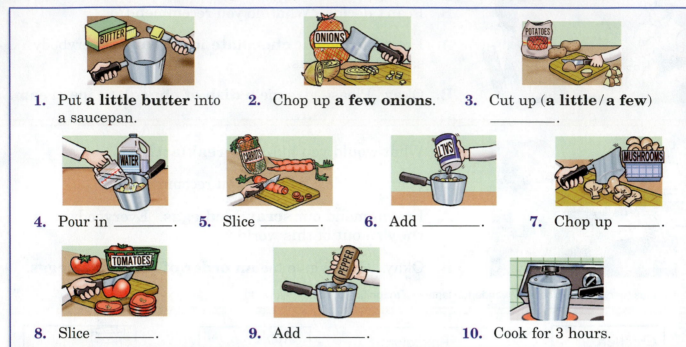

1. Put **a little butter** into a saucepan.
2. Chop up **a few onions**.
3. Cut up (**a little / a few**) _____.

4. Pour in _____.
5. Slice _____.
6. Add _____.
7. Chop up _____.

8. Slice _____.
9. Add _____.
10. Cook for 3 hours.

When is your English teacher's birthday? Do you want to bake a special cake? Stanley the chef recommends this recipe for FRUITCAKE. Everybody says it's out of this world!

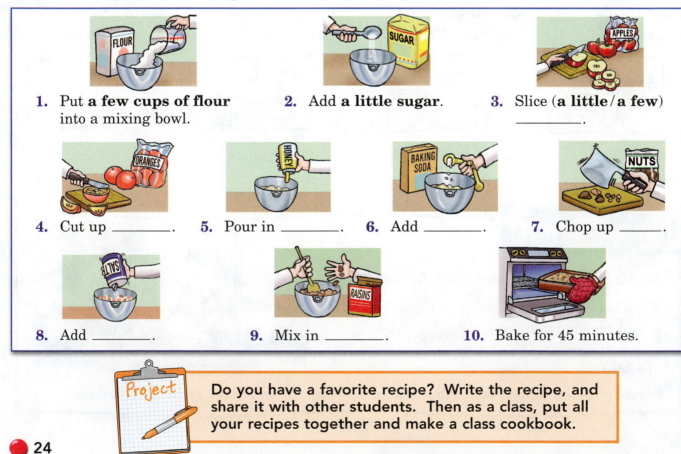

1. Put **a few cups of flour** into a mixing bowl.
2. Add **a little sugar**.
3. Slice (**a little / a few**) _____.

4. Cut up _____.
5. Pour in _____.
6. Add _____.
7. Chop up _____.

8. Add _____.
9. Mix in _____.
10. Bake for 45 minutes.

Project Do you have a favorite recipe? Write the recipe, and share it with other students. Then as a class, put all your recipes together and make a class cookbook.

AT THE CONTINENTAL RESTAURANT

Yesterday was Sherman and Dorothy Johnson's thirty-fifth wedding anniversary. They went to the Continental Restaurant for dinner. This restaurant is a very special place for Sherman and Dorothy because they went there on their first date thirty-six years ago.

Sherman and Dorothy sat at a quiet romantic table in the corner. They looked at the menu, and then they ordered dinner. For an appetizer, Dorothy ordered a bowl of vegetable soup, and Sherman ordered a glass of tomato juice. For the main course, Dorothy ordered baked chicken with rice, and Sherman ordered broiled fish with potatoes. For dessert, Dorothy ordered a piece of apple pie, and Sherman ordered a bowl of strawberries.

Sherman and Dorothy enjoyed their dinner very much. The soup was delicious, and the tomato juice was fresh. The chicken was wonderful, and the rice was tasty. The fish was fantastic, and the potatoes were excellent. The apple pie was magnificent, and the strawberries were out of this world.

Sherman and Dorothy had a wonderful evening at the Continental Restaurant. It was a very special anniversary.

ROLE PLAY

Sherman and Dorothy are ordering dinner from their waiter or waitress. Using these lines to begin, work in groups of three and create a role play based on the story.

- **A.** Would you like to order now?
- **B.** Yes. For an appetizer, I'd like . . .
- **C.** And I'd like . . .

Now, the waiter or waitress is asking about the dinner. Using this model, continue your role play based on all the foods in the story.

- **A.** How (is / are) the _____?
- **B.** (It's / They're) _____.
- **A.** I'm glad you like (it / them). And how (is / are) the _____?
- **C.** (It's / They're) _____.
- **A.** I'm glad you like (it / them).

PRONUNCIATION *Of Before Consonants and Vowels*

Listen. Then say it.

a bowl of soup

a head of lettuce

a piece of apple pie

a bag of onions

Say it. Then listen.

a glass of milk

a jar of jam

a pound of oranges

a dish of ice cream

SIDE by SIDE JOURNAL

In your journal, write about a special meal you enjoyed—in your home, in someone else's home, or at a restaurant. What foods did you have? Who was at the meal? Why was it special?

GRAMMAR FOCUS

COUNT / NON-COUNT NOUNS

Lettuce Butter Milk	is	very expensive.
Apples Carrots Onions	are	

Add	a little	salt. sugar. honey.
	a few	potatoes. nuts. raisins.

IMPERATIVES

Please **give me** a dish of ice cream.
Put a little butter into a saucepan.
Cook for 3 hours.

Choose the correct word.

1. Add a (little   few) salt.
2. Cheese (is   are) very expensive this week.
3. Put a (little   few) cups of flour into a bowl.
4. There (isn't   aren't) any more lettuce.

5. Slice a (little   few) tomatoes.
6. The fish (was   were) tasty.
7. The potatoes (was   were) excellent.
8. Chop up a (little   few) nuts.

PARTITIVES

a bag of flour	**a dozen** eggs	**a jar of** jam	**a bowl of** chicken soup
a bottle of ketchup	**a gallon of** milk	**a loaf of** bread	**a cup of** hot chocolate
a box of cereal	**a half pound (half a pound) of** cheese	**a pint of** ice cream	**a dish of** ice cream
a bunch of bananas		**a pound of** meat	**a glass of** milk
a can of soup	**a head of** lettuce	**a quart of** orange juice	**an order of** scrambled eggs
			a piece of apple pie

Complete the sentences.

9. I bought a _____ of lettuce.
10. Please get a _____ eggs.
11. We need two _____ of cereal.
12. I'm looking for a _____ of flour.

13. I had a _____ of chicken soup for lunch.
14. He had a _____ of pie for dessert.
15. Please give me an _____ of scrambled eggs.
16. I'd like a _____ of ice cream for dessert, please.

1 CONVERSATION   LOCATING ITEMS IN A SUPERMARKET

Practice conversations with a classmate. Use the directory to find the correct section and aisle for these items.

A. Excuse me. Where are the _____?

B. They're in the _____ section, Aisle ____.

A. Thank you.

A. Excuse me. Where's the _____?

B. It's in the _____ section, Aisle ____.

A. Thank you.

STORE DIRECTORY

Section	Aisle
Baked Goods	6
Beverages	4
Dairy	2
Frozen Foods	5
Meat	3
Produce	1

1.   2.   3.   4.

5.   6.   7.   8.

9.   10.   11.   12.

2 TEAMWORK   CATEGORIZING

Bring a supermarket ad to class. Work with a classmate. On a piece of paper, write the names of the six supermarket sections on this page. Then list items in your supermarket ad in the correct section.

26a

READING A SUPERMARKET RECEIPT

SAVE MORE SUPERMARKET

LETTUCE	1.80
WHOLE WHEAT BREAD	2.50
ORANGE JUICE 1 GAL.	3.19
MILK 1 QT.	1.29
3 LBS. @ $1.20 LB. CHICKEN	3.60
4 @ $1.00 TOMATOES	4.00
1/2 LB. @ $9.00 LB. SWISS CHEESE	4.50
8 @ 4 FOR $1.00 BANANAS	2.00
TOTAL	$22.88
CASH TENDERED	$25.00
CHANGE	$ 2.12

Look at the receipt and answer the questions.

1. How much is a loaf of whole wheat bread?
   A. $1.80   B. $2.50   C. $1.29

2. How much orange juice did the person buy?
   A. a pound   B. a quart   C. a gallon

3. How much does a pound of chicken cost?
   A. $1.20   B. $3.60   C. $2.00

4. How many tomatoes did the person buy?
   A. three   B. eight   C. four

5. How much do eight bananas cost?
   A. $1.00   B. $2.00   C. $3.00

6. How much does Swiss cheese cost?
   A. 4 for $1.00   B. $4.50 a pound   C. $9.00 a pound

Now find the answers to these questions. Circle the answers on the receipt.

1. How many pounds of chicken did the person buy?
2. How much does a head of lettuce cost?
3. How much Swiss cheese did the person buy?
4. How much milk did the person buy?
5. How much did the person pay for tomatoes?
6. How much did the person spend today?

READING A FOOD LABEL

COLUMBUS LOW FAT MILK 1% Milk Fat
Nutrition Facts
Serving Size 1 cup (240mL)
Servings per Container 4

Amount per Serving

Calories 110   Calories from Fat 20

	% Daily Value
Total Fat 3g	4%
Cholesterol 10mg	4%
Sodium 130 mg	5%
Total Carbohydrate 13mg	4%

Vitamin A 10%	•	Vitamin C	4%
Calcium 30%	•	Vitamin D	25%

Keep Refrigerated

Read the label. Decide if the following sentences are True (T) or False (F).

_____ 1. This milk doesn't have any fat.

_____ 2. There are four cups of milk in the container.

_____ 3. A cup of this milk has four grams of fat.

_____ 4. This milk contains three types of vitamins.

_____ 5. You can put this milk in your kitchen cabinet.

_____ 6. This milk has more fat than regular milk.

TEAMWORK Bring a supermarket receipt and a food label to class. Work with a classmate. Ask each other questions about your receipts and labels.

Look at the menu and answer the questions.

Annie's Place

Soups

Chicken Soup	Cup	$2.25
	Bowl	$3.00
Mushroom Soup	Cup	$2.50
	Bowl	$3.50

Salads

Greek Salad	Small	$3.00
	Large	$4.25
Chef's Salad		$3.50
with chicken		$5.00

Sandwiches

Chicken Salad	$4.00
Egg Salad	$2.75
Cheese	$2.50
Hamburger	$4.50

served with lettuce, tomato, and french fries

Lunch Specials

| Baked Chicken | $10.00 |

served with rice and choice of vegetable

| Broiled Fish of the Day | $12.00 |

served with any two side dishes

| Spaghetti with Annie's Tomato Sauce | $6.50 |

served with salad and choice of vegetable

| with meatballs | $8.50 |

Side Dishes ($1.50 each)

Baked Potato   French Fries   Rice
Mushrooms   Carrots   Green Beans

Beverages

| Soda | $1.50 | | Coffee | $2.00 |
| Juice | $2.00 | | Tea | $1.50 |

Desserts

Chocolate Cake $3.50   Apple Pie $4.00

---

1. A bowl of chicken soup and a cheese sandwich cost _____.
   A. $5.50   C. $6.25
   B. $6.00   D. $6.50

2. A cup of chicken soup and a large Greek salad cost _____.
   A. $6.00   C. $6.50
   B. $6.25   D. $7.25

3. A hamburger comes with _____.
   A. soup   C. soda
   B. salad   D. french fries

4. A chicken salad sandwich with french fries and a glass of juice costs _____.
   A. $6.50   C. $8.00
   B. $7.50   D. $8.50

5. When you order baked chicken with rice and green beans you pay _____.
   A. $10.00   C. $12.00
   B. $11.50   D. $13.00

6. Roberto only has two dollars. He can order _____.
   A. a salad   C. soup
   B. a sandwich   D. a beverage

7. Spaghetti and meatballs, a cup of tea, and a piece of apple pie cost _____.
   A. $13.00   C. $14.00
   B. $13.50   D. $15.00

8. Broiled fish does NOT come with _____.
   A. carrots   C. rice
   B. salad   D. a baked potato

9. A chef's salad with chicken, a glass of soda, and a piece of chocolate cake cost _____.
   A. $8.50   C. $10.00
   B. $9.50   D. $12.50

10. Baked chicken comes with rice and any _____.
    A. beverage   C. salad
    B. dessert   D. side dish

TEAMWORK Bring a restaurant menu to class. Work with a classmate. Ask each other questions about the food and the prices on the menus.

Choose the correct answer.

1. I ordered a _____ for dessert.
   A. bowl of soup
   B. bag of flour
   C. piece of pie
   D. loaf of bread

2. I'm slicing some _____.
   A. tomatoes
   B. sugar
   C. soup
   D. juice

3. I recommend our _____ for breakfast.
   A. flour
   B. chocolate ice cream
   C. lettuce
   D. pancakes

4. Next, chop up some _____.
   A. jam
   B. nuts
   C. flour
   D. milk

5. The recipe says to pour in some _____.
   A. fish
   B. bread
   C. cheese
   D. water

6. Oranges are in the _____ section.
   A. Produce
   B. Dairy
   C. Meat
   D. Beverages

Look at the supermarket receipt. Choose the correct answer.

7. The person bought _____ of milk.
   A. a pint
   B. a quart
   C. a gallon
   D. a pound

8. A pound of fish costs _____.
   A. $2.00
   B. $7.00
   C. $8.00
   D. $14.00

9. The person bought _____.
   A. a pound of cheese
   B. seven pounds of fish
   C. six onions
   D. six lemons

10. The person spent _____.
    A. $32.03
    B. $7.97
    C. $40.00
    D. $47.97

```
BUY & SAVE SUPERMARKET
          * * *
WHITE BREAD          2.20
SUGAR                1.80
MILK 1 GAL.          3.10
ORANGE JUICE 1 QT.   1.63
2 LBS @ $7.00 LB.
FISH                14.00
3 @ $1.10
ONIONS               3.30
1/2 LB.@ $8.00 LB.
CHEESE               4.00
6 @ 3 FOR $1.00
LEMONS               2.00
                  ---------
            TOTAL  $32.03
    CASH TENDERED  $40.00
           CHANGE  $ 7.97
```

SKILLS CHECK ✓

Words:

- [ ] apple
- [ ] apple pie
- [ ] baked chicken
- [ ] baking soda
- [ ] banana
- [ ] bread
- [ ] broiled fish
- [ ] carrot
- [ ] cereal
- [ ] cheese
- [ ] chicken
- [ ] eggs
- [ ] flour
- [ ] grapes
- [ ] honey
- [ ] hot chocolate

- [ ] ice cream
- [ ] jam
- [ ] ketchup
- [ ] lettuce
- [ ] meat
- [ ] milk
- [ ] mushrooms
- [ ] nuts
- [ ] onions
- [ ] orange juice
- [ ] pancakes
- [ ] raisins
- [ ] scrambled eggs
- [ ] soda
- [ ] soup
- [ ] strawberries

- [ ] sugar
- [ ] Swiss cheese
- [ ] tomato juice
- [ ] tomatoes
- [ ] vanilla ice cream
- [ ] water
- [ ] white bread
- [ ] whole wheat bread

- [ ] Baked Goods
- [ ] Beverages
- [ ] Dairy
- [ ] Frozen Foods
- [ ] Meat
- [ ] Produce

I can ask & answer:

- [ ] How much does *a head of lettuce* cost?
- [ ] What would you like for *dessert*?
- [ ] What do you recommend for *breakfast*?
- [ ] Excuse me. Where are the *apples*?

I can:

- [ ] identify supermarket sections
- [ ] interpret a supermarket receipt
- [ ] read a food label
- [ ] order from a restaurant menu

I can write:

- [ ] a shopping list
- [ ] recipe instructions

I can write about:

- [ ] a meal I enjoyed

Food Shopping

Everybody eats, and everybody shops for food!

In the past, people shopped for fruits, vegetables, bread, and meat at small food stores and at open markets. Before there were refrigerators, it was difficult to keep food fresh for a long time, so people shopped almost every day.

Life today is very different from the past. Refrigerators keep food fresh so people don't have to shop every day. People also have very busy lives. They have time to shop for food only once or twice a week.

People shop for food in different kinds of places—in small grocery stores, at large supermarkets, and sometimes at enormous wholesale stores that sell food and other items at very low prices. Some people even shop on the Internet. They order food online, and the company delivers it to their home. And in many places around the world, people still shop in little food stores and at open markets. There are certainly many different ways to shop for food these days!

FACT FILE

One Day's Food

Eggs: The world's hens produce more than 2 billion eggs a day—enough eggs to make an omelet the size of the island of Cyprus!

Chocolate: The world produces 8,818 tons of cocoa beans every day—enough to make 700 million chocolate bars!

Rice: The world produces 1.6 million tons of rice every day—an amount the size of Egypt's Great Pyramid!

BUILD YOUR VOCABULARY!

Ordering Fast Food

I'd like _____ , please.

- a hamburger
- a hot dog
- a sandwich
- a taco
- a bowl of chili
- a slice of pizza
- a donut
- a bagel
- a muffin

Where People Shop for Food

People in different places shop for food in different ways.

These people shop for food at an open market.

This person buys a fresh loaf of bread every day at this bakery.

These people go to a big supermarket once a week.

Where do people shop for food in countries you know? Where do YOU shop for food?

Global Exchange

Glen25: Hi, Maria. How are you today? I just had breakfast. I had a glass of orange juice, a bowl of cereal, and a muffin. At 12 noon I'm going to have lunch. For lunch I usually have a sandwich and a glass of milk. Our family's big meal of the day is dinner. We usually eat at about 6 P.M. We usually have meat, chicken, or fish, rice or potatoes, and vegetables. How about you? When do you usually eat? What do you have? What's your big meal of the day?

MariaV: Hi, Glen. It's the middle of the afternoon here. Our family just had our big meal of the day. Today we had meat, potatoes, and vegetables. For breakfast I usually have a roll and a cup of hot chocolate. We don't have a big dinner in the evening. We usually have a snack early in the evening and a light supper at about 9:30.

Send a message to a keypal. Tell about the meals you eat.

LISTENING

Attention, Food Shoppers!

_d_	**1** cereal	**a.**	$2.75
___	**2** bread	**b.**	$ .40
___	**3** orange juice	**c.**	$3.25
___	**4** ice cream	**d.**	$3.49
___	**5** bananas	**e.**	$1.79

What Are They Saying?

Future Tense: Will
Time Expressions
Might

- Telling About the Future
- Probability
- Possibility
- Warnings

- Social Interaction: Offers and Invitations
- Reading and Writing Invitations
- Cross-Cultural Expectations
- Reading Skill: Signal Words

VOCABULARY PREVIEW

1. begin
2. end
3. arrive
4. return
5. grow up
6. get married
7. name
8. move
9. helmet
10. safety glasses
11. warning

Will the Train Arrive Soon?

(I will)	I'll
(He will)	He'll
(She will)	She'll
(It will)	It'll } work.
(We will)	We'll
(You will)	You'll
(They will)	They'll

Will he work?
Yes, he will.

A. Will the train arrive soon?

B. Yes, it will. It'll arrive in five minutes.

1. Will the game begin soon?
at 7:00

2. Will Ms. Lopez return soon?
in an hour

3. Will you be ready soon?
in a few minutes

4. Will the guests be here soon?
in half an hour

5. Will your brother get home soon?
in a little while

6. Will you be back soon?
in a week

7. Will the storm end soon?
in a few hours

8. Will I get out of the hospital soon?
in two or three days

What Do You Think?

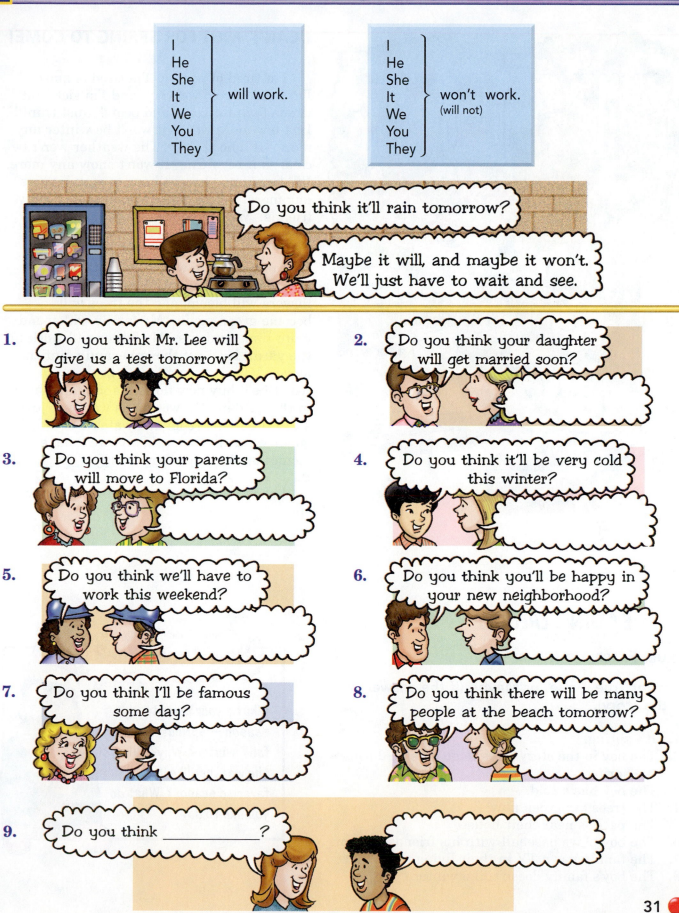

I / He / She / It / We / You / They } will work.

I / He / She / It / We / You / They } won't work. (will not)

Do you think it'll rain tomorrow?

Maybe it will, and maybe it won't. We'll just have to wait and see.

1. Do you think Mr. Lee will give us a test tomorrow?

2. Do you think your daughter will get married soon?

3. Do you think your parents will move to Florida?

4. Do you think it'll be very cold this winter?

5. Do you think we'll have to work this weekend?

6. Do you think you'll be happy in your new neighborhood?

7. Do you think I'll be famous some day?

8. Do you think there will be many people at the beach tomorrow?

9. Do you think _____ ?

31

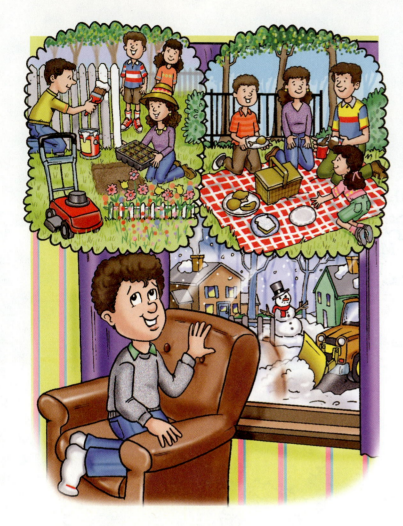

I CAN'T WAIT FOR SPRING TO COME!

I'm tired of winter. I'm tired of snow, I'm tired of cold weather, and I'm sick and tired of winter coats and boots! Just think! In a few more weeks it won't be winter any more. It'll be spring. The weather won't be cold. It'll be warm. It won't snow any more. It'll be sunny. I won't have to stay indoors any more. I'll go outside and play with my friends. We'll ride bicycles and play baseball again.

In a few more weeks our neighborhood won't look sad and gray any more. The flowers will bloom, and the trees will become green again. My family will spend more time outdoors. My father will work in the yard. He'll cut the grass and paint the fence. My mother will work in the yard, too. She'll buy new flowers and plant them in the garden. On weekends we won't just sit in the living room and watch TV. We'll go for walks in the park, and we'll have picnics on Sunday afternoons.

I can't wait for spring to come! Hurry, spring!

✔ ## READING *CHECK-UP*

TRUE, FALSE, OR MAYBE?

Answer True, False, or Maybe (if the answer isn't in the story).

1. It's spring.
2. The boy in the story likes to go outside during the spring.
3. The boy has a cold.
4. The trees are green now.
5. The park is near their house.
6. The boy plays baseball with his friends all year.
7. The family has a TV in their living room.
8. The boy's family doesn't like winter.

How About You?

What's your favorite season—spring? summer? fall? winter? Why? What's the weather like in your favorite season? What do you like to do?

They Really Can't Decide

| I |
| He |
| She |
| It | } might clean it today. |
| We |
| You |
| They |

A. When are you going to clean your apartment?

B. I don't know. I might clean it today, or I might clean it next Saturday. I really can't decide.

A. Where are you going to go for your vacation?

B. We don't know. We might go to Mexico, or we might go to Japan. We really can't decide.

1. What's he going to make for dinner tonight?

2. What color is she going to paint her bedroom?

3. What are they going to name their new daughter?

4. When are you two going to get married?

5. What are you going to buy your brother for his birthday?

6. What are they going to do tonight?

7. How are you going to get to school tomorrow?

8. What's he going to name his new puppy?

9. What are you going to be when you grow up?

33

Careful!

A. Careful! Put on your helmet!

B. I'm sorry. What did you say?

A. Put on your helmet! You might hurt your head.

B. Oh. Thanks for the warning.

1. Put on your safety glasses!
hurt your eyes

2. Don't stand there!
get hit

3. Watch your step!
fall

4. Don't touch that machine!
get hurt

5. Don't touch those wires!
get a shock

6.

How to Say It!

Asking for Repetition

A. *Careful! Watch your step!*

B. *I'm sorry.* { What did you say?
Could you please repeat that?
Could you say that again? }

Practice some conversations on this page again. Ask for repetition in different ways.

I'm Afraid I Might Drown

A. Would you like to go swimming with me?

B. No, I don't think so.

A. Why not?

B. I'm afraid I might drown.

A. Don't worry! You won't drown.

B. Are you sure?

A. I'm positive!

B. Okay. I'll go swimming with you.

1. go skiing
   break my leg

2. go to the beach
   get a sunburn

3. go dancing
   step on your feet

4. take a walk in the park
   catch a cold

5. go to the movies
   fall asleep

6. go to the company picnic
   have a terrible time

7. go on the roller coaster
   get sick

8. go sailing
   get seasick

9.

JUST IN CASE

Larry didn't go to work today, and he might not go to work tomorrow either. He might see his doctor instead. He's feeling absolutely terrible, and he thinks he might have the flu. Larry isn't positive, but he doesn't want to take any chances. He thinks it might be a good idea for him to see his doctor . . . just in case.

Mrs. Randall didn't go to the office today, and she might not go to the office tomorrow either. She might go to the doctor instead. She feels nauseous every morning, and she thinks she might be pregnant. Mrs. Randall isn't positive, but she doesn't want to take any chances. She thinks it might be a good idea for her to go to the doctor . . . just in case.

Tommy and Julie Harris didn't go to school today, and they might not go to school tomorrow either. They might stay home in bed instead. They have little red spots all over their arms and legs. Mr. and Mrs. Harris think their children might have the measles. They aren't positive, but they don't want to take any chances. They think it might be a good idea for Tommy and Julie to stay home in bed . . . just in case.

✔️ READING *CHECK-UP*

CHOOSE

Larry is "calling in sick." Choose the correct words and then practice the conversation.

A. Hello. This is Larry Parker. I'm afraid I (might   can't)¹ come to work today. I think I (will   might)² have the flu.

B. That's too bad. (Are you   Will you)³ going to see your doctor?

A. I think I (might   sure).⁴

B. (Not   Will)⁵ you be at work tomorrow?

A. I'm not sure. I (might not   might)⁶ go to work tomorrow either.

B. Well, I hope you feel better soon.

A. Thank you.

LISTENING

WHAT'S THE LINE?

Mrs. Harris (from the story on page 36) is calling Tommy and Julie's school. Listen and choose the correct lines.

1.
   a. Hello. This is Mrs. Harris.
   b. Hello. This is the Park Elementary School.
2.
   a. I can't.
   b. Tommy and Julie won't be in school today.
3.
   a. They might have the measles.
   b. Yes. This is their mother.
4.
   a. They aren't bad. They're just sick.
   b. Yes.
5.
   a. Thank you.
   b. It might be a good idea.

Good morning.
Park Elementary School.

WHAT'S THE WORD?

Listen and choose the word you hear.

1. a. can't	b. might	4. a. we'll	b. will	7. a. I	b. I'll
2. a. want to	b. won't	5. a. they'll	b. they	8. a. red	b. wet
3. a. here	b. there	6. a. hurt	b. hit	9. a. sick	b. seasick

Write a Note!

Your child didn't go to school yesterday. Write a note to the teacher and explain why.

.........., 20.......

Dear ....,

.... didn't go to school yesterday because

....

....

Sincerely,

....

PRONUNCIATION *Going to*

going to = gonna

Listen. Then say it.

When are you going to clean your room?
What color is she going to paint her bedroom?
How are they going to get to school?

Say it. Then listen.

When are you going to get married?
What's he going to name his cat?
When am I going to get out of the hospital?

Write in your journal about your future. Where do you think you might live? Where do you think you might work? What do you think might happen in your life?

FUTURE TENSE: WILL

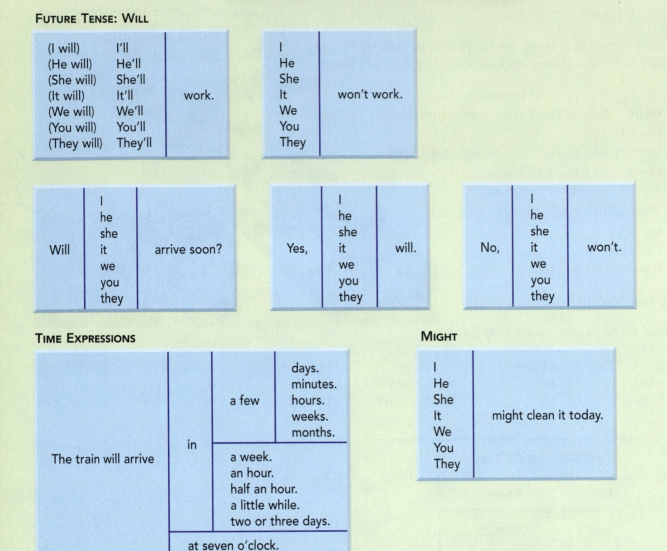

TIME EXPRESSIONS

MIGHT

Complete the sentences.

1. A. _____ Mrs. Sanchez return soon?

   B. Yes, _____ _____. _____ return in an hour.

2. A. _____ the flowers bloom soon?

   B. Yes, _____ _____. _____ bloom in a week.

3. A. _____ there be many people at the party tonight?

   B. No, _____ _____.

4. A. _____ you call me today?

   B. Yes, _____ _____. _____ call you soon.

5. A. _____ your brother be ready soon?

   B. No, _____ _____. He's still sleeping.

6. A. _____ you and your wife visit us soon?

   B. Yes, _____ _____. _____ visit you on Sunday.

7. A. Do you think it _____ be a nice day tomorrow?

   B. Maybe _____ _____, and maybe _____ _____.

8. A. Do you think _____ catch a cold?

   B. No, you _____. _____ be fine.

1 CONVERSATION   MAKING, ACCEPTING, & DECLINING OFFERS

Practice the conversations with a classmate.

A. Would you like some french fries?

B. Yes. Thanks.

Now work with other classmates.
Practice making, accepting, and declining offers.

A. Would you like some more coffee?

B. No, thank you.

A. Would you like _____?

B. { Yes. Thanks.
{ No, thank you.

2 CONVERSATION   MAKING, ACCEPTING, & DECLINING INVITATIONS

Practice the conversations with a classmate.

A. Would you like to have dinner with my family tomorrow?

B. Yes. I'd love to.

Now work with other classmates.
Practice making, accepting, and declining invitations.

A. Would you like to go out for lunch today?

B. I'm sorry. I can't. I have to work.

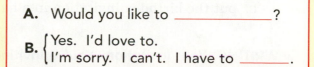

A. Would you like to _____?

B. { Yes. I'd love to.
{ I'm sorry. I can't. I have to _____.

38a

Look at the invitations and answer the questions.

IT'S A SURPRISE!

Shhh! "Keep it under your hat!"

Please join us as we celebrate
Mark Lane's 30th Birthday!

Sunday, March 5th
at Jeffrey Wagner's house
725 Garfield Street, Silverton

Be there at 6 P.M. Don't be late!

There will be hot dogs, hamburgers, and beverages for all.
Please bring an appetizer, a side dish, or dessert.

RSVP before March 1st
by e-mail only
jwagner@worldmail.com

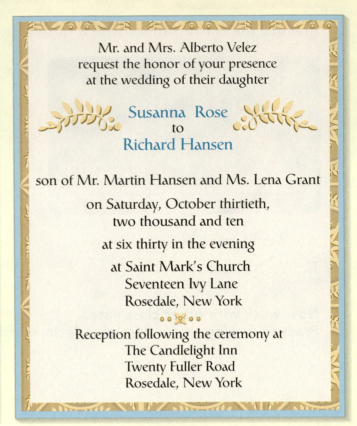

Mr. and Mrs. Alberto Velez
request the honor of your presence
at the wedding of their daughter

Susanna Rose
to
Richard Hansen

son of Mr. Martin Hansen and Ms. Lena Grant

on Saturday, October thirtieth,
two thousand and ten

at six thirty in the evening

at Saint Mark's Church
Seventeen Ivy Lane
Rosedale, New York

Reception following the ceremony at
The Candlelight Inn
Twenty Fuller Road
Rosedale, New York

1. The birthday invitation is from _____.
   A. Mr. and Mrs. Velez
   B. Jeffrey Wagner
   C. Mark Lane

2. Guests can bring _____ to the birthday party.
   A. hot dogs or hamburgers
   B. cookies or ice cream
   C. juice or soda

3. You need to answer the birthday invitation _____.
   A. before 6 o'clock
   B. after March fifth
   C. by e-mail

4. "Keep it under your hat" means _____.
   A. don't tell Mark Lane about the party
   B. wear a hat to the birthday party
   C. put the birthday invitation in a hat

5. The wedding ceremony is _____.
   A. at the Candlelight Inn
   B. at Saint Mark's Church
   C. on Saturday, October 13, 2010

6. _____ are getting married.
   A. Mr. and Mrs. Alberto Velez
   B. Mr. Martin Hansen and Ms. Lena Grant
   C. Susanna Rose Velez and Richard Hansen

7. The reception is _____.
   A. at six thirty in the evening
   B. after the wedding ceremony
   C. at 17 Ivy Lane

8. "Mr. and Mrs. Velez request the honor of your presence" means _____.
   A. Mr. and Mrs. Velez invite you to come
   B. please reply to this invitation
   C. Mr. and Mrs. Velez thank you for your gifts

WRITING Your Invitation You're inviting the students in your class to a party. What kind of party are you having? When is the party? Where is it going to be? Make an invitation.

Dinner Invitations Around the World

Some friends invited you to their home for dinner. When should you arrive? How much should you eat? When should you leave? The answers to these questions depend on the country you're in. Different countries have different rules and traditions.

In the United States, punctuality (being on time) is very important. When people invite you to their home for dinner, they usually give an exact time, for example, "We're having dinner at 6:30." You should plan to arrive on time or just a little late. If you're going to be more than fifteen minutes late, you need to call. Punctuality is also important in Sweden, Norway, and other Scandinavian countries. However, in countries in South America and in Italy and Spain, a guest can arrive half an hour late for a dinner invitation. In most countries, it isn't a good idea to arrive early in case the hosts who are making the dinner aren't ready for their guests.

Food is a very important part of any invitation to someone's home in the countries of the Middle East.

When someone offers you something to eat or drink, it's impolite to say "no". But you don't have to finish everything. In fact, when your plate is empty, your host will serve you more right away. So when you're full, stop eating and leave something on your plate. This is very different from France, Austria, and Japan, where it's important to finish everything on your plate to show your host that you liked the food. In Italy and Turkey, you don't have to finish everything, but if you do and you're still hungry, it's polite to ask for more.

It's important to know when to arrive for dinner, but it's also important to know when to leave! In India, Europe, and North America, it's very impolite to leave right after you eat. You don't want your hosts to think that you came to their home only for the food. On the other hand, in some Asian and Central American countries, it's polite to leave right after dessert. If you stay, the hosts might think you're still hungry and there wasn't enough food.

---

1. It's important to be on time in ____.
   A. Italy
   B. Spain
   C. Norway
   D. Brazil

2. It's polite to leave right after dinner in some countries in ____.
   A. Europe
   B. North America
   C. Scandinavia
   D. Central America

3. When dinner is at 7:30 P.M. in the United States, it's polite to arrive ____.
   A. more than fifteen minutes late
   B. at 7:40 P.M.
   C. at 7:50 P.M.
   D. at 7:15 P.M.

4. ____ is a Scandinavian country.
   A. India
   B. The United States
   C. Sweden
   D. Austria

5. Finish everything on your plate in ____, or your host will think you don't like the food.
   A. Austria
   B. Italy
   C. Turkey
   D. the Middle East

6. According to this article, in the Middle East, it's important to ____.
   A. be on time
   B. leave right after dinner
   C. eat everything on your plate
   D. say "yes" when someone offers food

Reading Tip

Signal words can help you understand the information in a reading. In this article, the author uses the words *however*, *but*, and *on the other hand* to show differences between information before these words and after them. Find these words in the reading. What differences do they help to show?

38c

Choose the correct answer.

1. The ____ will arrive in fifteen minutes.
   A. game
   B. train
   C. vacation
   D. measles

2. Remember to put on your ____.
   A. warning
   B. floor
   C. helmet
   D. feet

3. We're going on vacation. We'll be back ____.
   A. in a few minutes
   B. this afternoon
   C. in half an hour
   D. in a week

4. Don't touch that wire! You might ____.
   A. get a shock
   B. see your doctor
   C. get seasick
   D. drown

5. I'm going to call the doctor. I think my son might ____.
   A. bloom
   B. be sick and tired of the weather
   C. have the flu
   D. be famous

6. Watch your step! You might ____.
   A. fall asleep
   B. fall
   C. catch a cold
   D. get sick

7. ____ I can't have dinner with you tomorrow.
   A. I have to.
   B. I'd love to.
   C. I'm sorry.
   D. Yes. Thanks.

8. I received ____ to a wedding.
   A. an invitation
   B. a ceremony
   C. a reception
   D. a surprise

9. My friends ____ me to their home for dinner.
   A. arrived
   B. wanted
   C. returned
   D. invited

10. Dinner is almost ready. Will our guests ____ soon?
    A. get home
    B. be here
    C. get out
    D. end

SKILLS CHECK ✓

Words:
- □ arrive
- □ be back
- □ begin
- □ end
- □ get home
- □ return
- □ break *my* leg
- □ catch a cold
- □ fall
- □ get a shock
- □ get a sunburn
- □ get hit
- □ get hurt
- □ get seasick
- □ get sick
- □ hurt *your* head/eyes
- □ the flu
- □ the measles
- □ celebrate
- □ get married
- □ grow up
- □ move
- □ name (v)
- □ ceremony
- □ reception
- □ RSVP

I can ask & answer:
- □ Will I/we/you/they/he/she/it *be back soon*?
- □ Do you think I/we/you/they/he/she/it will *be back soon*?

I can ask for repetition:
- □ I'm sorry. What did you say?
- □ I'm sorry. Could you please repeat that?
- □ I'm sorry. Could you say that again?

I can make, accept, & decline an offer:
- □ Would you like *some french fries*?
   Yes. Thanks.
   No, thank you.

I can make, accept, & decline an invitation:
- □ Would you like to *go out for lunch*?
   Yes. I'd love to.
   I'm sorry. I can't. I have to *work*.

I can write:
- □ a note to a teacher to explain a child's absence from school
- □ a story about my future
- □ an invitation to a party

5

Comparatives
Should
Possessive Pronouns

- Making Comparisons
- Advice
- Expressing Opinions
- Agreement and Disagreement
- Shopping
- Advertisements
- Reading Skill: Inference Questions
- Civics: Letters to the Editor

VOCABULARY PREVIEW

1. cute
2. delicious
3. exciting
4. fashionable
5. friendly
6. hospitable
7. hot / spicy
8. intelligent / smart
9. lazy
10. light
11. polite
12. powerful
13. soft
14. talented
15. talkative

My New Bicycle Is Faster

soft – softer small – smaller	large – larger safe – safer	big – bigger hot – hotter	fancy – fancier pretty – prettier

A. I think you'll like my new bicycle.

B. But I liked your OLD bicycle. It was **fast**.

A. That's right. But my new bicycle is **faster**.

1. *rug*
   soft

2. *tennis racket*
   light

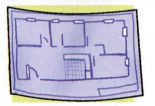

3. *apartment*
   large

4. *neighborhood*
   safe

5. *office*
   big

6. *recipe for chili*
   hot

7. *dog*
   friendly

8. *sports car*
   fancy

9. *dishwasher*
   quiet

10. *wig*
    pretty

11. *cell phone*
    small

12. *cat*
    cute

My New Rocking Chair Is More Comfortable

fast – faster nice – nicer big – bigger pretty – prettier	comfortable – more comfortable beautiful – more beautiful interesting – more interesting intelligent – more intelligent

A. I think you'll like my new rocking chair.

B. But I liked your OLD rocking chair. It was **comfortable**.

A. That's right. But my new rocking chair is **more comfortable**.

1. *apartment building*
   beautiful

2. *roommate*
   interesting

3. *girlfriend*
   intelligent

4. *boyfriend*
   handsome

5. *briefcase*
   attractive

6. *computer*
   powerful

7. *printer*
   fast

8. *English teacher*
   smart

9. *recipe for meatloaf*
   delicious

10. *boss*
    nice

11. *parrot*
    talkative

12.

Bicycles Are Safer Than Motorcycles

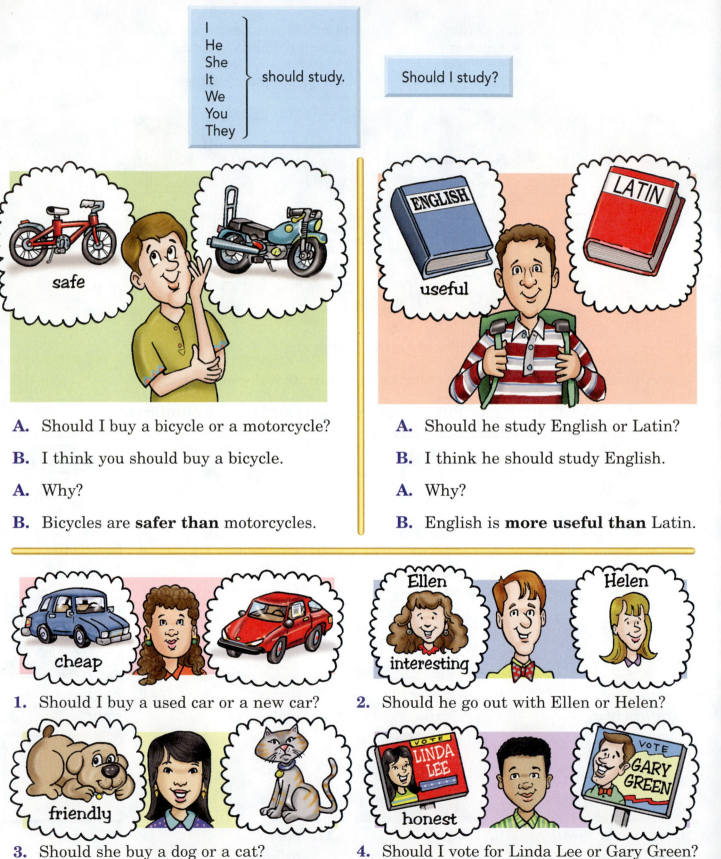

I
He
She
It
We
You
They

should study.

Should I study?

safe

A. Should I buy a bicycle or a motorcycle?

B. I think you should buy a bicycle.

A. Why?

B. Bicycles are **safer than** motorcycles.

useful

A. Should he study English or Latin?

B. I think he should study English.

A. Why?

B. English is **more useful than** Latin.

cheap

1. Should I buy a used car or a new car?

Ellen
interesting
Helen

2. Should he go out with Ellen or Helen?

friendly

3. Should she buy a dog or a cat?

honest

4. Should I vote for Linda Lee or Gary Green?

5. Should she take a course with Professor Blake or Professor Drake?

6. Should they plant flowers or vegetables this spring?

7. Should we buy this fan or that fan?

8. Should she buy these earrings or those earrings?

9. Should he take piano lessons with Mrs. Clark or Miss Smith?

10. Should I buy the hat in my left hand or the hat in my right hand?

11. Should she buy fur gloves or leather gloves?

12. Should I buy a notebook computer or a desktop computer?

13. Should I hire Ms. Parker or Ms. Jones?

14. Should I fire Mr. Mason or Mr. Grimes?

15. Should we rent this movie or that movie?

16.

READING

IT ISN'T EASY BEING A TEENAGER

I try to be a good son, but no matter how hard I try, my parents never seem to be satisfied. They think I should be a better* son. They think I should eat healthier food, I should wear nicer clothes, and I should get better grades. And according to them, my hair should be shorter, my room should be neater, and my friends should be more polite when they come to visit.

You know . . . it isn't easy being a teenager.

IT ISN'T EASY BEING PARENTS

We try to be good parents, but no matter how hard we try, our children never seem to be satisfied. They think we should be better parents. They think we should wear more fashionable clothes, we should drive a newer car, and we should listen to more interesting music. And according to them, we should be more sympathetic when they talk about their problems, we should be friendlier when their friends come to visit, and we should be more understanding when they come home late on Saturday night.

You know . . . it isn't easy being parents.

*good – better

✔ READING *CHECK-UP*

WHAT'S THE WORD?

According to this boy's parents, he doesn't eat <u>healthy</u>¹ food, he doesn't wear _____² clothes, he doesn't get _____³ grades, his hair isn't _____⁴, and his friends aren't _____⁵ when they come to visit.

According to their children, these parents don't wear _____⁶ clothes, they don't have a _____⁷ car, they don't listen to _____⁸ music, and they aren't _____⁹ when their children's friends come to visit.

LISTENING

Listen and choose what the people are talking about.

1. a. TV b. printer
2. a. chair b. recipe
3. a. hair b. apartment
4. a. offices b. friends
5. a. neighborhood b. briefcase
6. a. rug b. computer

Don't Be Ridiculous!

my – mine	our – ours
his – his	your – yours
her – hers	their – theirs

A. You know, my dog isn't as friendly as your dog.

B. Don't be ridiculous! Yours is MUCH friendlier than **mine**.

A. You know, my novels aren't as interesting as Ernest Hemingway's novels.

B. Don't be ridiculous! Yours are MUCH more interesting than **his**.

clean

1. *my apartment*
   your apartment

powerful

2. *my computer*
   Bob's computer

nice

3. *my boss*
   your boss

comfortable

4. *my furniture*
   your furniture

big

5. *my house*
   the Jacksons' house

She sells sea shells...
good

6. *my pronunciation*
   Maria's pronunciation

pretty

7. *my garden*
   your garden

FRUITCAKE
delicious

8. *my recipe for fruitcake*
   Stanley's recipe for fruitcake

9.

BROWNSVILLE

The Taylor family lived in Brownsville for many years. And for many years, Brownsville was a very good place to live. The streets were clean, the parks were safe, the bus system was reliable, and the schools were good.

But Brownsville changed. Today the streets aren't as clean as they used to be. The parks aren't as safe as they used to be. The bus system isn't as reliable as it used to be. And the schools aren't as good as they used to be.

Because of the changes in Brownsville, the Taylor family moved to Newport last year. In Newport the streets are cleaner, the parks are safer, the bus system is more reliable, and the schools are better. The Taylors are happy in Newport, but they were happier in Brownsville. Although Newport has cleaner streets, safer parks, a more reliable bus system, and better schools, Brownsville has friendlier people. They're nicer, more polite, and more hospitable than the people in Newport.

The Taylors miss Brownsville. Even though they're now living in Newport, Brownsville will always be their real home.

✔ READING *CHECK-UP*

Q & A

The people of Brownsville are calling Mayor Brown's radio talk show. They're upset about Brownsville's streets, parks, bus system, and schools. Using this model and the story, call Mayor Brown.

A. This is Mayor Brown. You're on the air.
B. Mayor Brown, I'm very upset about the *streets* here in Brownsville.
A. Why do you say that?
B. *They aren't* as *clean* as *they* used to be.
A. Do you really think so?
B. Definitely! You know . . . they say the *streets* in Newport *are cleaner*.
A. I'll see what I can do. Thank you for calling.

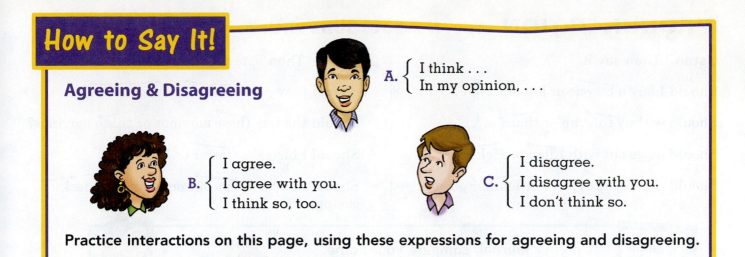

How to Say It!

Agreeing & Disagreeing

A. { I think . . .
     In my opinion, . . .

B. { I agree.
     I agree with you.
     I think so, too.

C. { I disagree.
     I disagree with you.
     I don't think so.

Practice interactions on this page, using these expressions for agreeing and disagreeing.

INTERACTIONS

_____er
more _____ } than

as _____ as
not as _____ as

I think New York is more interesting than Los Angeles.

I disagree. I think Los Angeles is MUCH more interesting than New York.

In my opinion, the weather in Honolulu is better than the weather in Miami.

I don't think so. I think the weather in Miami is better than the weather in Honolulu.

In my opinion, the people in Centerville aren't as friendly as the people in Greenville.

I agree. But the people in Centerville are more interesting.

I think so, too.

Practice conversations with other students. Compare different places you know. Talk about . . .

the streets (*quiet, safe, clean, wide, busy*)
the buildings (*tall, modern, attractive*)
the weather (*cold, cool, warm, hot, rainy, snowy*)
the people (*friendly, nice, polite, honest, happy, hospitable, talkative, healthy*)
the city in general (*large, interesting, exciting, expensive*)

47

Listen. Then say it.

Should I buy a bicycle or a motorcycle?

Should we buy this fan or that fan?

Should he go out with Ellen or Helen?

Should she buy fur gloves or leather gloves?

Say it. Then listen.

Should they plant flowers or vegetables?

Should she buy these earrings or those earrings?

Should I hire Ms. Carter or Mr. Price?

Should I buy a notebook computer or a desktop computer?

SIDE by SIDE JOURNAL

In your journal, compare your home town and the place you live now. Or compare any two places you know.

GRAMMAR FOCUS

COMPARATIVES

My new car is	faster larger bigger prettier	than my old car.
	more comfortable more attractive	

SHOULD

Should	I he she it we you they	study?

I He She It We You They	should study.

POSSESSIVE PRONOUNS

This dog is nicer than	mine. his. hers. ours. yours. theirs.

Complete the sentences.

1. A. Is your new computer fast?
   B. Yes. It's _____ than my old computer.

2. A. Is Jane's new neighborhood safe?
   B. Yes. It's _____ than her old neighborhood.

3. A. Is Livingston an interesting city?
   B. Yes. I think it's _____ than Centerville.

4. A. Is your new office big?
   B. Yes. It's _____ than my old office.

5. A. Is your new sofa comfortable?
   B. Yes. It's _____ than our old sofa.

6. A. Should my grandparents get a dog or a cat?
   B. They _____ get a dog. Dogs are very friendly. I think they're _____ than cats.

7. A. Should I order the chicken or the fish?
   B. I think you _____ order the fish. It's really good. It's _____ than the chicken.

Match the sentences.

____ 1. Is this your hat or your son's hat?   a. It isn't yours. It's mine.
____ 2. Is this your pen or your wife's pen?   b. It isn't hers. It's his.
____ 3. Is this my jacket or your jacket?   c. It isn't mine. It's hers.
____ 4. Is this your cat or your neighbors' cat?   d. It isn't mine. It's his.
____ 5. Is this Lucy's key or her brother's key?   e. It isn't ours. It's theirs.

1 CONVERSATION — ASKING FOR ADVICE WHEN SHOPPING

Practice conversations with a classmate. Use the comparative form of any word in the box below to compare the items.

A. Which refrigerator do you recommend—this one or that one?

B. I recommend this one. It's larger than that one.

cheap	energy-efficient	large	quiet
comfortable	fast	new	reliable
easy-to-use	good	powerful	small

1. dishwasher
2. computer
3. mattress
4. printer

5. cell phone
6. air conditioner
7. DVD player
8.

2 COMMUNITY CONNECTIONS — STORES

Go to a department store or a discount store. Compare two different types of the same item. Which one do you recommend? Why is it better? Do this for five products. Write the information and share it with the class.

3 TEAMWORK — ADVERTISEMENTS

Cut out some newspaper ads for the items on this page and other items. Bring the ads to class and work with a classmate. Compare two different types of each item. Which one is better? Why? Share your ads and opinions with the class.

Look at the advertisements. Choose the correct answer.

The 2011 Traveler
Larger, More Comfortable, & More Powerful than Last Year's Traveler!

- 7 inches longer — with two extra seats in the back.
- 1.5 inches higher means more headroom for taller drivers.
- 2 inches wider for more comfortable seating.
- New 330 horsepower engine — 50 pounds lighter and 10% more powerful than last year's engine.

From $30,000

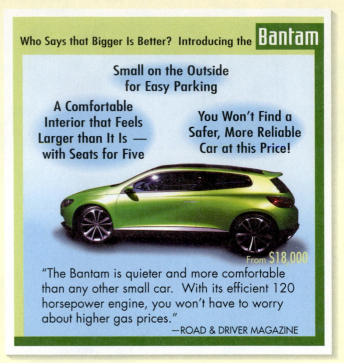

Who Says that Bigger Is Better? Introducing the **Bantam**

Small on the Outside for Easy Parking

A Comfortable Interior that Feels Larger than It Is — with Seats for Five

You Won't Find a Safer, More Reliable Car at this Price!

From $18,000

"The Bantam is quieter and more comfortable than any other small car. With its efficient 120 horsepower engine, you won't have to worry about higher gas prices."
—ROAD & DRIVER MAGAZINE

1. There are ____ more seats in the 2011 Traveler than in the 2010 Traveler.
   A. two
   B. three
   C. four
   D. five

2. The 2011 Traveler has more headroom because it is ____.
   A. more powerful
   B. longer
   C. wider
   D. higher

3. The 2011 Traveler is ____ than the 2010 Traveler.
   A. one and a half inches longer
   B. two inches wider
   C. ten percent larger
   D. seven inches higher

4. According to the ad, the engine in the 2010 Traveler ____.
   A. was lighter than this year's engine
   B. wasn't as heavy as this year's engine
   C. wasn't as powerful as this year's engine
   D. wasn't as quiet as this year's engine

5. According to the second ad, ____.
   A. bigger is better
   B. the Bantam is difficult to park
   C. five people can ride in the Bantam
   D. the Bantam is safer and more reliable than any car at any price

6. According to *Road & Driver*, the Bantam ____.
   A. isn't as noisy as other small cars
   B. is more reliable than other small cars
   C. is higher than other small cars
   D. is more expensive than other small cars

7. The Bantam is probably a good car for people ____.
   A. who read magazines
   B. who drive in the city
   C. with very large families
   D. with a lot of money

8. In the second ad, *efficient* means ____.
   A. the engine is quiet
   B. the engine is powerful
   C. the engine is light
   D. the engine doesn't use much gas

Reading Tip

One of these questions is an **inference question**. The answer isn't a fact in the reading. You have to think about the information and decide what the best answer is. Which question on this page is an inference question? Which word in the question tells you that this is an inference question?

Read the letters to the editor and answer the questions.

To the Editor:

Students at Clarksdale High School took tests in English, math, history, and science last month, and their test scores were lower than ever before. As a high school parent, I can tell you why.

Classes at Clarksdale High are much larger than they should be, with more than forty students in a class. Teachers are using textbooks that are more than ten years old. There isn't any money for newer books. Finally, many good teachers are leaving Clarksdale to teach at other schools for higher pay.

It's time to spend more money on our high school. We might have to pay higher taxes, but our children are our future.

Marion Kane

To the Editor:

I'm writing in response to the article by James Alan Perry, *Clarksdale: A Better City for All*. In my opinion, after three years with Mayor Burns, Clarksdale is better for rich people, but not for the poor.

It's true that in the more expensive neighborhoods, the buses are newer and more reliable and the parks and streets are cleaner and safer. However, in the poorer sections of town, like East Clarksdale, the buses are never on time, and the streets and parks are dirtier and aren't as safe. Why aren't there more police officers in East Clarksdale? Why aren't the buses there as reliable as they are in other parts of town?

Ming Lee

To the Editor:

I grew up in Clarksdale and moved away ten years ago. Last month, I finally returned to visit and was very happy to see all the wonderful changes.

Clarksdale is a much more interesting town today than it was when I lived there. Main Street, with its attractive new restaurants, hotel, and movie theater, is a much more exciting place. I was also glad to see that there's a new bookstore downtown and that the library is in a bigger and more modern building.

Clarksdale isn't as quiet as it used to be, but that's okay with me. It's a more beautiful town with a lot more things to do.

Helen Sanders

1. According to Marion Kane, textbooks at the high school should be _____.
   A. bigger
   B. longer
   C. more difficult
   D. newer

2. According to Marion Kane, good teachers are leaving the high school because _____.
   A. their students' test scores are low
   B. they don't want to pay higher taxes
   C. they want more money for the work they do
   D. classes have more than 50 students

3. According to Ming Lee, East Clarksdale _____.
   A. has cleaner parks than other parts of town
   B. isn't as safe as other parts of town
   C. has newer buses than other parts of town
   D. has more police officers than other parts of town

4. According to Ming Lee, the buses in the more expensive neighborhoods of Clarksdale _____.
   A. are never on time
   B. aren't as reliable as they used to be
   C. are more reliable than they used to be
   D. aren't as reliable as the buses in East Clarksdale

5. Helen Sanders thinks Clarksdale _____ it used to be.
   A. isn't as beautiful as
   B. is noisier than
   C. isn't as interesting as
   D. isn't as attractive as

6. We can infer that Helen Sanders _____.
   A. likes to read
   B. lives near Clarksdale
   C. is a quiet person
   D. moved away to get a better job

WRITING Your Letter to the Editor Write a letter to the editor. Give your opinion about something you like or don't like about your city or town.

Choose the correct answer.

1. Our new living room furniture is very _____.
   A. intelligent
   B. comfortable
   C. honest
   D. friendly

2. It's important to eat _____ food.
   A. bad
   B. sympathetic
   C. large
   D. healthy

3. The subway system in our city is very _____.
   A. polite
   B. talkative
   C. reliable
   D. understanding

4. You shouldn't buy that coat. It isn't very _____.
   A. attractive
   B. spicy
   C. short
   D. neat

5. I think we should hire Ramon. He'll be a _____ secretary.
   A. lazy
   B. capable
   C. light
   D. wide

6. I like this watch. It's _____ than that one.
   A. busier
   B. more talented
   C. cheaper
   D. more hospitable

7. It's easy to park our new car because it's _____.
   A. large
   B. convenient
   C. comfortable
   D. small

8. My new car is faster than my old car. It has a _____ engine.
   A. more powerful
   B. wider
   C. higher
   D. longer

9. We're upset because students' test scores were _____ this year than last year.
   A. higher
   B. lower
   C. more difficult
   D. better

10. We need more police officers so our city will be _____.
    A. more sympathetic
    B. more useful
    C. safer
    D. newer

SKILLS CHECK ✔

Words:

☐ attractive	☐ dirty	☐ happy	☐ neat	☐ small
☐ beautiful	☐ easy	☐ healthy	☐ new	☐ smart
☐ big	☐ easy-to-use	☐ high	☐ nice	☐ snowy
☐ busy	☐ efficient	☐ honest	☐ polite	☐ soft
☐ capable	☐ energy-efficient	☐ hospitable	☐ poor	☐ spicy
☐ cheap	☐ exciting	☐ hot	☐ powerful	☐ sympathetic
☐ clean	☐ expensive	☐ intelligent	☐ pretty	☐ talented
☐ cold	☐ fancy	☐ interesting	☐ quiet	☐ talkative
☐ comfortable	☐ fashionable	☐ large	☐ rainy	☐ tall
☐ convenient	☐ fast	☐ lazy	☐ reliable	☐ understanding
☐ cool	☐ friendly	☐ light	☐ rich	☐ useful
☐ cute	☐ good – better	☐ long	☐ safe	☐ warm
☐ delicious	☐ handsome	☐ modern	☐ short	☐ wide

I can ask for advice:
☐ Should I *buy a dog or a cat*?
☐ Which *computer* do you recommend?

I can express my opinion:
☐ I think . . ./In my opinion, . . .
☐ I agree./I agree with you.
☐ I disagree./I disagree with you.

I can:
☐ compare items in a store
☐ compare items in advertisements

I can write:
☐ a comparison of places I know
☐ a letter to the editor

Superlatives

- **Describing People, Places, and Things**
- **Shopping in a Department Store**
- **Expressing Opinions**

- **Store Directories**
- **Returning and Exchanging Items**
- **Using an ATM**
- **Checks**
- **Store Return Policies**

VOCABULARY PREVIEW

1. energetic
2. funny
3. generous
4. helpful
5. honest

6. lazy
7. mean
8. nice
9. noisy
10. obnoxious

11. patient
12. popular
13. rude
14. sloppy
15. stubborn

The Smartest Person I Know

smart – the smartest kind – the kindest	nice – the nicest safe – the safest
funny – the funniest pretty – the prettiest	big – the biggest hot – the hottest

A. I think your friend Margaret is very **smart**.

B. She certainly is. She's **the smartest** person I know.

1. *your Aunt Emma*
kind

2. *your friend Jim*
bright

3. *your parents*
nice

4. *your Uncle Ted*
funny

5. *your sister*
pretty

6. *your cousin Amy*
friendly

7. *Larry*
lazy

8. *your landlord*
mean

9. *your roommates*
sloppy

The Most Energetic Person I Know

smart – the smartest funny – the funniest nice – the nicest big – the biggest	energetic – the most energetic interesting – the most interesting patient – the most patient stubborn – the most stubborn

A. I think your grandmother is very **energetic**.

B. She certainly is. She's **the most energetic** person I know.

1. *your friend Carlos*
interesting

2. *your grandfather*
generous

3. *your cousins*
talented

4. *our English teacher*
patient

5. *your nephew Andrew*
stubborn

6. *your younger brother*
polite

7. *your older sister*
bright

8. *your upstairs neighbor*
noisy

9. *your downstairs neighbor*
rude

10. *Senator Smith*
honest

11. *our history professor*
boring

12.

THE NICEST PERSON

friendly | polite | smart | talented | pretty

Mr. and Mrs. Jackson are very proud of their daughter, Linda. She's a very nice person. She's friendly, she's polite, she's smart, and she's talented. She's also very pretty.

Mr. and Mrs. Jackson's friends and neighbors always compliment them about Linda. They say she's the nicest person they know. According to them, she's the friendliest, the most polite, the smartest, and the most talented girl in the neighborhood. They also think she's the prettiest.

Mr. and Mrs. Jackson agree. They think Linda is a wonderful girl, and they're proud to say she's their daughter.

THE MOST OBNOXIOUS DOG

noisy | stubborn | lazy | mean | ugly

Mr. and Mrs. Hubbard are very embarrassed by their dog, Rex. He's a very obnoxious dog. He's noisy, he's stubborn, he's lazy, and he's mean. He's also very ugly.

Mr. and Mrs. Hubbard's friends and neighbors always complain about Rex. They say he's the most obnoxious dog they know. According to them, he's the noisiest, the most stubborn, the laziest, and the meanest dog in the neighborhood. They also think he's the ugliest.

Mr. and Mrs. Hubbard agree. They think Rex is a horrible dog, and they're ashamed to say he's theirs.

✔ READING CHECK-UP

CHOOSE

1. Linda is the (most polite   smart) person I know.
2. She's the most (talented   friendliest) girl in the neighborhood.
3. She's a very (nicest   nice) person.
4. Rex is the most (stubborn   mean) dog in the neighborhood.
5. He's the (lazy   noisiest) dog I know.
6. He's also the most (ugliest   obnoxious) dog in town.

Q & A

The neighbors are talking. Using these models, create dialogs based on the stories.

A. You know . . . I think Linda is very *nice*.
B. I agree. She's the *nicest* girl in the neighborhood.

A. You know . . . I think Rex is very *obnoxious*.
B. You're right. He's the *most obnoxious* dog in the neighborhood.

How About You?

Tell about the nicest person you know.

How to Say It!

Expressing an Opinion

A. ⎰ In my opinion, . . .
  ⎱ As far as I'm concerned, . . .   *Linda is the most talented*
  ⎱ If you ask me, . . .   *student in our school.*
B. I agree. / I disagree.

Practice conversations with other students. Share opinions.

LISTENING

Listen to the sentence. Is the person saying something good or something bad about someone else?

1. a. good   b. bad
2. a. good   b. bad
3. a. good   b. bad
4. a. good   b. bad
5. a. good   b. bad
6. a. good   b. bad
7. a. good   b. bad
8. a. good   b. bad
9. a. good   b. bad

PRONUNCIATION   *Linking Words with Duplicated Consonants*

Listen. Then say it.

She's the nicest teacher in our school.

He's the most stubborn neighbor on our street.

They're the most talented dancers in the world.

Say it. Then listen.

He's the most generous student in our class.

This is the cheapest toothpaste in the store.

He's the most polite taxi driver in the city.

I Want to Buy a Small Radio

a small radio
a smaller radio
the smallest radio

a comfortable chair
a more comfortable chair
the most comfortable chair

a good car
a better car
the best car

A. May I help you?

B. Yes, please. I want to buy a **small** radio.

A. I think you'll like this one. It's VERY **small**.

B. Don't you have a **smaller** one?

A. No, I'm afraid not. This is **the smallest** one we have.

B. Thank you anyway.

A. Sorry we can't help you. Please come again.

1. *large TV*

2. *comfortable rocking chair*

3. *good CD player*

4. *cheap watch*

5. *fast printer*

6. *elegant evening gown*

7. *small cell phone*

8. *lightweight video camera*

9. *powerful computer*

10. *tall bookcase*

11. *short novel*

12.

BOB'S BARGAIN DEPARTMENT STORE

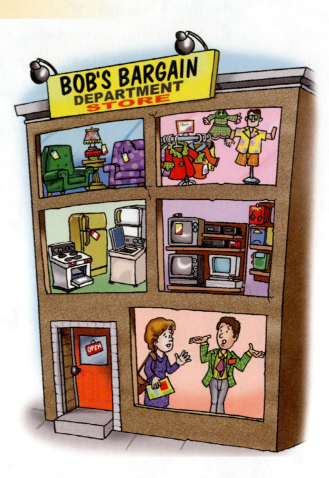

Bob's Bargain Department Store is the cheapest store in town. However, even though it's the cheapest, it isn't the most popular. People don't shop there very often because the products are bad.* In fact, some people say the products there are the worst in town.

The furniture isn't very comfortable, the clothes aren't very fashionable, the appliances aren't very dependable, and the home entertainment products aren't very good. Besides that, the location isn't very convenient, and the salespeople aren't very helpful.

That's why people don't shop at Bob's Bargain Department Store very often, even though it's the cheapest store in town.

THE LORD AND LADY DEPARTMENT STORE

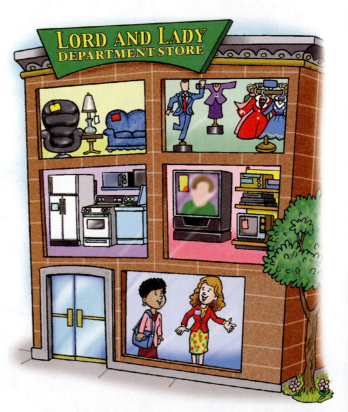

The Lord and Lady Department Store sells very good products. In fact, some people say the products there are the best in town.

They sell the most comfortable furniture, the most fashionable clothes, the most dependable appliances, and the best home entertainment products. And besides that, their location is the most convenient, and their salespeople are the most helpful in town.

However, even though the Lord and Lady Department Store is the best store in town, people don't shop there very often because it's also the most expensive.

* bad – worse – worst

THE SUPER SAVER DEPARTMENT STORE

The Super Saver Department Store is the most popular store in town. It isn't the cheapest, and it isn't the most expensive. It doesn't have the best products, and it doesn't have the worst.

The furniture isn't the most comfortable you can buy, but it's more comfortable than the furniture at many other stores. The clothes aren't the most fashionable you can buy, but they're more fashionable than the clothes at many other stores. The appliances aren't the most dependable you can buy, but they're more dependable than the appliances at many other stores. The home entertainment products aren't the best you can buy, but they're better than the home entertainment products at many other stores. In addition, the location is convenient, and the salespeople are helpful.

You can see why the Super Saver Department Store is the most popular store in town. The prices are reasonable, and the products are good. That's why people like to shop there.

✔ READING *CHECK-UP*

TRUE OR FALSE?

1. Bob's Bargain Department Store is the most popular store in town.
2. The salespeople at Lord and Lady are more helpful than the salespeople at Super Saver.
3. The location of Lord and Lady isn't as convenient as the location of Bob's.
4. The Super Saver Department Store has the best prices in town.
5. The home entertainment products at Super Saver are better than the home entertainment products at Bob's.
6. People in this town say the cheapest department store is the best.

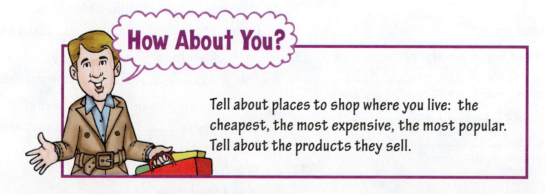

How About You?

Tell about places to shop where you live: the cheapest, the most expensive, the most popular. Tell about the products they sell.

Practice conversations with other students. Share opinions, and give reasons for your opinions.

In your opinion, . . .

1. Who is the most popular actor/actress in your country? Who is the most popular TV star? the best singer?

2. What is the most popular car in your country? the most popular sport? the best newspaper? the most popular magazine? the best TV program? the most popular food?

3. What is the best city in your country? What is the worst city? Why? What are the most interesting tourist sights in your country? What are the most popular vacation places?

4. Who is the most important person in your country now? Why? Who was the most important person in the history of your country? Why?

SIDE by **SIDE** **JOURNAL**

Who is the most important person in your life? Why? Write about this person in your journal.

GRAMMAR FOCUS

SUPERLATIVES

He's	the smartest the nicest the biggest the busiest	person I know.
	the most talented the most interesting	

Complete the sentences.

1. A. I'm looking for a fast computer.
   B. This is _____ computer we sell.

2. A. Your sister Susan is very intelligent.
   B. I agree. She's _____ person I know.

3. A. I'm looking for a big refrigerator.
   B. This is _____ refrigerator in the store.

4. A. Our cousins are very nice.
   B. I agree. They're _____ people in our family.

5. A. Is this camera lightweight?
   B. Yes. It's _____ camera you can find.

6. A. Our history teacher is very interesting.
   B. I agree. I think he's _____ teacher in the school.

7. A. This dress is very fashionable.
   B. I think it's _____ dress in the store.

8. A. I'm looking for a good DVD player.
   B. This is _____ one we sell.

9. A. Are your upstairs neighbors friendly?
   B. Yes. They're _____ people in our building.

10. A. Are the products at that store bad?
    B. Yes. I think they're _____ products in town.

1 CONVERSATION   LOCATING ITEMS IN A DEPARTMENT STORE

STORE DIRECTORY

DEPARTMENT	FLOOR
Children's Clothing	1
Women's Clothing	
Men's Clothing	2
Electronics	3
Housewares	
Furniture	4
Household Appliances	

Practice conversations with a classmate. Use the directory to find the correct department and floor for these items and others.

A. Excuse me. Where can I find refrigerators?

B. In the Household Appliances department on the fourth floor.

A. Thank you.

1.   2.   3.   4.   5.

2 CONVERSATION   RETURNING & EXCHANGING ITEMS

Practice conversations with a classmate.

A. I'd like to return this/these _____.

B. What's the matter with it/them?

A. It's/They're too _____.

B. Would you like to exchange it/them?

A. No, thank you. I'd like a refund, please.

B. Do you have your receipt?

A. Yes. Here it is.

1. sweater   2. jeans   3. pants   4. dress   5.
   tight   large   long   short

3 TEAMWORK   CATEGORIZING

Bring department store ads to class. Work with a classmate. On a piece of paper, write the names of the store departments on this page. Then list items in your ads in the correct department.

USING AN ATM

Look at the ATM screens and answer the questions.

1. *Insert your card* means _____.
   A. take your card
   B. put your card in the machine
   C. use your card
   D. return your card

2. Your PIN is your _____.
   A. social security number
   B. bank account number
   C. telephone number
   D. personal identification number

3. After you enter your PIN, you
   _____.
   A. enter the bank
   B. insert your ATM card
   C. select a transaction
   D. deposit money

4. To put $100 in your checking account, select _____.
   A. Deposit
   B. Balance Inquiry
   C. Fast Cash
   D. Withdrawal

5. To find out how much money is in your account, select _____.
   A. Transfers
   B. Balance Inquiry
   C. Deposit with Cash Back
   D. Withdrawal

6. To move money from one account to another, select _____.
   A. Fast Cash
   B. Balance Inquiry
   C. Transfers
   D. Deposit with Cash Back

READING CHECKS

Look at the check. Decide if the following sentences are True (T) or False (F).

| Mario Gomez | | 105 |
| Susan Gomez | Date _April 9, 2011_ | |

Pay to the order of _Northern Electric Company_ $ 56.34

Fifty-six and 34/100 ———————————— Dollars

Camden Savings Bank

For _electric bill 2/15-3/15 account #146056_   *Mario Gomez*

⑈311104017⑈:139057813⑏105⑈·

_____ 1. Northern Electric Company wrote this check on April 9, 2011.

_____ 2. The check is for fifty-six dollars and thirty-four cents.

_____ 3. Mario Gomez is paying the electric bill.

_____ 4. The bill is for the month of April.

_____ 5. Susan Gomez can also write checks with this checking account.

_____ 6. 146056 is the checking account number.

Read this sign in a Customer Service Department and answer the questions.

Gray's
Department Store
Our Return Policy

- We are happy to accept returns on most items within 90 days of the date of purchase.
- Exceptions to our 90-day return policy:
  - We will accept returns within 45 days of the date of purchase on computers, monitors, printers, and other computer components.
  - We will accept returns within 30 days of the date of purchase on CDs, DVDs, and computer software **ONLY** if they are unopened.
  - We will **NOT** accept returns on holiday items after the date of the holiday.
  - We will **NOT** accept returns on underwear, swimsuits, or items marked *Final Sale*.
- When you return items with a receipt, you can exchange the item or receive a refund. Your refund depends on your method of payment:

Method of Payment	Refund
Cash or debit card	Cash refund
Check (within the last 10 days)	Store credit
Check (more than 10 days ago)	Cash refund
Credit card	Credit to your account
Store credit card or gift card	Store credit

- Without a receipt, you can exchange the item for the same item in a different size or color, or you can receive a store credit for the lowest sale price of that item within the last 90 days. You need to present a photo I.D. at the time of the return. Gray's Department Store does not have to accept your return when there is no receipt.
- You can return items at any Gray's Department Store in the United States or Canada. The original price tag should be attached to the item.
- You can return defective items—items that are broken, ripped, or unsafe—at any time with or without a receipt. We will exchange or repair the defective item.

1. You have to return a computer monitor _____.
   A. within 30 days
   B. within 45 days
   C. within 90 days
   D. to the store where you bought it

2. You can return _____ 89 days after you buy it.
   A. a jacket
   B. a CD
   C. a swimsuit
   D. a printer

3. You CANNOT return _____.
   A. defective items
   B. unopened DVDs
   C. items marked *Final Sale*
   D. items with a price tag attached

4. You can receive a cash refund when you pay with _____.
   A. a credit card
   B. a check that is five days old
   C. a gift card
   D. a check that is eleven days old

5. When you don't have a receipt, _____.
   A. you have to show a photo I.D.
   B. you can't return the item
   C. you might receive a cash refund
   D. you can't exchange the item

6. You can return _____.
   A. a CD that you bought 2 months ago
   B. a computer that doesn't work
   C. computer software in an opened box
   D. a Christmas tree on January tenth

Choose the correct answer.

1. Everybody compliments us about our son. They say he's the ____ boy in the neighborhood.
   A. worst
   B. laziest
   C. friendliest
   D. most boring

2. The new shopping mall is in a very ____ location.
   A. short
   B. convenient
   C. lightweight
   D. energetic

3. George is a wonderful salesperson. He's always ____.
   A. helpful
   B. noisy
   C. rude
   D. sloppy

4. Our store sells the most ____ appliances in the city.
   A. patient
   B. generous
   C. honest
   D. dependable

5. Nobody in our building likes the man in Apartment 5. He's very ____.
   A. popular
   B. nice
   C. mean
   D. kind

6. My niece always says, "Thank you" and "You're welcome." She's the most ____ little girl I know.
   A. stubborn
   B. polite
   C. horrible
   D. obnoxious

7. To use the ATM, insert your ____ and enter your PIN.
   A. key
   B. money
   C. account
   D. card

8. I'm going to ____ money from my savings account to my checking account.
   A. transfer
   B. balance
   C. use
   D. select

9. I need to return this video camera to the store because ____.
   A. it was marked *Final Sale*
   B. it has the original price tag
   C. it's defective
   D. I paid with a credit card

10. Excuse me. Can you help me? I'd like to ____ this sports jacket for a larger size.
    A. accept
    B. exchange
    C. attach
    D. receive

SKILLS CHECK ✓

Words:
- ☐ bad–worse–worst
- ☐ boring
- ☐ bright
- ☐ cheap
- ☐ comfortable
- ☐ convenient
- ☐ dependable
- ☐ elegant
- ☐ energetic
- ☐ fashionable
- ☐ fast
- ☐ friendly
- ☐ funny
- ☐ generous
- ☐ good–better–best
- ☐ helpful
- ☐ honest
- ☐ horrible
- ☐ interesting
- ☐ kind
- ☐ large
- ☐ lazy
- ☐ lightweight
- ☐ long
- ☐ mean
- ☐ nice
- ☐ noisy
- ☐ obnoxious
- ☐ patient
- ☐ polite
- ☐ popular
- ☐ powerful
- ☐ pretty
- ☐ rude
- ☐ short
- ☐ sloppy
- ☐ small
- ☐ smart
- ☐ stubborn
- ☐ talented
- ☐ ugly
- ☐ wonderful
- ☐ deposit
- ☐ enter
- ☐ insert
- ☐ press
- ☐ balance
- ☐ card
- ☐ cash
- ☐ checking
- ☐ key
- ☐ PIN
- ☐ savings
- ☐ transfer
- ☐ withdrawal
- ☐ exchange
- ☐ return
- ☐ credit card
- ☐ debit card
- ☐ date of purchase
- ☐ defective
- ☐ final sale
- ☐ gift card
- ☐ price tag
- ☐ receipt
- ☐ refund
- ☐ store credit

I can ask & answer:
- ☐ May I help you?
  Yes, please. I want to buy *a small radio.*
- ☐ Where can I find *refrigerators*?
- ☐ I'd like to return this/these ____.
  What's the matter with it/them?

I can read:
- ☐ a department store directory
- ☐ ATM screens
- ☐ checks
- ☐ a department store return policy

I can write about:
- ☐ the most important person in my life

SIDE by SIDE Gazette

Did You Know?

The longest car in the world is 100 feet long. It has 26 wheels, a swimming pool, and a waterbed!

The world's biggest costume party is the Carnival celebration in Brazil. Every day during Carnival, more than 50,000 people walk through the streets in costumes.

The largest subway station in the world is Grand Central Terminal in New York City. Every day more than half a million people pass through the station.

The biggest igloo in the world is the Ice Hotel in Sweden. It has rooms for 150 guests. Every year workers have to rebuild the hotel because it melts in the spring!

FACT FILE

World Geography Facts

- The longest river in the world is the Nile. It is 4,180 miles (6,690 kilometers) long.

- The largest ocean in the world is the Pacific Ocean. It is 64,000,000 square miles (165,760,000 square kilometers).

- The highest mountain in the world is Mount Everest. It is 29,028 feet (8,848 meters) high.

- The biggest desert in the world is the Sahara. It is 3,500,270 square miles (9,065,000 square kilometers).

BUILD YOUR VOCABULARY!

Adjectives with Negative Prefixes

They're _____ .

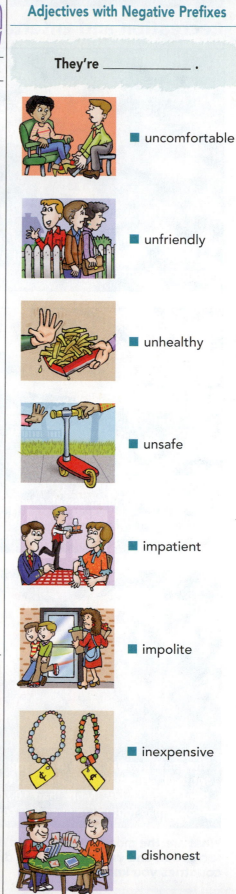

- uncomfortable
- unfriendly
- unhealthy
- unsafe
- impatient
- impolite
- inexpensive
- dishonest

Recreation and Entertainment

The most popular type of outdoor recreation in France is camping. Every night 3 million people in France sleep outside.

Movies are the most popular type of entertainment in India. Every day 15 million people in India go to the movies.

The most popular sport in the world is football. This game is called "soccer" in the United States. More than 100,000,000 people play football in over 150 countries.

What are the most popular types of recreation and entertainment in different countries you know?

Global Exchange

IvanaG: I'm going on vacation with my family tomorrow. We're going to the most popular beach in our country. We'll stay there for a week in a small hotel. It isn't the best hotel there, but it's the friendliest and the closest to the beach. We go there every year. It's a lot of fun! The water is clear, and the air is fresh. My sister and my brother and I swim all day, and we go to an amusement park in the evening. I think it has the largest roller–coaster in the world! So I'll write again when I get back and tell you all about our vacation.

P.S. Do you have a favorite vacation place? Where is it? When do you go there? What do you do?

Send a message to a keypal. Tell about a favorite vacation place in your country.

LISTENING

And Now a Word From Our Sponsors!

And Now a Word From Our Sponsors!

_b_	①	Rings & Things	**a.**	furniture
	②	Big Value Store	**b.**	jewelry
	③	Comfort Kingdom	**c.**	sports equipment
	④	Electric City	**d.**	appliances
	⑤	Recreation Station	**e.**	home entertainment products

What Are They Saying?

The biggest! The smallest! The fastest! The most exciting!

7

Imperatives
Directions

- Getting Around Town
- Public Transportation
- Schedules of Building Hours
- Bus Schedules
- Traffic and Safety Signs
- Safe Driving Practices

VOCABULARY PREVIEW

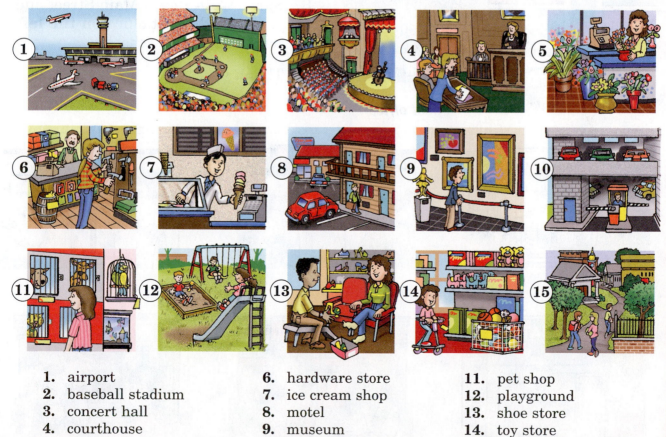

1.	airport	6.	hardware store	11.	pet shop
2.	baseball stadium	7.	ice cream shop	12.	playground
3.	concert hall	8.	motel	13.	shoe store
4.	courthouse	9.	museum	14.	toy store
5.	flower shop	10.	parking garage	15.	university

Can You Tell Me How to Get to . . . ?

walk up walk down	on the right on the left	across from next to between

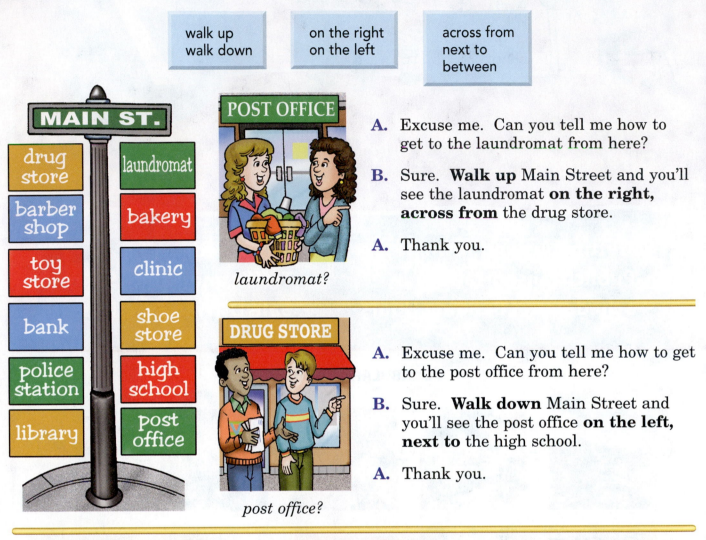

MAIN ST.

drug store	laundromat
barber shop	bakery
toy store	clinic
bank	shoe store
police station	high school
library	post office

laundromat?

A. Excuse me. Can you tell me how to get to the laundromat from here?

B. Sure. **Walk up** Main Street and you'll see the laundromat **on the right, across from** the drug store.

A. Thank you.

---

post office?

A. Excuse me. Can you tell me how to get to the post office from here?

B. Sure. **Walk down** Main Street and you'll see the post office **on the left, next to** the high school.

A. Thank you.

1. *clinic?*

2. *police station?*

3. *drug store?*

4. *library?*

5. *barber shop?*

6. *toy store?*

Could You Please Tell Me How to Get to . . . ?

| walk along | on the right
on the left | across from
next to
between |

A. Excuse me. Could you please tell me how to get to the hospital from here?

B. Sure. **Walk along** Central Avenue and you'll see the hospital **on the left, between** the museum and the park.

A. Thanks.

hospital?

1. *museum?*

2. *university?*

3. *park?*

4. *hotel?*

5. *parking lot?*

6. *zoo?*

Would You Please Tell Me How to Get to . . . ?

turn left   turn right

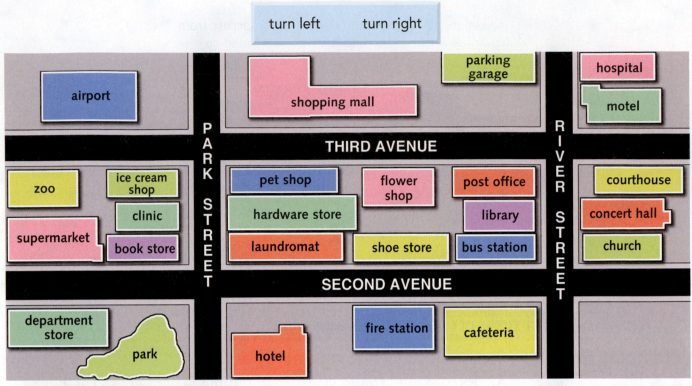

- PARK STREET
- RIVER STREET
- THIRD AVENUE
- SECOND AVENUE

airport | shopping mall | parking garage | hospital | motel
zoo | ice cream shop | pet shop | flower shop | post office | courthouse
clinic | hardware store | library | concert hall
supermarket | book store | laundromat | shoe store | bus station | church
department store | park | hotel | fire station | cafeteria

bus station?

A. Excuse me. Would you please tell me how to get to the bus station from here?

B. Certainly. **Walk up** Park Street to Second Avenue and **turn right**. **Walk along** Second Avenue and you'll see the bus station **on the left, across from** the cafeteria.

A. Thanks very much.

concert hall?

A. Excuse me. Would you please tell me how to get to the concert hall from here?

B. Certainly. **Drive along** Second Avenue to River Street and **turn left**. **Drive up** River Street and you'll see the concert hall **on the right, between** the courthouse and the church.

A. Thanks very much.

1. *hospital?*

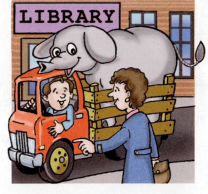

2. *zoo?*

3. *shoe store?*

4. *laundromat?*

5. *supermarket?*

6. *post office?*

7. *clinic?*

8. *airport?*

9.

How to Say It!

Asking for Repetition

A. I'm sorry. Could you please { repeat that? / say that again? }

B. Sure. *Walk along . . .*

Practice some conversations on this page again. Ask people to repeat the directions.

Take the Main Street Bus

A. Excuse me. What's the quickest way to get to Peter's Pet Shop?

B. **Take** the Main Street bus and **get off** at First Avenue. **Walk up** First Avenue and you'll see Peter's Pet Shop **on the right**.

A. Thank you very much.

B. You're welcome.

A. Excuse me. What's the easiest way to get to Harry's Barber Shop?

B. **Take** the subway and **get off** at Fourth Avenue. **Walk down** Fourth Avenue and you'll see Harry's Barber Shop **on the left**.

A. Thank you very much.

B. You're welcome.

1. What's the fastest way to get to the baseball stadium?

2. What's the best way to get to the library?

3. What's the most direct way to get to the zoo?

4. I'm in a hurry! What's the shortest way to get to the train station?

A. Can you recommend **a good hotel**?

B. Yes. The Bellview is **a good hotel**. I think it's **one of the best hotels** in town.

A. Can you tell me how to get there?

B. Sure. Take the subway and get off at Brighton Boulevard. You'll see the Bellview at the corner of Brighton Boulevard and Twelfth Street.

A. Thank you very much.

B. You're welcome.

These people are visiting your city. Recommend real places you know and like, and give directions.

Can you recommend a good restaurant?

Can you recommend a big department store?

Can you recommend an interesting tourist sight?

Can you recommend _____?

HAROLD NEVER GOT THERE!

Dear Students,

Here are directions to my house. I'll see you at the party.

Your English teacher

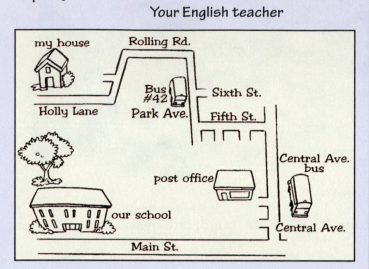

1. From our school, walk along Main St. to Central Ave. and turn left.

2. Walk up Central Ave. 2 blocks, and you'll see a bus stop at the corner, across from the post office.

3. Take the Central Ave. bus and get off at Fifth St.

4. Turn left and walk along Fifth St. 3 blocks to Park Ave. and turn right.

5. Walk up Park Ave. 1 block, and you'll see a bus stop at the corner of Park Ave. and Sixth St.

6. Take Bus #42 and get off at Rolling Rd.

7. Turn left and walk along Rolling Rd. 1 block.

8. Turn left again, and walk 2 blocks to Holly Lane and turn right.

9. Walk along Holly Lane. My house is the last one on the right.

Harold was very disappointed last night. All the other students in his English class went to a party at their teacher's house, but Harold never got there. He followed his teacher's directions, but he made one little mistake.

From their school, he walked along Main Street to Central Avenue and turned left. He walked up Central Avenue two blocks to the bus stop at the corner, across from the post office. He took the Central Avenue bus and got off at Fifth Street. He turned left and walked along Fifth Street three blocks to Park Avenue and turned right. He walked up Park Avenue one block to the bus stop at the corner of Park Avenue and Sixth Street.

He took Bus Number 42, but he got off at the wrong stop. He got off at River Road instead of Rolling Road. He turned left and walked along River Road one block. He turned left again and walked two blocks, turned right, and got completely lost.

Harold was very upset. He really wanted to go to the party last night, and he can't believe he made such a stupid mistake!

✓ READING CHECK-UP

TRUE OR FALSE?

1. Harold's English teacher lives on Holly Lane.
2. The Central Avenue bus stops across from the post office.
3. The teacher made one little mistake in the directions.
4. The school is on Main Street.
5. Harold took the wrong bus.
6. Bus Number 42 goes to Rolling Road.
7. Harold got off the bus at Rolling Road.
8. Harold didn't really want to go to the party last night.

WHAT'S THE WORD?

It's very easy to get _____¹ the zoo from here. Walk up this street _____² the corner and turn right. Walk two blocks and you'll see a bus stop _____³ the corner _____⁴ Grove Street and Fourth Avenue. Take the West Side bus and get _____⁵ _____⁶ Park Road. You'll see the zoo _____⁷ the left. It's next _____⁸ the library and across _____⁹ the museum.

LISTENING

WHAT'S THE WORD?

Listen and choose the word you hear.

1. a. right   b. left
2. a. right   b. left
3. a. down   b. up
4. a. along   b. down
5. a. to   b. on
6. a. off   b. of
7. a. on   b. at

WHERE ARE THEY?

Where are these people? Listen and choose the correct place.

1. a. department store   b. laundromat
2. a. pet shop   b. cafeteria
3. a. restaurant   b. library
4. a. hospital   b. hotel
5. a. barber shop   b. supermarket
6. a. parking lot   b. parking garage

IN YOUR OWN WORDS

FOR WRITING AND DISCUSSION

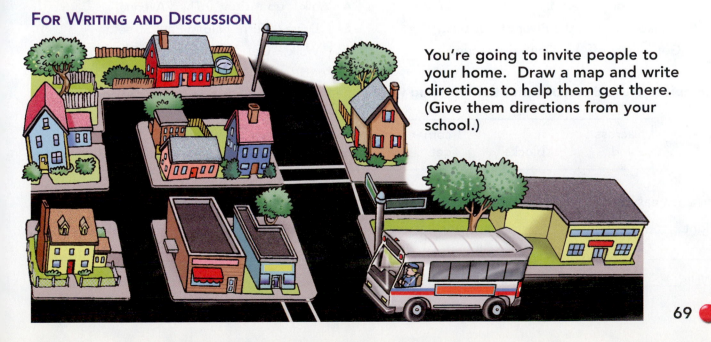

You're going to invite people to your home. Draw a map and write directions to help them get there. (Give them directions from your school.)

Listen. Then say it.

Could you please tell me how to get to the bank?

Could you please repeat that?

Would you please tell me how to get to the library?

Say it. Then listen.

Could you please tell me how to get to the park?

Could you please say that again?

Would you please tell me how to get to the zoo?

SIDE *by* SIDE
JOURNAL

How do you get to different places in your community? Do you walk? Do you drive? Do you take a bus, train, or subway? Is it easy or difficult to get to these places? Write about it in your journal.

BUS STOP

GRAMMAR FOCUS

IMPERATIVES

Walk up Main Street.	**Turn right.**	**Take** the Main Street bus.
Walk down Main Street.	**Turn left.**	**Get off** at First Avenue.
Walk along Central Avenue.		**Drive along** Second Avenue.

Choose the correct word.

1. Turn (along   left).
2. (Take   Walk) the River Street bus.
3. Get (up   off) at Central Avenue.

4. Walk (up   right) Third Avenue.
5. (Drive   Turn) along Park Street.
6. (Walk   Get) off the bus at Fourth Avenue.

Complete these directions with the following words.

across	at	corner	on	Take	turn	Walk
and	blocks	get	see	to	two	

It's easy to get to the hospital from here. Walk up this street _____¹ the corner and _____²

right. _____³ three _____⁴ and you'll _____⁵ a bus stop at the _____⁶ of Park Street

_____⁷ Tenth Avenue. _____⁸ the Park Street bus and _____⁹ off _____¹⁰ University Road.

Walk _____¹¹ blocks and you'll see the hospital _____¹² the right, _____¹³ from the bus station.

1 CONVERSATION ASKING FOR & GIVING SCHEDULE INFORMATION

CLINIC	
Mon–Fri	8:00 – 7:00
Sat	8:00 – 5:00
Sun	Closed

LIBRARY HOURS
M, W, F 9:00 AM – 6:30 PM
T, TH 9:00 AM – 9:00 PM
SAT, SUN 10:00 AM – 5:00 PM

POST OFFICE
M–F 8:00 – 4:00
Sat 8:00 – 1:00
Sun Closed

Practice the conversations with a classmate.

A. What time does the clinic open on Tuesday?

B. It opens at eight o'clock.

A. What time does the library close on Friday?

B. It closes at six thirty.

A. How many hours is the post office open on Saturday?

B. It's open for five hours.

Now walk around the classroom and practice new conversations with other students. Use the information in the signs above.

A. What time does the _____ open on _____?

B. It opens at _____.

A. What time does the _____ close on _____?

B. It closes at _____.

A. How many hours is the _____ open on _____?

B. It's open for _____ hours.

2 MAILBOX PICKUP TIMES USING POSTAL SERVICES

Look at the schedule and answer the questions.

How many times do they pick up the mail on weekday mornings? on weekday afternoons? on the weekend?

What time do they pick up the mail on Tuesday morning? on Friday afternoon? on Saturday?

UNITED STATES POSTAL SERVICE **COLLECTION TIMES**

Monday – Friday	Saturday	Sunday
8:30 AM 4:30 PM 11:30 AM	2:00 PM	Holiday

Location of Express Mail Drop: 250 Adams Street

For information call: (800) ASK-USPS

3 COMMUNITY CONNECTIONS SCHEDULES IN THE COMMUNITY

Find three schedule signs in your community. Draw the signs, bring them to class, and share with other students. Ask students questions about the schedule information on your signs.

THINK & SHARE Think about schedules of different places in your community. When are these places open? Are the schedules good or bad? Why? What can you do to change a schedule? Discuss with your classmates.

A BUS SCHEDULE

Look at the bus schedule and answer the questions. Circle the answers on the schedule.

High Street	State Street	Kellogg Road	Congress Street	Western Avenue
6:33 AM	6:41 AM	6:54 AM	7:01 AM	7:14 AM
7:48 AM	7:58 AM	8:12 AM	8:24 AM	8:37 AM
8:00 AM	8:10 AM	8:24 AM	8:36 AM	8:49 AM
9:10 AM	9:20 AM	9:33 AM	9:43 AM	9:54 AM
9:50 AM	10:00 AM	———	10:21 AM	10:32 AM
10:30 AM	10:40 AM	———	11:01 AM	11:12 AM
11:00 AM	11:10 AM	11:23 AM	11:33 AM	11:45 AM
11:55 AM	12:05 PM	12:18 PM	12:28 PM	12:39 PM

1. What time does the first bus arrive at Congress Street?

2. When does the 8:00 AM bus get to Kellogg Road?

3. What time does the 10:30 AM bus get to Western Avenue?

4. What time does the 9:50 AM bus arrive at State Street?

5. When does the last morning bus leave from High Street?

6. When does the 7:48 AM bus arrive at Western Avenue?

Choose the correct answers.

7. How long does it take to get from High Street to Kellogg Road at 11:00 AM?
   - A. 18 minutes
   - B. 23 minutes
   - C. 24 minutes
   - D. 33 minutes

8. You're at the Congress Street bus stop. It's a quarter to nine. When is the next bus?
   - A. 8:36 AM
   - B. 8:49 AM
   - C. 9:33 AM
   - D. 9:43 AM

9. You're at the State Street bus stop. It's 10:10 AM. How long do you have to wait for a bus?
   - A. ten minutes
   - B. twenty minutes
   - C. half an hour
   - D. an hour

10. You're meeting someone at the Western Avenue bus stop at 12 noon. When should you leave High Street?
    - A. 10:30 AM
    - B. 11:00 AM
    - C. 11:45 AM
    - D. 11:55 AM

TRAFFIC AND SAFETY SIGNS

Match each warning with the correct sign.

| A | B | C | D | E | F |

_____ 1. You can't make a left turn here.

_____ 2. Slow down. There's a school nearby. Watch for children crossing the road.

_____ 3. Traffic from another lane will enter the road.

_____ 4. Slow down. There's a crosswalk ahead. Watch for pedestrians crossing the road.

_____ 5. Be careful! The road ahead is slippery.

_____ 6. The road ahead is closed. Take this road instead.

COMMUNITY CONNECTIONS

Find different traffic signs in your community and draw them. Write down all the words and symbols on the signs. Bring your signs to class, and compare signs with other students.

Safe Driving

More than 3.5 million people get hurt in car accidents in the United States each year. Here are some things you can do so that you and your passengers are safe.

Always wear a seat belt. Also, make sure that all the passengers in your car wear their seat belts. Children under the age of five should ride in child safety seats that you attach to the back seat of the car. The center back seat is the safest.

Many accidents happen when cars are in bad condition. Take good care of your car. Check the brakes every week to be sure that you can stop the car when you need to. Keep the windshield clean so you can see the road ahead. Be sure the windshield wipers work in the rain.

Be a careful driver. Pay attention to traffic signs, road conditions, and other drivers. Look before you make a turn or change lanes on the highway. Don't "tailgate"—don't stay too close to the car in front of you. The driver might stop without warning. Be especially careful when the weather is bad. Slow down and use your headlights in the rain, snow, and fog. Pay attention to the speed limit. When the speed limit is sixty miles an hour, that's the fastest you should drive. On the other hand, don't be a slow driver. Slow drivers can cause accidents.

You can't pay attention to the road when you're tired or busy doing too many things. Don't eat, drink, or talk on your cell phone while you're driving. Don't take any medicine that can make you sleepy before you drive. The label on such medicine usually has the warning "May cause drowsiness." Remember, other drivers are not always as careful as you are. Be prepared for their mistakes. If you are in an accident, the police will ask to see your papers. Always have your license, car registration, and insurance card with you to show to the police.

1. The best place for a child safety seat is _____.
   A. in the front seat
   B. in the back seat next to the door
   C. in the center back seat
   D. next to the driver

2. According to this article, drivers should _____.
   A. use headlights when it's foggy
   B. always drive sixty miles per hour
   C. ride in safety seats
   D. make mistakes

3. According to this article, drivers should NOT _____.
   A. be prepared for other drivers' mistakes
   B. look before changing lanes
   C. use their windshield wipers in the rain
   D. use a cell phone while they're driving

4. A driver who *tailgates* _____.
   A. is a slow driver
   B. drives too close to the car ahead
   C. stops without warning
   D. is a careful driver

5. We can infer that *the windshield* in paragraph 3 _____.
   A. stops the car
   B. cleans the car
   C. is in the back of the car
   D. is in the front of the car

6. *May cause drowsiness* means the medicine _____.
   A. is old
   B. is bad for you
   C. might make you tired
   D. might make you nervous

Choose the correct answer.

1. I go to the _____ on Main Street to wash my shirts.
   A. shopping mall
   B. department store
   C. hardware store
   D. laundromat

2. They bake wonderful pies and cakes at the _____ down the street.
   A. bank
   B. bakery
   C. barber shop
   D. flower shop

3. I got off the bus at the wrong _____.
   A. stop
   B. map
   C. bus
   D. directions

4. We don't want to be late for the plane. What's the fastest way to get to the _____?
   A. train station
   B. airport
   C. bus station
   D. gas station

5. Can you _____ a good department store in a convenient location?
   A. tell me how
   B. directions
   C. how to get there
   D. recommend

6. What _____ does the clinic close on Monday?
   A. hours
   B. schedule
   C. time
   D. schedule sign

7. When you drive, you should always _____.
   A. ride in a child safety seat
   B. wear a seat belt
   C. tailgate
   D. be a slow driver

8. When you drive, don't _____.
   A. drive and talk on your cell phone
   B. use your headlights in the fog
   C. look before you change lanes
   D. pay attention to the speed limit

Look at the bus schedule. Choose the correct answer.

9. You're at the Lake Street bus stop. It's half past seven. The next bus is at _____.
   A. 6:15 AM
   B. 7:10 AM
   C. 7:55 AM
   D. 8:30 AM

10. You're at the Main Street bus stop. It's a quarter after eight. You have to wait _____ for the next bus.
    A. 6 minutes
    B. 21 minutes
    C. 8:21
    D. 8:51

Lake St.	First Ave.	Main St.	River Rd.
6:15 AM	6:24 AM	6:36 AM	6:42 AM
7:10 AM	7:21 AM	7:34 AM	7:42 AM
7:55 AM	8:07 AM	8:21 AM	8:29 AM
8:30 AM	8:40 AM	8:51AM	8:58 AM

SKILLS CHECK ✓

Words:

□ airport
□ bakery
□ bank
□ barber shop
□ baseball stadium
□ book store
□ bus station
□ cafeteria
□ church
□ clinic
□ concert hall
□ courthouse
□ department store

□ drug store
□ fire station
□ flower shop
□ gas station
□ hardware store
□ high school
□ hospital
□ hotel
□ ice cream shop
□ laundromat
□ library
□ motel
□ museum
□ park

□ parking garage
□ parking lot
□ pet shop
□ playground
□ police station
□ post office
□ restaurant
□ shoe store
□ shopping mall
□ supermarket
□ toy store
□ train station
□ university
□ zoo

□ back seat
□ brakes
□ child safety seat
□ headlights
□ passenger
□ road conditions
□ seat belt
□ speed limit
□ tailgate
□ traffic sign
□ windshield
□ windshield wipers

I can ask & answer:

□ Can you tell me/Could you please tell me/ Would you please tell me how to get *there*?
□ What's the quickest/easiest way to get to the *bank*?
□ What time does the *clinic* open/close on *Tuesday*?

I can read:

□ schedule information on signs
□ a bus schedule
□ traffic & safety signs

I can:

□ draw a map and write directions

I can write about:

□ ways I get to places in my community

8

- **Describing People's Actions**
- **Describing Plans and Intentions**
- **Consequences of Actions**
- **Job Interview**
- **Stating Skills and Work Experience**

- **Asking for Permission at Work**
- **Help Wanted Ads**
- **Reading a Paycheck and Pay Stub**
- **Employee Accident Report**

VOCABULARY PREVIEW

1. actor
2. dancer
3. driver
4. painter

5. player
6. runner
7. singer
8. skier

9. teacher
10. translator
11. worker

He Drives Very Carelessly

slow – slowly careless – carelessly	careful – carefully graceful – gracefully	fast – fast hard – hard	good – well

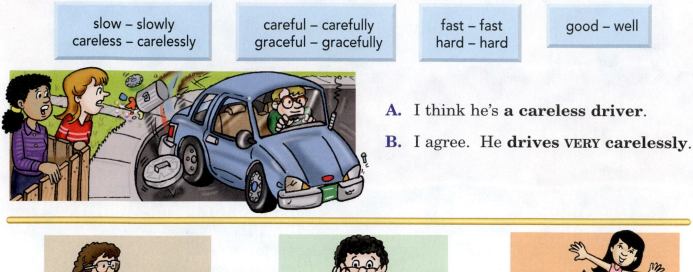

A. I think he's **a careless driver**.

B. I agree. He **drives** VERY **carelessly**.

1. *a careful worker*

2. *a slow chess player*

3. *a graceful dancer*

4. *good actors*

5. *a careless skier*

6. *a fast runner*

7. *a beautiful singer*

8. *bad painters*

9. *a good teacher*

10. *a hard worker*

11. *an accurate translator*

12. *dishonest card players*

You Should Work Faster

fast – faster quickly – quicker* loud(ly) – louder* slowly – slower*	carefully – more carefully gracefully – more gracefully accurately – more accurately	well – better

A. Am I working **fast** enough?

B. Actually, you should work **faster**.

A. Am I painting **carefully** enough?

B. Actually, you should paint **more carefully**.

1. Am I typing quickly enough?

2. Am I dancing gracefully enough?

3. Am I speaking loud enough?

4. Am I driving slowly enough?

5. Am I translating accurately enough?

6. Am I playing well enough?

* *quicker* or *more quickly*   *louder* or *more loudly*   *slower* or *more slowly*

73

He Should Try to Speak Slower

loud(ly) – louder*	slowly – slower*	carefully – more carefully	early – earlier
neatly – neater*	softly – softer*	politely – more politely	late – later
quickly – quicker*			well – better

A. Bob speaks VERY **quickly**.

B. You're right. He should try to speak **slower**.

1. Timothy types very slowly.

2. Carol skates very carelessly.

3. Howard speaks very softly.

4. Linda goes to bed very late.

5. Jimmy gets up very early.

6. They dress very sloppily.

7. Brenda plays her radio very loudly.

8. Richard speaks to his parents very impolitely.

9. Our next-door neighbor drives very badly.

How to Say It!

Expressing Agreement

You're right.   That's right.   That's true.   I know.   I agree.   I agree with you.

Practice the conversations on this page again. Express agreement in different ways.

* *louder* or *more loudly*   *neater* or *more neatly*   *quicker* or *more quickly*   *slower* or *more slowly*   *softer* or *more softly*

TRYING HARDER

Michael's boss talked with him today. In general, she doesn't think Michael is doing very well on the job. He has to do better. According to Michael's boss, he types too slowly. He should type faster. In addition, he files too carelessly. He should file more carefully. Furthermore, he speaks on the telephone too quickly. He should speak slower. Michael wants to do well on the job, and he knows now that he has to try a little harder.

Stella's director talked with her today. In general, he doesn't think Stella is doing very well in his play. She has to do better. According to Stella's director, she speaks too softly. She should speak louder. In addition, she walks too slowly. She should walk faster. Furthermore, she dances too awkwardly. She should dance more gracefully. Stella wants to do well in the play, and she knows now that she has to try a little harder.

Billy's teacher talked with him today. In general, she doesn't think Billy is doing very well in school. He has to do better. According to Billy's teacher, he arrives at school too late. He should arrive earlier. In addition, he dresses too sloppily. He should dress more neatly. Furthermore, he speaks too impolitely. He should speak more politely. Billy wants to do well in school, and he knows now that he has to try a little harder.

✔ READING *CHECK-UP*

Q & A

Michael is talking with his boss. Stella is talking with her director. Billy is talking with his teacher. Using this model, create dialogs based on the story.

A. Do I *type fast* enough?
B. No. You *type* too *slowly*.
A. Oh. I'll try to *type faster* in the future.

WHAT'S THE OPPOSITE?

1. quickly (*slowly*)
2. carefully
3. loudly
4. politely
5. badly
6. sloppily
7. awkwardly
8. earlier
9. faster

If

If _____ will _____

A. What are they going to name their new baby?

B. If they have a boy, they'll name him John.
If they have a girl, they'll name her Jane.

1. A. How are you going to get to school tomorrow?

B. If it rains, I'll _____.
If it's sunny, I'll _____.

2. A. What's Roger going to do this Saturday afternoon?

B. If the weather is good, he'll _____.
If the weather is bad, he'll _____.

3. A. What's Rosa going to have for dinner tonight?

B. If she's very hungry, _____.
If she isn't very hungry, _____.

4. A. What's Ken going to do tomorrow?

B. If he feels better, _____.
If he doesn't feel better, _____.

How About You?

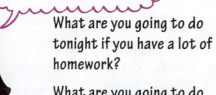

What are you going to do tonight if you have a lot of homework?

What are you going to do tonight if you DON'T have a lot of homework?

What are you going to wear tomorrow if it's warm and sunny?

What are you going to wear tomorrow if it's cool and raining?

What are you going to do this weekend if the weather is nice?

What are you going to do this weekend if the weather is bad?

If You Drive Too Fast, You Might Have an Accident

If _____ might _____

A. You know . . . you shouldn't drive so fast.

B. Oh?

A. Yes. If you drive too fast, you might have an accident.

B. Hmm. You're probably right.

1. *eat so quickly*
get a stomachache

2. *sing so loudly*
get a sore throat

3. *work so slowly*
lose your job

4. *go to bed so late*
be tired in the morning

5. *listen to loud music*
hurt your ears

6. *watch scary movies*
have nightmares

7. *do your homework*
*   so carelessly*
make mistakes

8. *sit at your computer*
*   so long*
get a backache

9.

GOOD DECISIONS

Ronald wants to stay up late to watch a movie tonight, but he knows he shouldn't. If he stays up late to watch a movie, he won't get to bed until after midnight. If he doesn't get to bed until after midnight, he'll be very tired in the morning. If he's very tired in the morning, he might oversleep. If he oversleeps, he'll be late for work. If he's late for work, his boss might get angry and fire him. So, even though Ronald wants to stay up late to watch a movie tonight, he isn't going to. Good decision, Ronald!

Barbara wants to buy a new car, but she knows she shouldn't. If she buys a new car, she'll have to take a lot of money out of her bank account. If she has to take a lot of money out of her bank account, she won't have much left. If she doesn't have much left, she won't have enough money to pay the rent. If she doesn't have enough money to pay the rent, her landlord might evict her from her apartment. So, even though Barbara wants to buy a new car, she isn't going to. Good decision, Barbara!

✔️ **READING** *CHECK-UP*

WHICH WORD IS CORRECT?

1. If Ronald (doesn't won't) go to bed early, he'll be (angry tired) in the morning.
2. If (he's he'll) late for work, his boss might (watch fire) him.
3. If Barbara (buy buys) a new car, she (won't doesn't) have much money left.
4. If she (should doesn't) pay her rent, her landlord might (account evict) her.
5. Even though Ronald and Barbara (won't want) to do these things, they (are aren't) going to.

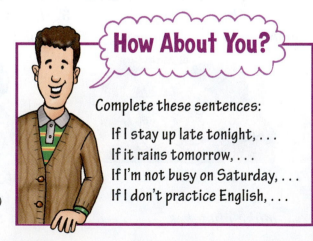

How About You?

Complete these sentences:

If I stay up late tonight, . . .

If it rains tomorrow, . . .

If I'm not busy on Saturday, . . .

If I don't practice English, . . .

LISTENING

Listen and choose the best answer to complete the sentence.

1. a. my teacher will be happy.
   b. my teacher won't be happy.

2. a. she won't go back to school.
   b. she'll go back to school.

3. a. you'll get a sore throat.
   b. you might get a backache.

4. a. I'll be early in the future.
   b. I'll be tired in the morning.

5. a. people will hear you.
   b. people won't hear you.

6. a. your boss might fire you.
   b. your landlord might evict you.

ON YOUR OWN *Superstitions*

Many people believe that you'll have GOOD luck . . .

> if you find a four-leaf clover.
> if you find a horseshoe.
> if you give a new pair of shoes to a poor person.

Many people believe that you'll have BAD luck . . .

> if a black cat walks in front of you.
> if you walk under a ladder.
> if you open an umbrella in your home.
> if you put your shoes on a table.

Here are some other superstitions:

> If your right eye itches, you'll laugh soon.
> If your left eye itches, you'll cry soon.

> If your right ear itches, somebody is saying good things about you.
> If your left ear itches, somebody is saying bad things about you.

> If a knife falls, a man will visit soon.
> If a fork falls, a woman will visit soon.
> If a spoon falls, a baby will visit soon.

> If you break a mirror, you'll have bad luck for seven years.

Do you know any superstitions? Share them with other students in your class.

Listen. Then say it.

If it rains, I'll go to the movies.
If it's sunny, I'll go to the beach.

If they have a boy, they'll name him John.
If they have a girl, they'll name her Jane.

If she's tired, she'll go to bed early.
If she isn't tired, she'll go to bed late.

Say it. Then listen.

If it's hot, I'll wear a tee shirt.
If it's cold, I'll wear a sweater.

If we work quickly, we'll finish early.
If we work slowly, we'll finish late.

If he speaks loudly, people will hear him.
If he doesn't speak loudly, people won't hear him.

SIDE by SIDE JOURNAL

Think about something you want to do.
If you do it, what will happen?
Write about it in your journal.

GRAMMAR FOCUS

ADVERBS

He works	slowly.
	carefully.
	sloppily.
	fast.
	hard.
	well.

COMPARATIVE OF ADVERBS

He should try to work	quicker.
	more quickly.
	more carefully.
	more accurately.
	faster.
	harder.
	better.

AGENT NOUNS

actor	singer
dancer	skier
driver	teacher
painter	translator
player	worker
runner	

Choose the correct word.

1. Roger is a (slow   slowly) driver. He drives very (slow   slowly).

2. Angela is a (careful   carefully) worker. She works very (careful   carefully).

3. Mrs. Chang teaches very (good   well). She's a (good   well) teacher.

4. Jim always arrives at the office too (late   later). He should arrive (later   earlier).

IF-CLAUSES

If	I / we / you / they	feel		I'll / we'll / you'll / they'll		go to work.
		better,				
	he / she / it	feels		he'll / she'll / it'll		

If	I'm / we're / you're / they're		I'll / we'll / you'll / they'll		go to sleep early.
		tired,			
	he's / she's / it's		he'll / she'll / it'll		

Choose the correct word.

5. If (I   I'm) hungry, (I'm   I'll) have a big dinner.

6. If (she   she'll) goes to bed late, (she   she'll) be tired tomorrow.

7. If (you'll   you) eat too fast, (you'll   you) get sick.

8. If it (rains   will rain) tomorrow, (we'll   we) go to the movies.

1 CONVERSATION DESCRIBING JOB INTEREST, SKILLS, & WORK HISTORY

Look at the job application forms. Practice conversations with your classmates.

A. What kind of job are you looking for?

B. I'm looking for a job as a/an _____.

A. Tell me about your skills.

B. I can _____, and I can _____.

A. Where do you work now?

B. I work at _____.

A. And where did you work before that?

B. I worked at _____.

1.

Position Desired:	waitress
Skills:	take orders, serve customers
EMPLOYMENT	
Current:	Jake's Restaurant
Previous:	the Main Street Diner

2.

Position Desired:	auto mechanic
Skills:	fix cars, tune up engines
EMPLOYMENT	
Current:	Ahmed's Car Repair
Previous:	County Line Auto Shop

3.

Position Desired:	electrician
Skills:	install light fixtures, wire a house
EMPLOYMENT	
Current:	Ajax Electrical Services
Previous:	City Light & Power Company

4.

Position Desired:	medical technician
Skills:	take blood samples, do lab tests
EMPLOYMENT	
Current:	Memorial Hospital
Previous:	Bay Shore Laboratory

2 TEAMWORK PREPARING FOR A JOB INTERVIEW

Work with a classmate. Fill out the form with your information. Then practice job interview conversations.

Position Desired:	_____
Skills:	_____
EMPLOYMENT	
Current:	_____
Previous:	_____

80a

3 CONVERSATION REQUESTING A SCHEDULE CHANGE

Practice this conversation between an employee and a supervisor at work.

A. Excuse me, Mr. Harris.

B. Yes?

A. Could I possibly leave early today? The reason is I have to take my mother to the doctor.

B. I understand. Yes. That'll be okay.

A. Thank you very much.

Now practice conversations with different classmates. Use your last names in the conversations.

1. take the day off next Monday
I have to go to court.

2. take a break
I don't feel well. I need to sit down.

3. leave now
The school nurse called. My daughter is sick.

4. come in an hour late on Friday morning
I have a parent-teacher conference at my son's school.

4 TEAMWORK CRITICAL THINKING

Work with a classmate. What are some good reasons to ask for a change in schedule or time off from work? What are some bad reasons? Make two lists. Then discuss with your classmates.

Good Reasons	Bad Reasons
_____	_____
_____	_____
_____	_____

Look at the help wanted ads and answer the questions.

CASHIER	RECEPTIONIST NEEDED
Donut shop needs PT cashier. 2 weekday nights, 7 P.M.–11 P.M. & 2 weekend days, 8 A.M.–4 P.M. $9+/hr. Apply in person at Mr. Donut, 850 Willow Avenue.	PT, $7.50–$8/hr. Answer phones, file, get customer information. Must have high school diploma. Good English language and telephone skills req. Spanish speaker pref. Call Rita at 760-846-3700.
CHEF	**RESTAURANT HELP**
Fine restaurant needs FT chef. Prepare & cook appetizers, soups, vegetables, desserts. Supervise 5 employees. 2 yrs. exper. req. Excel. salary & benefits. Send 2 copies of resume to Carrington Restaurant, 53 Ames St., Bridgeport, CA.	New restaurant now hiring FT dishwashers, PT waitpersons. Exper. pref., but not req. Will train. Apply in person. Harbor Restaurant, 350 Ocean Drive. No phone calls, please.
CUSTODIAN	**SALESPEOPLE**
FT. $8.00/hr. M–F, 10 P.M.–5 A.M. Clean offices, vacuum carpets, operate floor machines, clean restrooms. 1 yr. exper. pref. Call 760-467-9000. Ask for Gordon.	FT & PT positions starting at $9/hr. Work days or eves. No exper. req. Call 760-965-3400 ext. 47 or apply in person at P. T. Jones and Company, 457 Forest Ave.
DRIVERS WANTED	**SECRETARY**
Looking for drivers to deliver the Bridgeport Herald. PT, 7 days/wk early morning. $950–$1,050/mo. Must have reliable car, valid CA driver's license, & clean driving record. Call Mark. 760-983-1945.	FT position in busy doctors' office. Excel. computer skills & 2+ yrs. exper. req. Excel. salary & medical benefits. Send resume to Mt. Pleasant Medical Associates, 1240 Main St., Bridgeport, CA.

1. The Harbor Restaurant needs _____.
   A. part-time dishwashers
   B. a full-time chef
   C. part-time waiters and waitresses
   D. a part-time cashier

2. The custodian does NOT have to _____.
   A. clean offices
   B. vacuum carpets
   C. operate floor machines
   D. have a clean driving record

3. The drivers work _____.
   A. forty hours a week
   B. seven mornings a week
   C. eight hours a day
   D. evenings

4. The cashier at Mr. Donut has to work _____.
   A. Sunday morning
   B. Wednesday evening
   C. Saturday night
   D. Monday afternoon

5. Apply in person for the job as _____.
   A. a driver
   B. a secretary
   C. a receptionist
   D. a dishwasher

6. Send two copies of your resume to _____.
   A. P.T. Jones and Company
   B. Mt. Pleasant Medical Associates
   C. Carrington Restaurant
   D. Harbor Restaurant

7. Experience is required for the job _____.
   A. at Harbor Restaurant
   B. at P.T. Jones and Company
   C. as a custodian
   D. at Mt. Pleasant Medical Associates

8. The receptionist does NOT have to _____.
   A. have a high school diploma
   B. speak Spanish
   C. have good English language skills
   D. have good telephone skills

TEAMWORK Cut out some help wanted ads from the newspaper and bring them to class. Work with a classmate. Compare ads for different jobs. What information is in the ads? How should people apply for the jobs?

Look at the paycheck and pay stub and answer the questions.

FOSTER COMPANY LAM M. EMP. NO. 46803
PAY PERIOD **PAY DATE:**
06/30/10 – 07/06/10 07/11/10

EARNINGS	RATE	HOURS	THIS PERIOD	YEAR TO DATE
REGULAR	11.00	32	352.00	11,440.00
OVERTIME	16.50	2	33.00	319.00
HOLIDAY	22.00	8	176.00	528.00
GROSS PAY			561.00	12,287.00

	THIS PERIOD	YEAR TO DATE	GROSS PAY	561.00
FED TAX	37.84	975.92	TAXES	92.94
FICA/MED	36.18	933.22	DEDUCTIONS	42.25
STATE TAX	18.92	487.96		
HEALTH	42.25	1,140.75		
			NET PAY	425.81

Fc FOSTER COMPANY

Check No. 2689412

Date Issued 07/11/10

Pay to MEI LAM

FOUR HUNDRED TWENTY-FIVE DOLLARS AND EIGHTY-ONE CENTS ***$425.81

Rosemary Martinez

1. Mei's regular pay is _____.
   A. $8.00 an hour   C. $16.50 an hour
   B. $11.00 an hour   D. $32.00 an hour

2. Mei earned _____ when she worked on the July 4th holiday during this pay period.
   A. $11.00 an hour   C. $176.00
   B. $16.50 an hour   D. $528.00

3. Mei worked _____ this pay period.
   A. 32 hours   C. 40 hours
   B. 34 hours   D. 42 hours

4. A pay period at this company is _____.
   A. a week   C. a month
   B. a day   D. a year

5. Mei earned _____ before taxes and other deductions.
   A. $92.94   C. $425.81
   B. $352.00   D. $561.00

6. The deduction for state taxes was _____.
   A. $18.92   C. $37.84
   B. $36.18   D. $42.25

7. Mei paid $1,140.75 this year for _____.
   A. federal taxes   C. state taxes
   B. health insurance   D. overtime

8. Mei earned _____ from 1/1/10 to 7/6/10.
   A. $975.92   C. $11,440.00
   B. $1,140.75   D. $12,287.00

THINK & SHARE What taxes and deductions do you see on the pay stub in this lesson? What do these taxes and deductions pay for? Discuss as a class.

Look at the employee accident report and answer the questions.

━━━━━ HILLER HOTEL EMPLOYEE ACCIDENT REPORT ━━━━━

PLEASE COMPLETE AND SUBMIT TO THE PERSONNEL DEPARTMENT.

Name of injured employee: Orlando Cortina   **SS#** 289-43-6708   **SEX:** ✔ M ☐ F

Home address of employee: 89 Carleton Road, Cloverleaf, TX 77015   **Date of Birth:** 5/22/80

Job Title: Custodian   **Department:** Maintenance   **Date of Report:** 10/01/12

Where did accident occur? Laundry room, basement   **Date of Accident:** 9/23/12

Time of Accident: 11:30 (A.M.) P.M.   **Names of Witnesses:** Paula Sanders, Jane Ling

Nature of injury and part(s) of body injured: I broke my left arm.

How did the employee get injured? I went to the laundry room to fix a broken shelf. I was on a ladder. The ladder moved, and I fell off.

What safety equipment, if any, did employee use? None

What factors contributed to the accident? The floor was wet and slippery. There wasn't enough light.

Did employee lose time from work? Yes   **How much time?** One week

Physician's name: Dr. Rafael Garcia   **Address:** 78 Forest Avenue, Cloverleaf, TX 77015

Immediate Supervisor signature: Alice Winter   **Date signed:** 10/01/12

Department Head signature: Carlo Marconi   **Date signed:** 10/01/12

Employee signature: Orlando Cortina   **Date signed:** 10/01/12

---

1. What is Orlando Cortina's job?
   A. He's a laundry worker.
   B. He's a physician.
   C. He's a supervisor.
   D. He's a custodian.

2. When was the accident?
   A. On May twenty-second.
   B. On September twenty-third.
   C. On October first.
   D. At 11:30 at night.

3. Who saw the accident?
   A. Alice Winter.
   B. Carlo Marconi.
   C. Dr. Rafael Garcia.
   D. Paula Sanders and Jane Ling.

4. Why did Orlando go to the laundry room?
   A. To fix a shelf.
   B. To do the laundry.
   C. To move a ladder.
   D. To fix a ladder.

5. Who should Orlando give this report to?
   A. The maintenance department.
   B. The personnel department.
   C. His physician.
   D. His supervisor.

6. What DIDN'T Orlando do?
   A. He didn't break his left arm.
   B. He didn't fall off a ladder.
   C. He didn't use safety equipment.
   D. He didn't sign the accident report.

THINK & SHARE What kinds of accidents and injuries can happen at different workplaces you know? How can employers and employees prevent these accidents and injuries? Share ideas as a class.

Choose the correct answer.

1. Timothy isn't a good dancer. He dances _____.
   A. awkwardly
   B. beautifully
   C. gracefully
   D. very well

2. If you want to finish this report today, you'll have to work more _____.
   A. slowly
   B. quickly
   C. carelessly
   D. sloppily

3. I'm sorry. I can't hear you. You aren't speaking _____ enough.
   A. softly
   B. fast
   C. quickly
   D. loud

4. Barry's boss likes him because he always _____.
   A. arrives late for work
   B. speaks impolitely
   C. dresses sloppily
   D. gets to work early

5. I can fix cars and tune up engines. I have good _____ to be a mechanic.
   A. work
   B. job
   C. skills
   D. employment

6. _____, Ms. Carson. Could I possibly leave work early today?
   A. Excuse me
   B. The reason is
   C. That'll be okay
   D. Thank you very much

7. Marcela earned _____ this pay period.
   A. 40 hours
   B. $127.50
   C. federal taxes
   D. health insurance

8. Anna had an accident at work. She completed and submitted _____.
   A. her supervisor
   B. three witnesses
   C. her physician
   D. an accident report

Look at the help wanted ads. Choose the correct answer.

9. The salesperson doesn't have to _____.
   A. work in the morning
   B. apply in person
   C. work on Sunday
   D. go to Washington Street

10. Experience is required for the _____.
    A. full-time job
    B. job at the Maxwell Company
    C. job as a cashier
    D. job as a salesperson

CASHIER
Drug store needs PT cashier 3 weekday afts. 1 P.M.–5:30 P.M. & 2 weekend mornings 8:00 A.M.–11:30 A.M. $11/hr. Exper. pref., but not req. Call Ms. Lee at 775-220-4574.

CUSTODIAN
PT. $9.00/hr. 4 weekday mornings 8:00 A.M.–11:00 A.M. & 2 weekend afternoons 2:00 P.M.–5:00 P.M. 2 yrs. exper. req. Apply in person at the Maxwell Company, 451 Winter St.

SALESPERSON
FT position starting at $10/hr. 9:30 A.M.–6:00 P.M. M–Sat. No exper. req. Apply in person. Saxony Department Store, 943 Washington St.

SKILLS CHECK ✓

Words:
- ☐ accurate – accurately
- ☐ awkward – awkwardly
- ☐ bad – badly
- ☐ beautiful – beautifully
- ☐ careful – carefully
- ☐ careless – carelessly
- ☐ dishonest – dishonestly
- ☐ fast – fast
- ☐ good – well
- ☐ graceful – gracefully

- ☐ hard – hard
- ☐ impolite – impolitely
- ☐ loud – loud(ly)
- ☐ neat – neat(ly)
- ☐ polite – politely
- ☐ quick – quickly
- ☐ sloppy – sloppily
- ☐ slow – slowly
- ☐ soft – softly

I can ask & answer:
- ☐ Am I *working fast* enough? Actually, you should *work faster*.
- ☐ What are you going to do *tomorrow*? If _____, I'll _____.
- ☐ What kind of job are you looking for?
- ☐ Tell me about your skills.
- ☐ Where do you work now?
- ☐ And where did you work before that?
- ☐ Could I possibly *leave early today*? The reason is _____.

I can express agreement:
- ☐ You're right./That's right./ That's true./I know./I agree./ I agree with you.

I can write about:
- ☐ consequences of my actions

I can interpret:
- ☐ help wanted ads
- ☐ a paycheck and pay stub
- ☐ an employee accident report

BUILD YOUR VOCABULARY!
Occupations

You're Hired!

Ten tips for a successful job interview!

We asked personnel officers at companies in New York, Los Angeles, Toronto, Miami, Chicago, and Vancouver: What should job applicants do to have a successful job interview? Here is their advice:

1. Dress neatly. Don't dress sloppily. Comb your hair neatly.
2. Arrive promptly. Don't be late for your interview. Try to arrive early.
3. Shake hands firmly. A firm handshake shows that you are a friendly and confident person.
4. Look at the interviewer directly. Make "eye contact." Smile!
5. Listen carefully to the interviewer. Listen to the questions carefully so you can answer accurately.
6. Speak politely. Don't speak too quickly, and don't speak too loudly or softly.
7. Answer questions honestly. Tell the truth.
8. Speak confidently. Describe your skills and experience completely. If you don't have experience, you should talk about how you can learn quickly.
9. Speak enthusiastically. Show that you really want the job!
10. Send a thank-you note promptly. Thank the interviewer for his or her time and express again your interest in the job.

Some of these tips might not be correct in some cultures—for example, a firm handshake or eye contact. Are these tips correct in different cultures you know? What are other tips for job interviews in these cultures?

I'm a/an _____ .

- assembler
- designer
- director
- gardener
- inspector
- photographer
- programmer
- supervisor
- welder
- writer

Men and Women at Work

The jobs that men and women have are changing in many countries around the world.

a construction worker in Vietnam

a nurse in Costa Rica

a teacher in Bangladesh

a company president in France

an airline pilot in England

a homemaker in the United States

What jobs do men and women usually have in different countries you know? Is this changing?

Global Exchange

Glen25: In your last message, you asked me to tell you more about myself. So I will. I'm very athletic. I get up early every morning, and I run for an hour. My friends say I'm a fast runner. I'm also a hard worker. I work very hard at school. I'm a good driver. I drive very carefully. I'm not a good dancer. I don't dance very well. I'm not really a very shy person, but everybody tells me I speak softly. And I like to play the piano. I play pretty well, but I want to play better, so I have a piano lesson every week. How about you? Tell me more about yourself.

Send a message to a keypal. Tell a little about yourself. (Remember: Don't give your full name or other personal information when you communicate with people online.)

LISTENING

Attention, All Employees!

_d_	**1** Workplace 1	**a.** neatly
___	**2** Workplace 2	**b.** early
___	**3** Workplace 3	**c.** quickly
___	**4** Workplace 4	**d.** carefully
___	**5** Workplace 5	**e.** loudly

What Are They Saying?

Past Continuous Tense
Reflexive Pronouns
While-Clauses

- Describing Ongoing Past Activities
- Reporting a Home Emergency
- Emergency Preparedness
- First-Aid Instructions

- Warning Labels on Household Products
- Safety Procedures: Earthquakes and Hurricanes

VOCABULARY PREVIEW

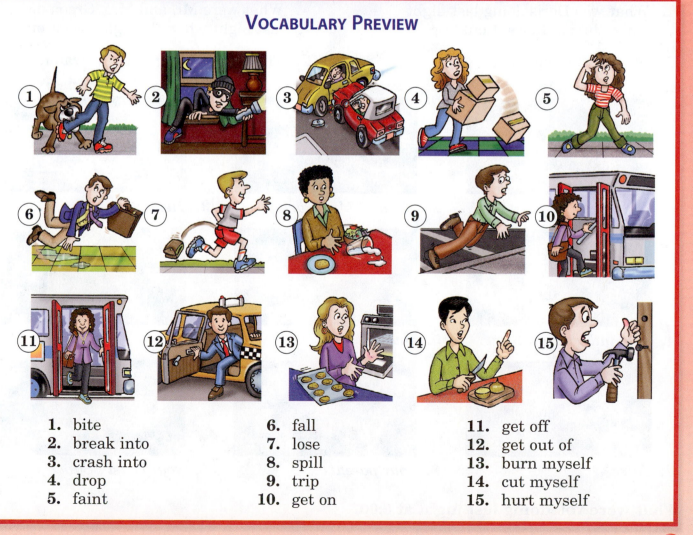

1. bite
2. break into
3. crash into
4. drop
5. faint
6. fall
7. lose
8. spill
9. trip
10. get on
11. get off
12. get out of
13. burn myself
14. cut myself
15. hurt myself

The Blackout

I
He
She
It
} was

working.

We
You
They
} were

Last night at 8:00 there was a blackout in Centerville. The lights went out all over town.

A. What was Doris doing last night when the lights went out?

B. She was taking a bath.

A. What were Mr. and Mrs. Green doing last night when the lights went out?

B. They were riding in the elevator.

1. *David*

2. *Mr. and Mrs. Park*

3. *Helen*

4. *you and your brother*

5. *you*

6. *Larry*

7. *Alice*

8. *your parents*

9. *your cousin Sam*

What were YOU doing last night at 8:00?

I Saw You Yesterday, but You Didn't See Me

A. I saw you yesterday, but you didn't see me.

B. Really? When?

A. At about 2:30. You were **getting out of a taxi on Main Street**.

B. That wasn't me. Yesterday at 2:30 I was **cooking dinner**.

A. Hmm. I guess I made a mistake.

1. *walking into the laundromat*
working at my office

2. *walking out of the library*
taking a history test

3. *getting on a bus*
visiting my grandparents

4. *getting off a merry-go-round*
practicing the piano

5. *jogging through the park*
fixing my bathroom sink

6.

A ROBBERY

There was a robbery at 151 River Street yesterday afternoon. Burglars broke* into every apartment in the building while all the tenants were out.

The man in Apartment 1 wasn't home. He was washing his clothes at the laundromat. The woman in Apartment 2 wasn't home either. She was visiting a friend in the hospital. The people in Apartment 3 were gone. They were having a picnic at the beach. The man in Apartment 4 was out. He was playing tennis in the park. The college students in Apartment 5 were away. They were attending a football game. And the elderly lady in Apartment 6 was out of town. She was visiting her grandchildren in Ohio.

Yesterday certainly was an unfortunate day for the people at 151 River Street. They had no idea that while they were away, burglars broke into every apartment in the building.

* break – broke

✔ READING CHECK-UP

Q & A

The tenants at 151 River Street are talking to the police. Using this model, create dialogs based on the story.

A. Which apartment do you live in?
B. Apartment *1.*
A. Were you home at the time of the robbery?
B. No, *I wasn't. I was washing my clothes at the laundromat.*
A. What did the burglars take from your apartment?
B. They took *my VCR, my computer,* and some money *I had in a drawer in my bedroom.*
A. How much money did they take?
B. About *three hundred dollars.*

He Went to the Movies by Himself

I	myself
you	yourself
he	himself
she	herself
it	itself
we	ourselves
you	yourselves
they	themselves

A. What did **John** do yesterday?

B. He went to the movies.

A. Oh. Who did he go to the movies with?

B. Nobody. He went to the movies **by himself**.

1. *Aunt Ethel*
go to the circus

2. *your parents*
go sailing

3. *you and your wife*
have a picnic

4. *Ann*
drive to the mountains

5. *you*
go bowling

6. *your brother and sister*
play volleyball

7. *Grandma*
take a walk in the park

8. *Uncle Joe*
go fishing

9.

I Had a Bad Day Today

while

A. You look upset.

B. I had a bad day today.

A. Why? What happened?

B. I lost my wallet while I was jogging through the park.

A. I'm sorry to hear that.

A. Harry looks upset.

B. He had a bad day today.

A. Why? What happened?

B. He cut* himself while he was shaving.

A. I'm sorry to hear that.

1. *you*
hurt* myself
fixing my fence

(second picture - center)

2. *Emma*
dropped her packages
walking out of the supermarket

3. *your parents*
got a flat tire
driving over a bridge

* cut – cut   hurt – hurt

4. Henry
   tripped and fell*
   walking down the stairs

5. you
   burned myself
   cooking on the barbecue

6. Wilma
   fainted
   waiting for the bus

7. you and your husband
   somebody stole our car
   shopping

8. you
   a can of paint fell on me
   walking under a ladder

9. the mail carrier
   a dog bit* him
   delivering the mail

How to Say It!

Reacting to Bad News

I'm sorry to hear that. That's too bad! That's terrible! That's a shame! What a shame! What a pity! How awful!

Practice the conversations in this lesson again. React to the bad news in different ways.

How About You?

Everybody has a bad day once in a while. Can you remember when something bad happened to you? What happened, and what were you doing when it happened?

* fall – fell   bite – bit

FRIDAY THE 13TH

Yesterday was Friday the 13th. Many people believe that Friday the 13th is a very unlucky day. I, myself, didn't think so . . . until yesterday.

Yesterday I burned myself while I was cooking breakfast.

My wife cut herself while she was opening a package.

My son poked himself in the eye while he was putting on his glasses.

Our daughter spilled milk all over herself while she was eating lunch.

Both our children fell and hurt themselves while they were roller-blading.

And we all got wet paint all over ourselves while we were sitting on a bench in the park.

I'm not usually superstitious, but yesterday was a very unlucky day. So, the next time it's Friday the 13th, do yourself a favor! Take care of yourself!

✔️ READING CHECK-UP

Q & A

The man in the story is talking with a friend. Using this model, create dialogs based on the story.

A. *My wife* had a bad day yesterday.
B. Oh? What happened?
A. *She cut herself* while *she was opening a package.*
B. That's too bad!

WHICH WORD IS CORRECT?

1. He _____ himself while he was cooking.
   a. burned   b. cut

2. His daughter spilled ____.
   a. paint   b. milk

3. His son poked himself in the _____.
   a. eye   b. glasses

4. His children fell and hurt _____.
   a. ourselves   b. themselves

5. We got wet paint all over _____.
   a. ourselves   b. themselves

LISTENING

Listen to the conversations. What happened to these people? Listen and choose the correct answer.

1. a. He cut himself.
   b. He dropped his packages.
2. a. She tripped.
   b. She got a flat tire.
3. a. He burned himself.
   b. He fainted.

4. a. Somebody stole his wallet.
   b. He got paint on his pants.
5. a. They fell on the sidewalk.
   b. They hurt themselves in the basement.
6. a. He fell in the water.
   b. He spilled the water.

READING

AN ACCIDENT

   I saw an accident this morning while I was standing at the corner of Park Street and Central Avenue. A man in a small red sports car was driving down Park Street very fast. While he was driving, he was talking on his cell phone. At the same time, a woman in a large green pick-up truck was driving along Central Avenue very slowly. While she was driving, she was drinking a cup of coffee and eating a donut. While the woman was driving through the intersection, the man in the sports car didn't stop at a stop sign, and he crashed into the pick-up truck. The man and the woman were very upset. While they were shouting at each other, the police came.* Fortunately, nobody was hurt badly.

* come – came

✔ READING CHECK-UP

TRUE, FALSE, OR MAYBE?

Answer True, False, or Maybe (if the answer isn't in the story).

1. The accident happened at the corner of Park Street and Central Avenue.
2. The man was driving a small green sports car.
3. While the woman was driving, she was talking on her cell phone.
4. The man likes donuts.
5. The sports car crashed into the truck.
6. The woman was driving to work.
7. The police came after the accident.

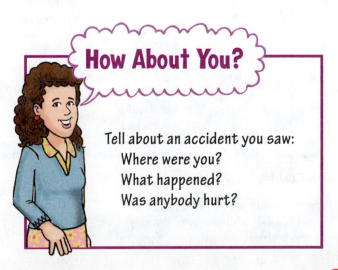

How About You?

Tell about an accident you saw:
Where were you?
What happened?
Was anybody hurt?

Listen. Then say it.

What **did** he do?

Who **did** he go with?

What **was** he doing?

Where **was** she driving?

Say it. Then listen.

How **did** he hurt himself?

Where **did** he fall?

Where **was** she going?

Where **did** it happen?

Some people like to go places and do things by themselves. Others like to do things with family members and friends. How about you? Do you like to do things alone or with other people? Write about it in your journal.

GRAMMAR FOCUS

PAST CONTINUOUS TENSE

What	was	I he she it	doing?
	were	we you they	

I He She It	was	eating.
We You They	were	

Complete the sentences with the correct form of the verb.

bake	listen	read	take	watch

What was everybody doing at 8:00 last night?

1. Monica _____ the newspaper.
2. Michael _____ a shower.
3. My parents _____ TV.
4. You _____ to music.
5. My wife and I _____ cookies.

REFLEXIVE PRONOUNS

I You He She It We You They	took a walk by	myself. yourself. himself. herself. itself. ourselves. yourselves. themselves.

WHILE-CLAUSES

I lost my wallet **while I was jogging.**
He cut himself **while he was shaving.**

Complete the sentences with a reflexive pronoun and the correct form of the verb.

give	make	open	play	slice	sit

6. My brother hurt _____ while he _____ basketball.
7. I cut _____ while I _____ a package.
8. My sister burned _____ while she _____ pancakes.
9. My son and I got paint all over _____ while we _____ on a bench in the park.
10. My cousins spilled water all over _____ while they _____ their dog a bath.
11. Dad, did you cut _____ while you _____ carrots?

1 CONVERSATION CALLING 911

Practice conversations to report these emergencies.

A. Emergency operator.

B. _____

A. What's the address?

B. _____

A. What's your name?

B. _____

A. Telephone number?

B. _____

A. Okay. We'll be there right away.

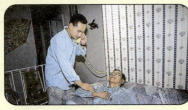

1. I think my father is having a heart attack!

2. My baby is very sick! She isn't breathing!

3. There's a fire in my apartment building!

4. My son overdosed on some medicine! He isn't waking up!

5. Someone is breaking into my apartment!

6. There's a man with a gun in front of our building!

2 TEAMWORK PREPARING FOR EMERGENCIES AT HOME

Practice these interviews.

How are you prepared for an emergency at home?

 I have a list of emergency numbers near the telephone.

I keep a first-aid kit in a convenient place.

 I keep a fire extinguisher in my kitchen.

I change the batteries in my smoke detectors twice a year.

 I know how to turn off the utilities.

 I taught my children how to dial 911.

Now interview your classmates. Are they prepared for emergencies at home?
Then discuss as a class: What else can you do to prepare for emergencies?

READING FIRST-AID INSTRUCTIONS

Look at the first-aid chart and answer the questions.

EMERGENCY FIRST AID

Animal Bites: Wash the wound with soap and water for 5 minutes or more. Put a clean dry bandage on the wound. See a doctor as soon as possible.	**Burns:** Cool the burn. Put it in cool water for 5 minutes or more. Do not use ice. Do not use any ointments or soap. Cover with a sterile dressing.
Bee Stings: Try to remove the stinger with a clean knife. Clean the wound with soap and water and apply ice. Get medical help if the person is dizzy, nauseous, or can't breathe.	**Choking:** If the person can speak, tell him or her to cough. If the person can't speak or cough, ask someone to call 911. Then get behind the person and perform the Heimlich maneuver.
Bleeding: Apply direct pressure on the wound for 10 minutes with a clean cloth or a sterile dressing. If possible, raise the wound higher than the person's heart.	**Electric Shock:** Do not touch the person. Turn off the power. Call 911. If the person has no pulse, begin CPR (cardiopulmonary resuscitation).

1. Perform the Heimlich maneuver when _____.
   A. someone is bleeding
   B. someone has an animal bite
   C. someone received an electric shock
   D. someone is choking

2. You should put _____ on a burn.
   A. ointment
   B. a sterile dressing
   C. ice
   D. soap

3. When someone is bleeding a lot, _____.
   A. try to remove the stinger
   B. clean the wound for 10 minutes
   C. apply pressure on the wound
   D. begin CPR

4. Wash _____ for 5 minutes or more.
   A. an animal bite
   B. a burn
   C. a bee sting
   D. a sterile dressing

5. Get medical help for a bee sting if _____.
   A. you don't have a clean knife
   B. the wound is dirty
   C. the person is dizzy or nauseous
   D. there isn't any ice

6. If someone gets an electric shock, DON'T _____.
   A. give the person CPR
   B. turn off the electricity
   C. call 911
   D. touch the person right away

READING A WARNING LABEL ON A HOUSEHOLD PRODUCT

DANGER: Avoid contact with eyes or skin. Wash thoroughly with soap after handling. Harmful if swallowed. Do not breathe vapors or fumes.

First-Aid Treatment: If swallowed, give a glassful of water or milk and call a Poison Control Center immediately. If in eyes, rinse with water for 15 minutes. Get medical attention. If on skin, wash with soap and water.

KEEP OUT OF REACH OF CHILDREN.

Decide if these sentences are True (T) or False (F).

_____ 1. Do not get this product in your eyes or on your hands, face, or other parts of your body.

_____ 2. Wash carefully with soap before you use this product.

_____ 3. It's dangerous to eat or drink this product.

_____ 4. Close the windows when you use this product.

_____ 5. Call the Poison Control Center if someone eats or drinks this product.

_____ 6. See a doctor if this product gets in your eyes.

Read the safety posters and answer the questions.

Duck, Cover, and Hold!
What to Do During an Earthquake

IN THE CLASSROOM:

Duck! Get down under a desk or table and drop to your knees. Turn away from the windows. Avoid heavy objects, like bookcases, that might fall.

Cover! Cover your head with the desk or table. Cover your eyes. (Put your face into your arm.)

Hold! Hold on to the desk or table. If it starts to move, hold on, move with it, and keep it over your head.

OUTSIDE: Find an area without buildings or trees. Stay away from electrical wires and poles on the ground. Get down on your knees and cover your head with a book or other object.

IN THE HALL: Duck down on the floor next to an inside wall and get on your knees. Cover your head and neck with your arms. Put your face down.

NEAR A BUILDING: Duck! Get into a doorway. Get down on your knees. Cover your head with one hand. Hold on to the doorway.

Preparing for a Hurricane

A hurricane watch means that a hurricane might arrive within 36 hours. When there is a hurricane watch, you should do the following:

- Have an emergency evacuation plan. If you have to evacuate, where will you go, and how will you get there?

- Have an emergency kit ready to take with you. It should contain a first-aid kit, flashlights and batteries, prescription medicine, sleeping bags, important documents, cash and credit cards, a non-electric can opener, and enough canned food, water, and clothes for five days.

- Listen to the radio or TV for weather reports and evacuation instructions.

- Fill your car with gas.

- Cover windows and doors with wood or tape.

- Move trash cans, bicycles, barbecue grills, and other objects inside or secure them so they'll stay in place during strong winds.

- Fill clean bottles and other containers with water for drinking.

- Fill sinks and bathtubs with water for washing.

---

1. If you're in the classroom during an earthquake, _____.
   A. get under a bookcase
   B. hold on to a window
   C. cover your head with your knees
   D. get under a desk or a table

2. If you're outside during an earthquake, _____.
   A. get under a tree
   B. look for a building
   C. drop to your knees
   D. get under an electrical pole

3. In the first instruction in the earthquake safety poster, *avoid* means _____.
   A. cover
   B. stay away from
   C. stay near
   D. hold on to

4. Evacuation instructions tell you _____.
   A. what to do at home during a hurricane
   B. how to prepare for a hurricane
   C. what to do after a hurricane
   D. what to do if you have to leave your home

5. You probably WON'T need _____ during a hurricane.
   A. an electric can opener
   B. a flashlight
   C. canned food
   D. drinking water

6. When there is a hurricane watch, you should NOT _____.
   A. fill your car with gas
   B. listen to the radio or TV
   C. move bicycles and trash cans outside
   D. fill sinks and bathtubs with water

Choose the correct answer.

1. Careful! Don't _____ yourself!
   A. spill
   B. hurt
   C. put
   D. faint

2. I saw you while you were _____ the library.
   A. getting off
   B. walking off
   C. walking into
   D. getting on

3. I _____ all my packages while I was walking down the stairs.
   A. fell
   B. tripped
   C. bit
   D. dropped

4. I had a terrible day today. I _____ myself in the eye.
   A. poked
   B. poured
   C. fixed
   D. hurt

5. There was an accident at the intersection. A car _____ into a truck.
   A. fell
   B. crashed
   C. broke
   D. spilled

6. I change the batteries in my _____ twice a year.
   A. first-aid kit
   B. utilities
   C. fire extinguishers
   D. smoke detectors

7. I always look at the _____ on a household product.
   A. first aid
   B. wound
   C. warning label
   D. bandage

8. If someone eats or drinks this product, call the _____ Control Center.
   A. Heimlich
   B. Poison
   C. CPR
   D. 911

9. In the classroom during an earthquake, get under your desk and _____ your eyes.
   A. duck
   B. move
   C. get on
   D. cover

10. I have flashlights in my emergency _____.
    A. kit
    B. report
    C. medicine
    D. watch

SKILLS CHECK ✓

Words:
- ☐ attend
- ☐ bite
- ☐ break into
- ☐ burn *myself*
- ☐ crash into
- ☐ cut *myself*
- ☐ deliver
- ☐ drop
- ☐ faint
- ☐ fall
- ☐ get a flat tire
- ☐ get off

- ☐ get on
- ☐ get out of
- ☐ hurt *myself*
- ☐ lose
- ☐ open
- ☐ poke *myself*
- ☐ practice
- ☐ spill
- ☐ stop
- ☐ take a test
- ☐ take a walk
- ☐ trip

I can ask & answer:
- ☐ What were we/you/they doing?
    We/You/They were working.
- ☐ What was he/she/it doing?
    He/She/It was working.
- ☐ Who did I/he/she/we/you/they go with?
    I went by myself./He went by himself./
    She went by herself./We went by ourselves./
    You went by yourself./You went by yourselves./
    They went by themselves.
- ☐ What happened?

I can react to bad news:
- ☐ I'm sorry to hear that.
- ☐ That's too bad!
- ☐ That's terrible!
- ☐ That's a shame!
- ☐ What a shame!
- ☐ What a pity!
- ☐ How awful!

I can:
- ☐ call 911 to report an emergency at home
- ☐ identify ways to prepare for emergencies at home

I can interpret:
- ☐ first-aid instructions
- ☐ warning labels on household products
- ☐ safety procedures for earthquakes and hurricanes

I can write about:
- ☐ doing things alone or with other people

Could
Be Able to

Have Got to
Too + Adjective

- Expressing Past and Future Ability
- Expressing Past and Future Obligation
- Giving an Excuse

- Renting an Apartment
- Housing Ads
- Reading a Floor Plan
- Requesting Maintenance and Repairs
- Building Rules and Regulations

VOCABULARY PREVIEW

1. busy
2. disappointed
3. frustrated
4. full
5. nervous

6. shy
7. sick
8. tired
9. upset
10. weak

11. crowded
12. difficult
13. heavy
14. spicy
15. windy

They Couldn't

| I He She It We You They | could / couldn't study. |

Could he study?
Yes, he could.
No, he couldn't.

A. Could Peter play on the basketball team when he was a little boy?

B. No, he couldn't. He was too short.

1. Could Lisa go to lunch with her co-workers today?
busy

2. Could Sasha finish his homework last night?
tired

3. Could Max and Ruth finish their dinner yesterday?
full

4. Could you and your brother go to school yesterday?
sick

5. Could you walk the day after your operation?
weak

6. Could Timmy get into the movie last night?
young

7. Could Ben tell the police officer about the accident?
upset

8. Could Rita perform in school plays when she was young?
shy

9. Could Stuart and Gloria eat at their wedding?
nervous

They Weren't Able to

$$could = \begin{cases} \text{was} \\ \text{were} \end{cases} \text{able to}$$

$$couldn't = \begin{cases} \text{wasn't} \\ \text{weren't} \end{cases} \text{able to}$$

A. Was Jimmy able to lift his grandmother's suitcase?

B. No, he wasn't able to. It was too **heavy**.

1. Was Diane able to sit down on the subway this morning?

crowded

2. Was Charlie able to eat the food at the restaurant last night?

spicy

3. Were Nancy and Mark able to go camping last weekend?

windy

4. Were you able to solve the math problem last night?

difficult

5. Was Cathy able to find her cat last night?

dark

6. Were your parents able to swim in the ocean during their vacation?

cold

7. Was Tracy able to put her hair in a ponytail?

short

8. Was Ricky able to wear his brother's tuxedo to the prom?

small

95

She Had to Study for an Examination

A. Did Barbara enjoy herself at the concert last night?

B. Unfortunately, she { wasn't able to / couldn't } go to the concert last night. She had to **study for an examination**.

1. Did Paul enjoy himself at the tennis match last week?

visit his boss in the hospital

2. Did Amanda enjoy herself at the soccer game yesterday afternoon?

go to the eye doctor

3. Did you and your co-workers enjoy yourselves at the movies last night?

work overtime

4. Did Mr. and Mrs. Lee enjoy themselves at the symphony yesterday?

wait for the plumber

5. Did you enjoy yourself at the picnic last weekend?

work on my science project

6. Did Ralph enjoy himself at the amusement park last Sunday?

fix a flat tire

7. Did Carla enjoy herself at the school dance last Saturday night?

baby-sit for her neighbors

8.

READING

MRS. MURPHY'S STUDENTS COULDN'T DO THEIR HOMEWORK

Mrs. Murphy doesn't know what to do with her students today. They didn't do their homework last night, and now she can't teach the lesson she prepared.

Bob couldn't do his homework because he had a stomachache. Sally couldn't do her homework because she was tired and fell asleep early. John couldn't do his homework because he had to visit his grandmother in the hospital. Donna couldn't do her homework because she had to take care of her baby sister while her mother worked late at the office. And all the other students couldn't do their homework because there was a blackout in their neighborhood last night.

All the students promise Mrs. Murphy they'll be able to do their homework tonight. She certainly hopes so.

✔ READING *CHECK-UP*

Q & A

Mrs. Murphy is asking her students about their homework. Using this model, create dialogs based on the story.

A. *Bob*? Where's your homework?
B. I'm sorry, Mrs. Murphy. I couldn't do it.
A. You couldn't? Why not?
B. *I had a stomachache.*
A. Will you do your homework tonight?
B. Yes. I promise.

LISTENING

Listen and choose the correct answer.

1. a. It was too noisy.
   b. It was too crowded.
2. a. It was too windy.
   b. It was too upset.
3. a. It was too tired.
   b. It was too dark.
4. a. It was too full.
   b. It was too spicy.
5. a. They were too busy.
   b. They were too difficult.
6. a. I was too sick.
   b. I was too small.

I'm Afraid I Won't Be Able to Help You

will / won't be able to

(I have)	I've	
(We have)	We've	
(You have)	You've	
(They have)	They've	got to work.
(He has)	He's	
(She has)	She's	
(It has)	It's	

A. I'm afraid I won't be able to help you **move to your new apartment** tomorrow.

B. You won't? Why not?

A. I've got to **take my son to the doctor**.

B. Don't worry about it! I'm sure I'll be able to **move to my new apartment** by myself.

1. *paint your apartment*
drive my parents to the airport

2. *repair your fence*
take care of my niece and nephew

3. *study for the math test*
go to football practice

4. *set up your new computer*
fly to Denver

5. *hook up your new VCR*
take my daughter to her ballet lesson

6. *assemble Bobby's bicycle*
work late at the mall

7. *take Rover to the vet*
visit my mother in the hospital

8.

How to Say It!

Expressing Obligation

A. $\begin{cases} \text{I've got to} \\ \text{I have to} \\ \text{I need to} \end{cases}$ *take my son to the doctor.*

B. Don't worry about it.

Practice the conversations in this lesson again.
Express obligation in different ways.

THE BATHROOM PIPE IS BROKEN

Mr. and Mrs. Wilson are very frustrated. A pipe broke in their bathroom yesterday while Mr. Wilson was taking a shower. They called the plumber, but she couldn't come yesterday. She was sick. She can't come today either. She's too busy. And, unfortunately, she won't be able to come tomorrow because tomorrow is Sunday, and she doesn't work on Sundays. Mr. and Mrs. Wilson are afraid they won't be able to use their shower for quite a while. That's why they're so frustrated.

THE TELEVISION IS BROKEN

Timmy Brown and his brother and sister are very frustrated. Their television broke yesterday while they were watching their favorite TV program. Their parents called the TV repairperson, but he couldn't come yesterday. He was fixing televisions on the other side of town. He can't come today either. His repair truck is broken. And, unfortunately, he won't be able to come tomorrow because he'll be out of town. Timmy Brown and his brother and sister are afraid they won't be able to watch TV for quite a while. That's why they're so frustrated.

✔ READING CHECK-UP

ANSWER THESE QUESTIONS

1. Could the plumber come to the Wilsons' house yesterday? Why not?
2. Can she come to their house today? Why not?
3. Will she be able to come to their house tomorrow? Why not?
4. Could the TV repairperson come to the Browns' house yesterday? Why not?
5. Can he come to their house today? Why not?
6. Will he be able to come to their house tomorrow? Why not?

CHOOSE

Mr. Wilson is calling the plumber again. Choose the correct words and then practice the conversation.

A. Hello. This is Mr. Wilson. You (have to   got to)[1] send someone to fix our bathroom pipe. I've (have to   got to)[2] take a shower!

B. I'm sorry, Mr. Wilson. You've (have to   got to)[3] understand. We (can't   aren't)[4] able to send a plumber right now. I (have to   have)[5] a big job to do on the other side of town, and my assistant (has   has to)[6] got to help me. We won't (can't   be able to)[7] come over for a few more days.

Martha is upset. She got a flat tire, and she won't be able to get to the airport on time.

Frank is frustrated. He lost his key, and he can't get into his apartment.

Emily is upset. Her computer crashed, and she lost all her work. Now she won't be able to hand in her term paper tomorrow.

Ted was really disappointed last year. He couldn't dance in the school play. His teacher said he was too clumsy.

Are you frustrated, disappointed, or upset about something? Talk about it with other students in your class.

Think about a time you were frustrated, disappointed, or upset about something. What was the problem? How did you feel about it? What did you do about it? Write about it in your journal.

Listen. Then say it.

I **have to** work.

He **has to** go.

They've **got to** wait.

He's **got to** eat.

Say it. Then listen.

We **have to** study.

She **has to** leave.

You've **got to** practice.

She's **got to** drive.

GRAMMAR FOCUS

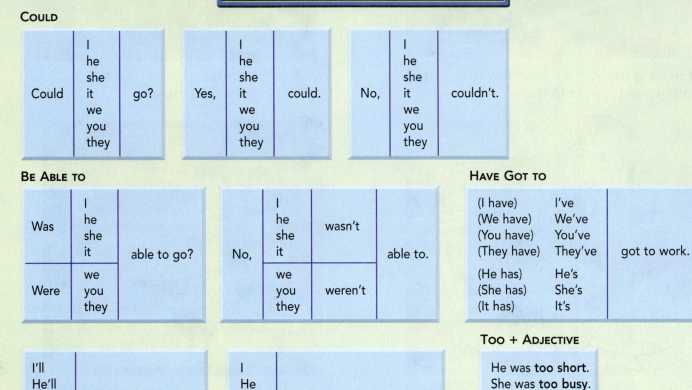

COULD

Could	I he she it we you they	go?

Yes,	I he she it we you they	could.

No,	I he she it we you they	couldn't.

BE ABLE TO

Was	I he she it	able to go?
Were	we you they	

No,	I he she it	wasn't	able to.
	we you they	weren't	

HAVE GOT TO

(I have)	I've	
(We have)	We've	
(You have)	You've	
(They have)	They've	got to work.
(He has)	He's	
(She has)	She's	
(It has)	It's	

TOO + ADJECTIVE

He was **too short**.
She was **too busy**.

I'll He'll She'll It'll We'll You'll They'll	be able to help you.

I He She It We You They	won't be able to help you.

Complete the sentences with the correct words.

able to   be able to   couldn't   got to   wasn't   won't

1. I _____ be able to help you fix your car tomorrow.

2. My daughter _____ go to school. She was too sick.

3. Mr. and Mrs. Ortega weren't _____ go to the concert.

4. Alex _____ able to finish his homework last night.

5. I've _____ work overtime today.

6. I'm sure I'll _____ fix my computer by myself.

1 CONVERSATION INQUIRING ABOUT RENTALS

Practice conversations in an apartment rental office.

A. I'm looking for a _____*-bedroom apartment.

B. We have a _____*-bedroom apartment available.

A. Great. How much is the rent?

B. The rent is $_____ a month.

A. Does that include utilities?

B. Yes, it does. / No, it doesn't.

A. _____

B. _____

Would you like to see the apartment?

A. Yes, please.

* number of bedrooms

1. Is there a security deposit?
Yes. We require one month rent as a deposit.

2. Are pets allowed in the building?
Cats and small dogs are allowed. Large dogs are not permitted.

3. Is parking included in the rent?
No. You have to pay extra for parking.

4. Is there public transportation nearby?
Yes. There's a bus stop in front of the building.

TEAMWORK Work with a classmate. Make a list of other questions to ask about an apartment. Practice more conversations using these questions.

2 CONVERSATION REQUESTING MAINTENANCE & REPAIRS

Practice with a classmate. Call about these apartment problems and others.

A. Hello. This is _____ in apartment _____. I have a problem in my apartment.

B. What's the problem?

A. _____

B. Okay. We'll send someone to fix it.

A. Thank you.

1. The stove doesn't turn on.
2. The refrigerator isn't working.
3. The dishwasher is leaking.
4. The kitchen sink is clogged.
5. The toilet keeps running.
6. _____
7. _____

READING HOUSING ADS

Look at the housing ads. Do you know all the abbreviations? Work with a classmate and read the ads aloud. Then answer the questions.

ARLINGTON Sunny 2 BR apt. Lg. eat-in kit., 1.5 BA, 3rd flr. mod. bldg. w/ elev. & washer/dryer. Pkg. for 2 cars. $900. Gas heat and hot water incl. Avail. June 16. Call landlord. 812-356-9872.	**DANBURY** 2 BR apt. in 2 fam. hse. Din. rm., lg. liv. rm., 1.5 BA, washer/dryer in bsmt. Pkg. on street. Nr. Danbury Park and #3 Bus. $700 mo. plus util. Call owner. 812-897-2469.
BAYSIDE 3 BR apt. w/ balc. on quiet st. Liv. rm., din. rm., 2.5 BA, kit. w/ new appliances. Walk to stores. Avail. immed. $875 mo. Call bldg. mgr. 812-724-0968.	**DEARING** Beaut. 3 BR apt. New refrig. & d/w. in kit., 2 BA, a/c. Laundry rm. in bsmt. Nr. excel. schls. Avail. 7/1. $900 mo. Call supt. 812-497-2741.

1. If you want to rent the apartment in Dearing, you should call the _____.
   A. building manager
   B. superintendent
   C. landlord

2. The apartment in Arlington has _____.
   A. three bedrooms
   B. a small kitchen
   C. one and a half bathrooms

3. You can move into the apartment in _____ right away.
   A. Arlington
   B. Bayside
   C. Dearing

4. You don't have to pay extra for heat if you rent the apartment in _____.
   A. Arlington
   B. Danbury
   C. Dearing

5. The apartment in Danbury does NOT have _____.
   A. a garage
   B. a washing machine in the basement
   C. a dining room

6. We can infer that the apartment in Bayside _____.
   A. has a large kitchen
   B. is on the first floor
   C. has a new refrigerator

TEAMWORK Cut out some housing ads from the newspaper and bring them to class. Work with a classmate. Compare ads for different places. What information do you see? List the abbreviations in the ads. Discuss which places you like and why.

READING A FLOOR PLAN

Look at the floor plan. Decide if these sentences are True (T) or False (F).

_____ **1.** The apartment has three bedrooms.

_____ **2.** The apartment has five closets.

_____ **3.** One of the closets is in the dining room.

_____ **4.** There are one and a half bathrooms.

_____ **5.** There's a fireplace in the bedroom.

PROJECT Draw a floor plan of your apartment or home. Show all the rooms, bathrooms, and closets. Then write a housing ad for your apartment or home, using abbreviations.

Read the apartment building regulations and answer the questions.

Building Rules and Regulations

Rent: Rent is due on or before the first day of each month. Pay with a check or a money order.

Noise: Do not make noise that disturbs other people in the building. There will be no noisy parties or loud playing of radios, stereos, musical instruments, or TVs, especially between 10 P.M. and 8 A.M.

Security: Do not give guests the key to your apartment. Do not let non-tenants who you do not know into the building. When you leave the building, lock the door to your apartment. Tell the building manager if your apartment is going to be empty for more than five days.

Health and Safety: Keep your apartment safe and clean. Keep hallways, stairs, laundry room, and other common areas clear. You can store bicycles and other personal belongings in the storage room in the basement.

Smoke Detectors/Bathroom Fans: Do not disconnect smoke detectors or bathroom fans. Tell the building manager when there is a problem with a smoke detector. If we find a smoke detector that isn't working, we will repair it and charge you for the repair.

Laundry: The laundry room is for residents only. It is open from 8 A.M. to 9:30 P.M. Remove all laundry from machines promptly, and keep the laundry area neat and clean.

Pets: There will be no pets in any of the apartments.

Balconies: Do not hang laundry or keep boxes, trash, or other items on your balcony. For safety reasons, do not use a barbecue grill on the balcony.

Parking: Park in the parking spaces provided for you and your guests. There is no parking on the grass or in the driveway.

Satellite Dishes/TV Antennas: Do not install satellite dishes or TV antennas without asking the landlord.

Hanging Items: Use small nails or picture hangers to hang items on the walls.

Changes to Rules and Regulations: We have the right to change these rules and regulations at any time.

1. Tenants have to _____.
   A. store their bicycles in the hallway
   B. park in the driveway
   C. install satellite dishes or antennas
   D. pay rent with a check or money order

2. Tenants have to ask the landlord before they can _____.
   A. hang pictures on the walls
   B. install satellite dishes
   C. store bicycles
   D. let someone into the building

3. Tenants can _____.
   A. store books in the basement
   B. use the laundry room at 10 P.M.
   C. change the rules and regulations
   D. store boxes on their balconies

4. Tenants should _____ when they leave the building.
   A. tell the building manager
   B. disconnect bathroom fans
   C. lock their doors
   D. give the building manager their keys

5. It is unsafe to _____.
   A. hang items on the walls
   B. remove laundry from machines promptly
   C. keep common areas clear
   D. use barbecues on the balconies

6. In the sixth rule, the word *residents* refers to _____.
   A. laundry workers
   B. guests
   C. tenants
   D. employees

Choose the correct answer.

1. Nobody was able to _____ the math problem. It was too difficult.
   A. perform
   B. solve
   C. go
   D. have

2. I couldn't lift the box because it was too _____.
   A. weak
   B. tired
   C. light
   D. heavy

3. I'll be happy to help you _____ your new computer.
   A. hand in
   B. crash
   C. set up
   D. break

4. We couldn't sit down on the bus because it was too _____.
   A. frustrated
   B. crowded
   C. clumsy
   D. disappointed

5. Were you able to _____ your son's bicycle by yourself?
   A. get into
   B. hook up
   C. assemble
   D. baby-sit

6. We require one month rent as _____.
   A. a security deposit
   B. utilities
   C. extra
   D. available

7. The _____ in our apartment isn't working. We have to repair it.
   A. satellite dish
   B. laundry
   C. parking space
   D. smoke detector

8. If you make a lot of noise, you'll _____ other tenants in the building.
   A. disturb
   B. disconnect
   C. remove
   D. install

BRADBURY 1 BR apt. Kit. w/ new stove, lge. liv. rm., 1.5 BA, laundry rm. in bsmt. $750 mo. plus utilities. Parking on street. Avail. Sept 15. Call supt. 310-659-4581.

BRANFORD 3 BR apt. in mod. apt. bldg., 2 BA, lge. liv. rm., kit. w/ dishwasher. Garage. Walk to stores. $900 plus utils. Call bldg. mgr. 310-393-2277.

DEXTER 2 BR apt. 1 BA, liv. rm. w/ frplc., lge. din. rm., balc. No pkg. Nr. mall. $800. Utils. incl. Avail. immed. Call landlord. 310-274-9836.

Look at the apartment ads. Choose the correct answer.

9. According to the ad, the apartment in Branford has _____.
   A. a new stove in the kitchen
   B. a large dining room
   C. one and a half bathrooms
   D. parking

10. According to the ad, if you rent the two-bedroom apartment, _____.
   A. you'll have to pay extra for heat
   B. you'll have two bathrooms
   C. you can move in right away
   D. you'll have to pay extra for electricity

SKILLS CHECK ✓

Words:
- ☐ busy
- ☐ clumsy
- ☐ cold
- ☐ crowded
- ☐ dark
- ☐ difficult
- ☐ disappointed
- ☐ frustrated
- ☐ full
- ☐ heavy
- ☐ nervous
- ☐ short
- ☐ shy
- ☐ sick
- ☐ small

- ☐ spicy
- ☐ tired
- ☐ upset
- ☐ weak
- ☐ windy
- ☐ young
- ☐ apartment
- ☐ appliances
- ☐ balcony
- ☐ bathroom fan
- ☐ building manager
- ☐ hallway
- ☐ heat
- ☐ hot water
- ☐ landlord

- ☐ laundry room
- ☐ owner
- ☐ parking
- ☐ parking space
- ☐ personal belongings
- ☐ rent
- ☐ resident
- ☐ rules and regulations
- ☐ security deposit
- ☐ smoke detector
- ☐ storage room
- ☐ tenant
- ☐ utilities

I can ask & answer:
- ☐ Could you *go*?
  Yes, I could.
  No, I couldn't.
- ☐ Were you able to *go*?
  Yes, I was able to.
  No, I wasn't able to.
- ☐ How much is the rent?
- ☐ Does that include utilities?
- ☐ Is there a security deposit?
- ☐ Are pets allowed in the building?
- ☐ Is parking included in the rent?
- ☐ Is there public transportation nearby?

I can express obligation:
- ☐ I've got to/I have to/I need to *study*.

I can:
- ☐ inquire about apartment rentals
- ☐ request maintenance and repairs

I can interpret:
- ☐ housing ads
- ☐ a floor plan
- ☐ apartment building rules and regulations

I can write about:
- ☐ a problem I experienced

● 102d

Families and Time

Families have less time together

It seems that everywhere around the world, people are spending more time at work or alone and less time with their families and friends. People are busier than ever before!

In the past in many countries, the father worked and the mother stayed home, took care of the children, and did the food shopping, cooking, and cleaning. Nowadays in many families, both parents work, so they both have to do the shopping, cooking, and cleaning in their free time. Parents, therefore, don't have as much time with their children as they used to have in the past. There are also many single-parent families. In these families, the single parent has to do everything.

These days, many children come home from school to an empty apartment or house. A lot of children spend many hours each day in front of the television. Even when families are together, it is common for family members to do things by themselves. For example, they watch programs on separate TVs in different rooms, they use the Internet, they talk with friends on the telephone, and they do other individual activities.

Isn't it strange? Thanks to technology, people are able to communicate so easily with people far away, but sometimes they don't communicate as well as before with people in their own homes.

Is this happening in your country? What's your opinion about this?

FACT FILE

Countries Where People Spend the Most Time at Work

COUNTRY	HOURS OF WORK PER YEAR
Thailand	2,200
United States	1,966
Japan	1,889
France	1,656
Germany	1,560

BUILD YOUR VOCABULARY!

Home Appliances

I think the _____ is broken!

■ coffee maker

■ dishwasher

■ dryer

■ garbage disposal

■ iron

■ microwave

■ toaster

■ vacuum cleaner

■ washing machine / washer

Child Care

While parents around the world are working, who takes care of their young children? There are many different types of child care for pre-school children around the world.

These children are in a day-care center in their community.

These children are in a day-care center in a factory where their parents work.

This child stays home during the day with his grandmother.

What different types of child care are there in countries you know?

Global Exchange

KoolKid2: Hi. It's me. I'm sorry I didn't answer your last e-mail. You won't believe what happened this week! My computer crashed, and I lost all my files—my e-mail messages, my address book, and all my schoolwork. I wasn't able to hand in the term paper for my science class yesterday because it was on my computer. I couldn't study very well for a history test because all my study notes for the exam were also on the computer. And besides all that, I tripped and fell yesterday while I was practicing for the school play. What a week! I'm glad it's over! Tell me, how was YOUR week? (I hope it was better than mine!)

Send a message to a keypal. Tell a little about your week.

LISTENING

You have five messages!

You Have Five Messages!

_d_ **1** Pete has to	**a.** fix his car.
____ **2** Susie has to	**b.** stay in bed.
____ **3** Marty has to	**c.** wait for the plumber.
____ **4** Judy has to	**d.** work overtime.
____ **5** Tom had to	**e.** visit her grandparents.

What Are They Saying?

11

Past Tense Review
Count/Non-Count Noun Review

Must
Mustn't vs. Don't Have to
Must vs. Should

- **Medical Examinations**
- **Medical Advice**
- **Health**
- **Nutrition**
- **Making a Doctor Appointment**

- **Calling in Sick**
- **Reporting Absence from School**
- **Medicine Labels**
- **Medicine Safety Tips**
- **Nutrition and Recipes**

VOCABULARY PREVIEW

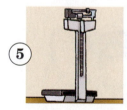
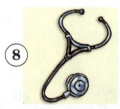
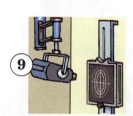

1. doctor
2. nurse
3. lab technician
4. X-ray technician

5. scale
6. weight
7. height
8. stethoscope

9. chest X-ray
10. cardiogram
11. blood pressure
12. blood test

The Checkup

I want to get a medical checkup. Can you recommend a good doctor?

Yes. You should go to MY doctor. She'll give you a very complete examination.

You'll stand* on a scale, and the nurse will measure your height and your weight.

The nurse will take your blood pressure.

The lab technician will do some blood tests.

The X-ray technician will take a chest X-ray.

Then the nurse will lead* you into an examination room.

The doctor will come in, shake* your hand, and say "hello."

She'll ask you some questions about your health.

Then, she'll examine your eyes, ears, nose, and throat.

Next, she'll listen to your heart with a stethoscope.

After that, she'll take your pulse.

Then, she'll do a cardiogram.

Finally, the doctor will talk with you about your health.

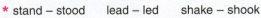

* stand – stood   lead – led   shake – shook

Your Checkup

How was your medical checkup?

The doctor gave me a very complete examination.

1. I stood on a scale _____

_____

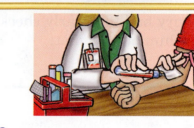

2. _____

_____

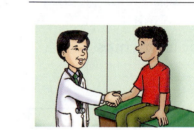

3. _____

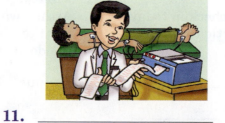

4. _____

_____

5. _____

6. _____

_____

7. _____

_____

8. _____

9. _____

_____

10. _____

_____

11. _____

_____

12. _____

_____

Diets

I He She It We You They	must work.

more / less	more / fewer
bread	cookies
fish	potatoes
fruit	eggs
rice	vegetables

Henry had his yearly checkup today. The doctor told him he's a little too heavy and put him on this diet:

Henry's Diet

⊖	⊕
bread	fish
cookies	vegetables
candy	fruit
potato chips	

You must eat **less** bread, **fewer** cookies, **less** candy, and **fewer** potato chips. Also, you must eat **more** fish, **more** vegetables, and **more** fruit.

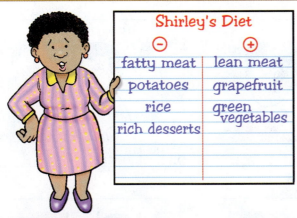

Shirley's Diet

⊖	⊕
fatty meat	lean meat
potatoes	grapefruit
rice	green vegetables
rich desserts	

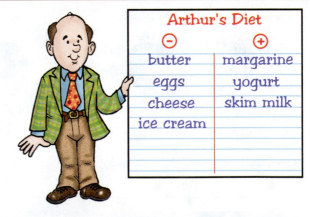

Arthur's Diet

⊖	⊕
butter	margarine
eggs	yogurt
cheese	skim milk
ice cream	

1. Shirley also had her annual checkup today. The doctor told her she's a little too heavy and put her on this diet:

   She must eat _____

   _____

   _____.

2. Arthur was worried about his heart. He went to his doctor for an examination, and the doctor told him to eat fewer fatty foods.

   He must eat/drink _____

   _____

   _____.

Buster's Diet	
⊖	⊕
fatty meat	lean meat
dog biscuits	water

My Diet	
⊖	⊕

3. Buster went to the vet yesterday for his yearly checkup. The vet told him he's a little too heavy and put him on this diet:

He must eat/drink _____

_____

_____ .

4. You went to the doctor today for your annual physical examination. The doctor told you you're a little overweight and said you must go on a diet.

I must eat/drink _____

_____

_____ .

LISTENING

Listen and choose the correct word to complete the sentence.

1. a. cake
   b. cookies
2. a. bread
   b. vegetables
3. a. soda
   b. grapefruit
4. a. rice
   b. desserts
5. a. fatty meat
   b. eggs
6. a. cheese
   b. potato chips

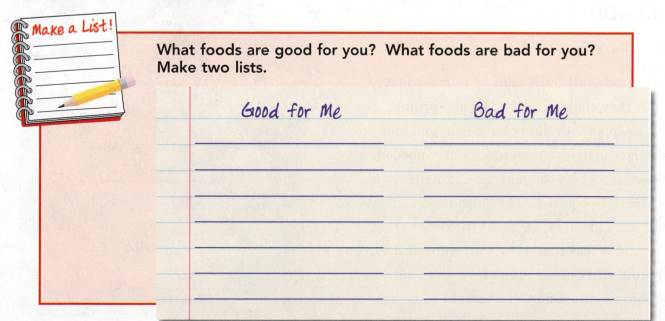

Make a List!

What foods are good for you? What foods are bad for you? Make two lists.

Good for Me	Bad for Me

CAROL'S APPLE CAKE

Carol baked an apple cake yesterday, but she couldn't follow all the instructions in her cookbook because she didn't have enough of the ingredients. She used less flour and fewer eggs than the recipe required. She also used less butter, fewer apples, fewer raisins, and less sugar than she was supposed to. As a result, Carol's apple cake didn't taste very good. As a matter of fact, it tasted terrible!

PAUL'S BEEF STEW

Paul cooked beef stew yesterday, but he couldn't follow all the instructions in his cookbook because he didn't have enough of the ingredients. He used less meat and fewer tomatoes than the recipe required. He also used fewer potatoes, less salt, less pepper, and fewer onions than he was supposed to. As a result, Paul's beef stew didn't taste very good. As a matter of fact, it tasted awful!

✔ READING CHECK-UP

WHAT'S THE WORD?

Steve and Judy built their own house last year, but they couldn't follow the blueprints exactly because they didn't have enough money to buy all the construction materials they needed. They used _____ 1 wood and _____ 2 nails than the blueprints required. They also used _____ 3 cement, _____ 4 pipes, _____ 5 electrical wiring, and _____ 6 bricks than they were supposed to. As a result, their house didn't last very long. As a matter of fact, it fell down last week!

They Must Lose Some Weight

| mustn't (must not) | don't doesn't } have to |

A. I had my yearly checkup today.

B. What did the doctor say?

A. He said I'm a little too heavy and I must lose some weight.

B. Do you have to stop eating **ice cream**?

A. No. I don't have to stop eating **ice cream**. But I mustn't eat as much **ice cream** as I did before.

A. Grandpa had his yearly checkup today.

B. What did the doctor say?

A. She said he's a little too heavy and he must lose some weight.

B. Does he have to stop eating **cookies**?

A. No. He doesn't have to stop eating **cookies**. But he mustn't eat as many **cookies** as he did before.

1. I had my yearly checkup today.

2. Billy had his yearly checkup today.

3. Grandma had her yearly checkup today.

4. Rover had his yearly checkup today.

Really, Doctor?

should   must

A. I'm really worried about your heart.

B. Really, Doctor? Should I stop eating rich desserts?

A. Mr. Jones! You MUST stop eating rich desserts! If you don't, you're going to have serious problems with your heart some day.

A. I'm really worried about your _____.

B. Really, Doctor? Should I _____?

A. (Mr./Miss/Mrs./Ms.) _____! You MUST _____! If you don't, you're going to have serious problems with your _____ some day.

1. *knees
stop jogging*

2. *back
start doing exercises*

3. *stomach
stop eating spicy foods*

4. *blood pressure
take life a little easier*

5. *hearing
stop listening to loud
rock music*

6.

Asking for Advice

A. *I have a cold.* {
    What should I do?
    Do you have any advice?
    Do you have any suggestions?
}

B. I think you should *drink some hot tea.*

Practice the conversations on this page, using these expressions for asking for advice.

INTERACTIONS

HOME REMEDIES

Different people have different remedies for medical problems that aren't very serious. For example, people do different things when they burn a finger.

Some people rub butter on their finger.

Other people put a piece of ice on their finger.

Other people put their finger under cold water.

Practice conversations with other students. Ask for advice about these medical problems, and give advice about "home remedies" you know.

I have a cold.

I have a toothache.

I have a stomachache.

I have a bloody nose.

I have the hiccups.

PRONUNCIATION *Must & Mustn't*

Listen. Then say it.

I **must** eat more fruit.

He **must** eat fewer cookies.

You **mustn't** eat cake.

They **mustn't** eat ice cream.

Say it. Then listen.

We **must** eat less cheese.

She **must** eat more vegetables.

I **mustn't** eat butter.

They **mustn't** eat potato chips.

There are a lot of rules in daily life—things you must do and things you mustn't do. Think about the rules in YOUR life—at school, on the job, in your home, and in your community. Write about these rules in your journal.

GRAMMAR FOCUS

MUST

I He She It We You They	must work.

I He She It We You They	mustn't eat candy.

MUSTN'T VS. DON'T HAVE TO

I **don't have to** stop eating cookies.
But I **mustn't** eat as many cookies as I did before.

MUST VS. SHOULD

Should I stop eating rich desserts?
You **must** stop eating rich desserts.

COUNT/NON-COUNT NOUNS:
NON-COUNT

He must eat	more less	bread. fish. meat.

COUNT

He must eat	more fewer	cookies. potatoes. eggs.

Choose the correct word.

1. I'm a little heavy. I know I (**must** mustn't) lose some weight.

2. You (**must** shouldn't) stop jogging. If you don't, you're going to have problems with your knees.

3. My doctor says I must eat (fewer **less**) eggs and (fewer **less**) butter.

4. You (must **mustn't**) eat as (many **much**) candy or as (many **much**) cookies as you did before.

5. I (**don't have to** must) stop eating ice cream, but I (have to **mustn't**) have it every day.

6. I know I should eat (**fewer** less) french fries, but I love them. My doctor says I (must **mustn't**) eat as many as I do now.

7. My husband has high blood pressure. I always tell him he (mustn't **should**) stop putting so (**much** many) salt on his food.

8. Michael's cookies didn't taste very good. He used (fewer **less**) flour and (**fewer** less) raisins than the recipe required. He knows that next time he (**must** mustn't) follow the recipe more carefully.

LIFE SKILLS

- **Making a doctor appointment**
- **Calling in sick**
- **Reporting a child's absence from school**

1 CONVERSATION MAKING A DOCTOR APPOINTMENT

Practice with a classmate. Make appointments for these medical problems. Use your name and any time you wish.

A. Doctor's office.

B. Hello. This is _____(first & last name)_____. I'd like to make an appointment.

A. What's the problem?

B. I have a bad _____.

A. Can you come in tomorrow at _(time)_?

B. Tomorrow at _(time)_? Yes. Thank you.

1. stomachache   **2. headache**   **3. backache**   **4. cough**

5. earache   **6. sore throat**   **7. fever**   **8. stiff neck**

2 CONVERSATION CALLING IN SICK

Practice with a classmate.

A. Hello. This is _____(first & last name)_____. I'm sorry, but I can't come to work today. I'm sick.

B. I'm sorry to hear that. What's the matter?

A. _____.

B. Okay. I hope you feel better soon.

A. Thank you.

3 CONVERSATION & WRITING REPORTING ABSENCE FROM SCHOOL

Practice with a classmate.

A. Hello. This is _(first & last name)_. My son/daughter _(child's name)_ will be absent from school today. He's/She's sick.

B. Okay. Thank you for calling.

Write a note to the teacher the next day.

_____(date)_____

Dear _____(teacher's name)_____,

My son/daughter _____(name)_____ was absent from school yesterday because _____.

Sincerely,

_____(your name)_____

Read the medicine labels. Decide if the sentences are True (T) or False (F).

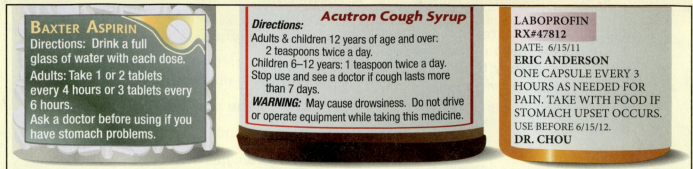

BAXTER ASPIRIN
Directions: Drink a full glass of water with each dose.
Adults: Take 1 or 2 tablets every 4 hours or 3 tablets every 6 hours.
Ask a doctor before using if you have stomach problems.

Acutron Cough Syrup
Directions:
Adults & children 12 years of age and over: 2 teaspoons twice a day.
Children 6–12 years: 1 teaspoon twice a day.
Stop use and see a doctor if cough lasts more than 7 days.
WARNING: May cause drowsiness. Do not drive or operate equipment while taking this medicine.

LABOPROFIN
RX#47812
DATE: 6/15/11
ERIC ANDERSON
ONE CAPSULE EVERY 3 HOURS AS NEEDED FOR PAIN. TAKE WITH FOOD IF STOMACH UPSET OCCURS.
USE BEFORE 6/15/12.
DR. CHOU

_____ 1. You should stop taking Acutron Cough Syrup if your cough doesn't get better after seven days.

_____ 2. Dr. Chou wrote a prescription for Laboprofin on June fifteenth, 2012.

_____ 3. An adult can take three Baxter Aspirin tablets every four hours.

_____ 4. Eleven-year old children can take two teaspoons of Acutron Cough Syrup a day.

_____ 5. When you take two Baxter Aspirin tablets you should drink a glass of water.

_____ 6. Eric Anderson should stop taking Laboprofin if he gets a stomachache.

Read the magazine article. Decide if the sentences are True (T) or False (F).

Medicine Safety Tips

Pharmacies have many aisles of medicine for every kind of ailment. There are decongestants and nose drops for stuffy noses, throat lozenges for sore throats, aspirin and other pain relievers for headaches, antihistamines for allergies, and antacids for stomachaches. Although you don't need a prescription for any of these over-the-counter drugs, they can hurt you if don't use them correctly.

Before you take a non-prescription medicine, be sure to read the label carefully. The label tells you what the medicine is for, its ingredients, the correct dosage (how much to take and how often), and the expiration date. If you take two or more medicines at the same time, read the labels carefully to make sure you don't take too much of an ingredient. Throw away the medicine if it is past the expiration date.

The warning on the label tells you when *not* to use the medicine, when to stop taking it, and possible problems or side effects you might have such as stomach pains. This information can help you decide if this is the right medicine for you. If you don't understand the label, talk to the pharmacist or your doctor. If you take the medicine and you don't feel better, see a doctor. You might have a more serious health problem that requires stronger medication.

Your doctor might write a prescription for medicine you will get at a pharmacy. Tell the doctor about any other medications you are taking because it can be dangerous to mix medicines. Prescription medicine has more possible side effects than over-the-counter medicine, so it's especially important to understand the directions and warnings on the label and to ask your doctor and pharmacist questions.

_____ 1. Antihistamines are for stomachaches.

_____ 2. Doctors prescribe over-the-counter drugs.

_____ 3. Non-prescription medicine isn't as strong as prescription medicine.

_____ 4. It's good to mix medicines.

_____ 5. Dosage instructions tell you how many times a day to take the medicine.

_____ 6. Stomachaches are a possible side effect.

_____ 7. The warning on the label tells you what the medicine is for.

Read the magazine article and answer the questions.

A Healthy Diet

Are you overweight? Do you feel tired all the time? Eating healthier foods will give you energy and will help you lose those extra pounds. It will also protect you from high blood pressure, heart problems, and other diseases.

Eat small amounts of many different kinds of food each day. It's important to eat food that is high in vitamins, minerals, and other nutrients and low in sugar, salt, and unhealthy fats. Eat fruits, vegetables, whole grains (whole wheat bread, brown rice, whole grain cereal), and low-fat dairy products (low-fat milk, low-fat yogurt). These foods provide most of the vitamins and minerals that you need, such as calcium and potassium. Include protein in your diet. You can get protein from meat, chicken, fish, eggs, beans, and nuts. Protein is important, but you should eat more fruits, vegetables, grains, and dairy products than protein.

Most of the fat you eat should come from fish, nuts, and vegetable oil. Fat from meat, chicken, butter, margarine, cream, mayonnaise, fried foods, and snack foods is bad for your heart.

Lemon Chicken

Ingredients	
1 chicken, cut up	Place the chicken in a baking pan. Mix the
2 Tbsp. vegetable oil	vegetable oil, mustard,
2 Tbsp. lemon juice	and lemon juice and pour
1 tsp. mustard	it over the chicken.
pepper	Add pepper to taste.
Tbsp.= tablespoon	Bake at 375° for
tsp.= teaspoon	45 minutes.

Buy fish or lean meat. If there is fat on the meat, cut off the fat before you cook it. For example, cook chicken without the skin. Don't cook with a lot of oil. It's better to grill, broil, or microwave food than to fry it.

Sugar doesn't have any nutrients, and it's bad for your teeth. Drink water or diet soda instead of soda, and eat very few sweet snacks and desserts. Try to eat less than a teaspoon of salt a day. Too much salt can give you high blood pressure.

Food that is low in salt, sugar, and fat can be delicious! There are many wonderful spices and other ingredients that you can add for flavor. Learn how to cook and eat the healthy way!

1. According to this article, you should _____.
   A. eat a lot of salt
   B. eat more protein foods than grains
   C. fry foods
   D. eat fewer desserts

2. _____ is a protein food.
   A. Butter
   B. Lettuce
   C. Fish
   D. Whole wheat bread

3. Whole grain products DON'T include _____.
   A. brown rice
   B. whole milk
   C. whole grain cereal
   D. whole wheat bread

4. Fat from _____ is unhealthy fat.
   A. fish
   B. mayonnaise
   C. nuts
   D. vegetable oil

5. To prepare lemon chicken, you _____.
   A. add two tablespoons of mustard
   B. broil the chicken for forty-five minutes
   C. cut up the chicken before you cook it
   D. microwave it

6. We can infer that chicken skin _____.
   A. is fatty
   B. has too much salt
   C. is sweet
   D. is lean

WRITING   Your Favorite Healthy Foods

What fruits do you like? What are your favorite vegetables? What are your favorite protein foods? What other healthy foods do you like? Write about them.

PROJECT   A Class Recipe Book

Write a recipe for your favorite healthy food. Share your recipe with the class. Then work together and make a class recipe book!

Choose the correct answer.

1. The doctor measured my _____.
   A. height
   B. heart
   C. health
   D. tests

2. The technician will take _____.
   A. an examination room
   B. your eyes, ears, nose, and throat
   C. an X-ray
   D. a medical checkup

3. My doctor is concerned about my weight. She put me on a _____.
   A. physical examination
   B. diet
   C. stethoscope
   D. suggestion

4. My pie wasn't very good. I didn't follow the _____ in the cookbook.
   A. blueprints
   B. construction
   C. exercises
   D. instructions

5. Do you know any _____ for a cold?
   A. recipes
   B. remedies
   C. questions
   D. problems

6. My doctor says I must lose some _____.
   A. energy
   B. advice
   C. weight
   D. blood pressure

7. I always read the label carefully. Many medicines have _____.
   A. side effects
   B. pharmacies
   C. ailments
   D. ingredients

8. This food is healthy because it has a lot of _____.
   A. fat
   B. salt
   C. sugar
   D. vitamins

Look at the medicine labels. Choose the correct answer.

Paxton's Pain Medicine
Directions
Adults: Take 2 tablets every 4 hours, or 3 tablets every 6 hours.
Children 6 years to under 12 years: 1 tablet every 6 hours.
Use before 11/15/12

Comfort Cold Medicine
Directions
Adults: Take 2 capsules 4 times a day.
Children 6 years to under 12 years: 1 capsule twice a day.
Use before 9/15/12

Victor's Cough Syrup
Directions:
Adults & children 12 years of age and over: 4 teaspoons twice a day. | Children 6 years to under 12 years: 2 teaspoons twice a day
Stop use and see a doctor if cough lasts more than 5 days.

9. Adults can take _____.
   A. 16 teaspoons of Victor's Cough Syrup a day
   B. 8 Comfort Cold capsules a day
   C. 15 Comfort Cold capsules a day
   D. 3 Paxton's Pain tablets every 4 hours

10. Nine-year-old children can take _____ a day.
   A. 12 Paxton's Pain tablets
   B. 8 teaspoons of Victor's Cough Syrup
   C. 4 Paxton Pain tablets
   D. 4 Comfort Cold capsules

12

Future Continuous Tense
Time Expressions

- **Describing Future Activities**
- **Expressing Time and Duration**
- **Making Plans by Telephone**
- **Handling Wrong-Number Calls**
- **Leaving and Taking Phone Messages**
- **Telephone Directory: White Pages, Government Pages, and Yellow Pages**
- **Using a Telephone Response System**

VOCABULARY PREVIEW

1. bathe the dog
2. clean out the garage
3. exercise
4. iron
5. knit
6. mop the floor
7. pay bills
8. rearrange furniture
9. repaint the kitchen
10. sew
11. borrow
12. return

Will They Be Home This Evening?

(I will)	I'll
(He will)	He'll
(She will)	She'll
(It will)	It'll
(We will)	We'll
(You will)	You'll
(They will)	They'll

be working.

A. Will you be home this evening?

B. Yes, I will. I'll be reading.

1. Amanda
ironing

2. Jack
sewing

3. Mr. and Mrs. Kramer
exercising

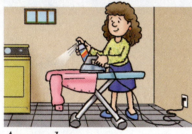

4. Omar
paying bills

5. you
knitting

6. Harriet
mopping the floor

7. you and your wife
bathing the dog

8. your parents
rearranging furniture

9.

When Can You Come Over?

Complete this conversation and practice with another student.

Hello.

Hi, _____.
This is _____.

Hi, _____. What's up?

I'm having some problems with the homework for tomorrow.

Oh. I'll be glad to help.

Thanks. I can come over at _____ o'clock. Is that okay?

I'm afraid I won't be home at _____ o'clock. I'll be _____ing. How about _____ o'clock?

No, I won't be able to come over at _____ o'clock. I'll be _____ing. How about _____ o'clock?

Fine. I'll see you then.

Will You Be Home Today at About Five O'Clock?

A. Hello, Richard. This is Julie. I want to return the tennis racket I borrowed from you last week. Will you be home today at about five o'clock?

B. Yes, I will. I'll be cooking dinner.

A. Oh. Then I won't come over at five.

B. Why not?

A. I don't want to disturb you. You'll be cooking dinner!

B. Don't worry. You won't disturb me.

A. Okay. See you at five.

A. Hello, _____. This is _____. I want to return the _____ I borrowed from you last week. Will you be home today at about _____ o'clock?

B. Yes, I will. I'll be _____ing.

A. Oh. Then I won't come over at _____.

B. Why not?

A. I don't want to disturb you. You'll be _____ing!

B. Don't worry. You won't disturb me.

A. Okay. See you at _____.

1. *videotape*
   repainting the kitchen

2. *hammer*
   cleaning out the garage

3. *football*
   ironing

4.

Calling People on the Telephone

The person you're calling is there.

A. Hello.

B. Hello. This is *David*. May I please speak to *Carol*?

A. Yes. Hold on a moment.

The person you're calling isn't there. A different person answers.

A. Hello.

B. Hello. This is *Maria*. May I please speak to *Kate*?

A. I'm sorry. *Kate* isn't here right now. Can I take a message?

B. Yes. Please tell *Kate* that *Maria* called.

A. Okay.

B. Thank you.

The person you're calling has an answering machine.

A. Hello. This is *Roger*. I'm not here right now. Please leave your name, telephone number, and a brief message after the beep, and I'll call you back. [*beep*]

B. Hi, *Roger*. This is *Eric*. . . .

Practice making telephone calls.

LISTENING

YOU HAVE EIGHT MESSAGES!

Listen to the messages on Bob's machine. Match the messages.

____ **1.** Aunt Betty   a. will be repainting the living room.

____ **2.** Melanie   b. will be exercising at the health club.

____ **3.** Alan   c. will be paying bills.

____ **4.** Ms. Wong   d. will be ironing her clothes.

____ **5.** Rick and Nancy   e. will be visiting Russia.

____ **6.** Denise   f. will be studying for a big test.

____ **7.** Dr. Garcia   g. will be working until 8 P.M.

____ **8.** Mom and Dad   h. will be attending a wedding.

GROWING UP

Jessica is growing up. Very soon she'll be walking, she'll be talking, and she'll be playing with the other children in the neighborhood. Jessica can't believe how quickly time flies! She won't be a baby very much longer. Soon she'll be a little girl.

Tommy is growing up. Very soon he'll be shaving, he'll be driving, and he'll be going out on dates. Tommy can't believe how quickly time flies! He won't be a little boy very much longer. Soon he'll be a teenager.

Kathy is growing up. Very soon she'll be going to college, she'll be living away from home, and she'll be starting a career. Kathy can't believe how quickly time flies! She won't be a teenager very much longer. Soon she'll be a young adult.

Peter and Sally are getting older. Very soon they'll be getting married, they'll be having children, and they'll be buying a house. Peter and Sally can't believe how quickly time flies! They won't be young adults very much longer. Soon they'll be middle-aged.

Walter is getting older. Very soon he'll be reaching the age of sixty-five, he'll be retiring, and he'll be taking it easy for the first time in his life. Walter can't believe how quickly time flies! He won't be middle-aged very much longer. Soon he'll be a senior citizen.

✔ **READING** *CHECK-UP*

TRUE OR FALSE?

1. Jessica will be talking soon.
2. Kathy doesn't go to college.
3. Peter and Sally are married.
4. Walter will stop working soon.
5. Tommy is a teenager.
6. Jessica won't be going out on dates very soon.

How About You?

What do you think you'll be doing ten years from now? Tell about your future.

She'll Be Staying with Us for a Few Months

A. How long will your Aunt Gertrude be staying with us?

B. She'll be staying with us **for a few months**.

1. How long will they be staying in Vancouver?
until Friday

2. How much longer will you be working on my car?
for a few more hours

3. How late will your son be studying this evening?
until 8 o'clock

4. How much longer will you be practicing the trombone?
for a few more minutes

5. When will we be arriving in Sydney?
at 7 A.M.

6. How far will we be driving today?
until we reach Milwaukee

7. How much longer will you be chatting online with your friends?
for ten more minutes

8. How soon will Santa Claus be coming?
in a few days

HAPPY THANKSGIVING!

Thanksgiving is this week, and several of our relatives from out of town will be staying with us during the long holiday weekend. Uncle Frank will be staying for a few days. He'll be sleeping in the room over the garage. Grandma and Grandpa will be staying until next Monday. They'll be sleeping in the master bedroom. Cousin Ben will be staying until Saturday. He'll be sleeping in the guest room. Cousin Bertha will be staying for a week. She'll be sleeping on a cot in the children's bedroom. (My wife and I will be sleeping downstairs on the convertible sofa in the living room.)

Our family will be busy for the next few days. My wife and I will be preparing Thanksgiving dinner, and our children will be cleaning the house from top to bottom. We're looking forward to the holiday, but we know we'll be happy when it's over.

Happy Thanksgiving!

✔ READING *CHECK-UP*

Q & A

Uncle Frank, Grandma, Grandpa, Cousin Ben, and Cousin Bertha are calling to ask about the plans for Thanksgiving. Using this model, create dialogs based on the story.

A. Hi! This is *Uncle Frank*!
B. Hi, *Uncle Frank*! How are you?
A. Fine!
B. We're looking forward to seeing you for Thanksgiving.
A. Actually, that's why I'm calling. Are you sure there will be enough room for me?
B. Don't worry! We'll have plenty of room. You'll be sleeping *in the room over the garage*. Will that be okay?
A. That'll be fine.
B. By the way, *Uncle Frank*, how long will you be staying with us?
A. *For a few days.*
B. That's great! We're really looking forward to seeing you.

Listen. Then say it.

Yes, I will. I'll be cooking.

Yes, he will. He'll be baking.

Yes, it will. It'll be raining.

Yes, we will. We'll be reading.

Say it. Then listen.

Yes, I will. I'll be cleaning.

Yes, she will. She'll be studying.

Yes, you will. You'll be working.

Yes, they will. They'll be sleeping.

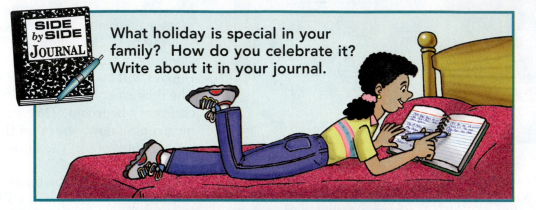

SIDE by SIDE JOURNAL

What holiday is special in your family? How do you celebrate it? Write about it in your journal.

GRAMMAR FOCUS

FUTURE CONTINUOUS TENSE

(I will)	I'll	
(He will)	He'll	
(She will)	She'll	
(It will)	It'll	be working.
(We will)	We'll	
(You will)	You'll	
(They will)	They'll	

TIME EXPRESSIONS

		a few months.
	for	a few more hours.
I'll be staying		a few more minutes.
	until	Friday.
		10 o'clock.
		we reach Milwaukee.

| We'll be arriving | at 7 A.M. |
| | in a few days. |

Complete the sentences with the future continuous tense and *for*, *until*, or *at*.

1. A. How long _____ your parents _____ staying in Montreal?
   B. _____ staying there _____ a week.

2. A. How late _____ you and your wife _____ cleaning your garage?
   B. _____ cleaning it _____ six o'clock.

3. A. When _____ Uncle George _____ arriving?
   B. _____ arriving _____ 10:45 this morning.

4. A. _____ you be home tonight?
   B. Yes, _____. _____ reading _____ I get tired.

5. A. When _____ the train _____ leaving?
   B. _____ leaving _____ exactly 9:19.

6. A. How much longer _____ your daughter _____ practicing the piano?
   B. _____ practicing _____ ten more minutes.

1 CONVERSATION   WRONG NUMBERS

Practice conversations with your classmates. Dial a wrong number!

A. Hello.

B. Hello. Is this ___(name)___?

A. I'm sorry. There's nobody here named ___(name)___.

B. Is this ___(phone number)___?

A. No, it isn't.

B. I apologize. I dialed the wrong number.

2 CONVERSATION   LEAVING A MESSAGE

Practice the conversation with a classmate.

Carla—

David called

417-624-9358

A. Hello.

B. Hello. This is David. May I speak with Carla?

A. Just a moment. Let me see if she's here.

B. Thanks.

. . .

A. Sorry. She isn't here right now. Can I take a message?

B. Yes. Please tell her that David called. My telephone number is 417-624-9358.

A. Okay.

B. Thank you.

3 CONVERSATION & WRITING   TAKING PHONE MESSAGES

Practice with a classmate. Write down the messages.

A. Hello.

B. Hello. This is _____. May I speak with _____?

A. Just a moment. Let me see if he's/she's here.

B. Thanks.

. . .

A. Sorry. He/She isn't here right now. Can I take a message?

B. Yes. Please tell him/her that _____ called. My telephone number is _____.

A. Okay.

B. Thank you.

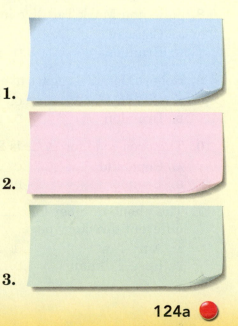

1.

2.

3.

124a

TABB—TAYLOR	213

TAFT Diane 472 Maple Lit 252 478-3296
Jane & Mark 15 Hill Con 252 853-9701
M A 86 Walnut Lit 252 478-5783
Peter 174 Rogers Bri 252 876-0021
TAGGART Robert D 19 Davis Bra 336 793-0065
Robert P 1655 E Pine Con 252 853-7428
Tammie 425 College Cop 336 516-6735
TAI Lan 262 Birch Lin ....(336 392-6163)
TALBOT Beth 243 Mill Bri 252 876-5218
Mark 32 Green Cop 336 793-2804
Vera & George 222 Congress Bri 252 478-6635
TALIENTO A & S 466 Ridge Lin 336 392-1306
Carlo 94 Laurel Lin 336 392-2854

BRANDON TOWN OF
AMBULANCE/FIRE & RESCUE
EMERGENCY CALLS ONLY 911
For All Other Business 336 793-3670
Animal Control Office 336 638-8621
Board of Health 336 638-3792
Building Inspector 336 793-4611
Highway Department 336 793-5900
Library 253 Park Bran 336 638-8156
Parks & Recreation 336 638-6258
POLICE —
EMERGENCY CALLS ONLY 911
For All Other Business 336 793-4500
Recycling 336 638-5415
SCHOOLS —
King Elementary School 336 634-1200
Lincoln Middle School 336 634-1400
Brandon High School 336 634-1600

Circle the answers on the telephone directory page above.

1. What is Lan Tai's phone number?

2. What is Carlo Taliento's address?

3. What is Robert Paul Taggart's phone number?

4. What is Mark Talbot's phone number?

5. What is Mary Ann Taft's address?

6. What is Armando and Sandra Taliento's telephone number?

7. What is George Talbot's address?

Choose the correct answer.

8. Jane and Mark Taft live in _____.
   A. Conway
   B. Brandon
   C. Copeland
   D. Littleton

9. Robert Daniel Taggart lives in _____.
   A. Conway
   B. Brandon
   C. Copeland
   D. Bridgeton

10. The area code for _____ is 252.
    A. Copeland
    B. Brandon
    C. Littleton
    D. Linwood

11. The phone number for _____ is on a different directory page.
    A. Amy Tan
    B. Rose Tallman
    C. Arthur Tenny
    D. Lisa Tate

12. Call _____ if someone is having a heart attack.
    A. 336 793-3670
    B. 911
    C. 336 793-4500
    D. 336 638-3792

13. Call _____ if there's a dangerous dog in the neighborhood.
    A. 336 638-3792
    B. 336 793-3670
    C. 336 793-5900
    D. 336 638-8621

14. Call _____ if someone just stole your wallet.
    A. 336 793-3670
    B. 336 638-3792
    C. 336 793-4500
    D. 911

15. Call _____ to ask about free flu shots.
    A. 336 793-4500
    B. 336 638-3792
    C. 336 638-5415
    D. 336 638-8156

16. Call _____ if a traffic light isn't working.
    A. 336 793-5900
    B. 336 793-3670
    C. 336 638-6258
    D. 911

17. Call _____ if your landlord won't repair the stairs in your building.
    A. 336 793-4500
    B. 336 638-3792
    C. 336 793-4611
    D. 336 793-3670

18. Call _____ if you have an old refrigerator you don't need anymore.
    A. 336 638-3792
    B. 336 793-4611
    C. 336 638-5415
    D. 336 793-3670

19. Call _____ to register your 5-year-old daughter for kindergarten next year.
    A. 336 634-1200
    B. 336 634-1400
    C. 336 634-1600
    D. 336 638-8156

YELLOW PAGES

HOSPITALS

King Medical Center
250 Central Mul 765 269–1580

Mount Hope Hospital
586 Riverway Mid
General Information 812 379–4200
Emergency Department 812 379–4300
Clinic 812 379–3054
Pharmacy 812 379–4703

HOTELS & MOTELS

BROOKSIDE HOTEL   —see our ad this page
93 South Med 765 516–6702

Hillside Motel
15 Waterview Mul 765 246–3065

Oakwood Hotel
772 Brighton Mil 765 921–5724

VILLAGE GREEN HOTEL   —see our ad this page
715 Raymond Mit 812 489–8831

WHITE PINES INN   —see our ad this page
212 Grove Mul 765 269–7050

BROOKSIDE HOTEL
93 South Street, Medford
Indoor Heated Pool
Restaurants, shops nearby
Open Year Round
765 516-6702
H

VILLAGE GREEN HOTEL Pets Welcome
· Outdoor Pool and Exercise Room
· A/C, Cable TV, refrigerators
· Pets Welcome
Open June to December
715 Raymond Street, Mitchell
812 489–8831

White Pines Inn
212 Grove Street, Mulberry
50 Comfortable Guest Rooms
Enjoy Our Fine Restaurant
765 269–7050
Open May to October

Circle the following information in the telephone directory listings above.

1. The address of a hospital in Mulberry.
2. The phone number of a hotel in Milton.
3. The address of a hotel with an outdoor pool.
4. The phone number of a hotel with a restaurant.
5. The phone number of a clinic in Midland.
6. The address of a hotel that is open in April.
7. The phone number of a hospital pharmacy.
8. The phone number of a hotel where you can bring your dog.

A TELEPHONE RESPONSE SYSTEM

When you call the Save-Mart store, an automated response system answers. Follow the instructions and answer the questions.

Thank you for calling Save-Mart Department Store.
• For gift card information, press 1.
• To locate a Save-Mart near you, press 2.
• To place an order, press 3.
• To check the delivery date of an order, press 4.
• If you are calling with a question about your credit card account, press 5.
• To add your name to our mailing list, press 6.
• For customer service, press 7.

1. Jeffrey wants to talk to a customer service representative. He should press _____.
   A. 2   B. 3   C. 6   D. 7

2. Susan thinks there's a mistake on her credit card bill. She should press _____.
   A. 1   B. 4   C. 5   D. 6

3. Monica wants to know the day her TV is going to arrive. She should press _____.
   A. 2   B. 3   C. 4   D. 6

4. Bruno is looking for the nearest Save-Mart store. He should press _____.
   A. 2   B. 3   C. 6   D. 7

5. Edna wants to order a computer. She should press _____.
   A. 1   B. 3   C. 4   D. 5

Choose the correct answer.

1. I'll be mopping the ____ this evening.
   A. clothes
   B. floor
   C. dog
   D. cot

2. I'm sorry. Ms. Wong isn't here right now. Can I take ____?
   A. a moment
   B. a beep
   C. a message
   D. an answering machine

3. Here's the plate I ____ from you last week.
   A. returned
   B. lent
   C. gave
   D. borrowed

4. We'll be ____ in Chicago until Sunday.
   A. staying
   B. arriving
   C. looking forward
   D. disturbing

5. William is middle-aged. Soon he'll be a ____.
   A. young adult
   B. teenager
   C. senior citizen
   D. little boy

6. I'll be busy on Saturday. I'll be attending ____.
   A. bills
   B. the garage
   C. furniture
   D. a wedding

Look at this page from a telephone directory. Choose the correct answer.

183 SANBORN—SATO	
SANBORN Erica 917 Main Gre	**573 544-2975**
T R 43 Pine Gle	**314 232-7736**
SANCHEZ D & N 16 High Can	**573 675-8920**
David N 573 Broadway Map	**314 899-4467**
P & M 425 First Cla	**314 337-2927**
SANDLER D M 75 Maple Can	**573 675-0098**
D & N 32 Green Cla	**314 337-2278**
Norman 32 Green Mal	**573 454-4187**
SANDS Louisa 357 Willow Gre	**573 544-1989**
Robert L 223 Grove Cla	**314 337-3378**
SANTANA L 468 King Mal	**573 454-4212**
R & L 773 West Map	**314 899-4926**
SANTOS Ramon 115 Kent Gle	**314 232-7721**

7. Daniel and Norma Sandler live in ____.
   A. Glendale
   B. Canton
   C. Clayton
   D. Greenville

8. The phone number for Rosa and Luis Santana is ____.
   A. 314-337-3378
   B. 314-899-4926
   C. 573-454-4212
   D. 573-544-1989

9. The area code for ____ is 314.
   A. Greenville
   B. Malden
   C. Glendale
   D. Canton

10. The phone number for ____ is on a different directory page.
   A. Marian Saunders
   B. J. P. Sarrouf
   C. Angela Sarmiento
   D. Kenji Sasaki

SKILLS CHECK ✓

Words:

☐ bathe
☐ borrow
☐ clean out
☐ come over
☐ disturb
☐ exercise
☐ grow up
☐ iron
☐ knit
☐ mop
☐ pay bills
☐ rearrange
☐ repaint
☐ retire

☐ return
☐ sew
☐ message
☐ telephone directory
☐ wrong number
☐ ambulance
☐ animal control office
☐ board of health

☐ building inspector
☐ fire & rescue
☐ highway department
☐ library
☐ parks & recreation
☐ police
☐ recycling
☐ schools

I can ask & answer:

☐ Will *you* be home *this evening*? Yes, *I* will. *I'll* be *reading*.
☐ Will you be home today at about *five o'clock*?
☐ Can I come over and visit *this evening*?
☐ How long/How much longer/How late will *you* be *studying*?
☐ When/How soon will *we* be *arriving*?
☐ How far will *we* be *driving*?

I can write about:

☐ how my family celebrates a holiday

I can leave and take telephone messages:

☐ Hello. This is *David*. May I (please) speak to/with *Carol*? Just a moment. Let me see if *she's* here.
   Yes. Hold on a moment.
   Sorry./I'm sorry. *Carol* isn't here right now. Can I take a message? Please tell *Carol* that *David* called.

I can:

☐ use the white pages, yellow pages, and government pages in the telephone directory
☐ use an automated telephone response system

13

Some/Any
Pronoun Review
Verb Tense Review

- Offering Help
- Indicating Ownership
- Household Problems
- Requesting Maintenance and Repairs

- Reading a Rental Agreement
- Tenants' Rights
- Friends

VOCABULARY PREVIEW

1. electrician
2. locksmith
3. mechanic
4. plumber
5. repairperson

6. downstairs neighbor
7. upstairs neighbor
8. next-door neighbor

9. dishwasher
10. faucet
11. garbage disposal
12. lock
13. video camera / camcorder

I'll Be Glad to Help

I	me	my	mine	myself
you	you	your	yours	yourself
he	him	his	his	himself
she	her	her	hers	herself
it	it	its	—	itself
we	us	our	ours	ourselves
you	you	your	yours	yourselves
they	them	their	theirs	themselves

A. What's **Johnny** doing?

B. **He's** getting dressed.

A. Does **he** need any help? I'll be glad to help **him**.

B. No, that's okay. **He** can get dressed by **himself**.

1. *your daughter feed the canary*

2. *your husband clean the garage*

3. *your children make lunch*

4. *you do my homework*

5. *your sister wash her car*

6. *Jim and Nancy rake the leaves*

7. *Tom paint the fence*

8. *you and your husband bathe the dog*

9.

I Just Found This Watch

Fred

A. I just found this watch. Is it yours?

B. No, it isn't mine. But it might be **Fred's**. **He** lost **his** a few days ago.

A. Really? I'll call **him** right away.

B. When you talk to **him**, tell **him** I said "Hello."

Kate

1. umbrella

Alan

2. wallet

Grace

3. notebook

Mr. and Mrs. Ryan

4. camera

Ruth

5. calculator

George

6. headphones

Robert

7. ring

Jessica

8. sunglasses

Mr. and Mrs. Price

9. cell phone

Henry

10. address book

Janet

11. briefcase

12.

127

I Couldn't Fall Asleep Last Night

A. You look tired today.

B. Yes, I know. I couldn't fall asleep last night.

A. Why not?

B. My **neighbors** were **arguing**.

A. How late did they **argue**?

B. Believe it or not, they **argued** until 3 A.M.!

A. That's terrible! Did you call and complain?

B. No, I didn't. I don't like to complain.

A. Well, I hope you sleep better tonight.

B. I'm sure I will. My **neighbors** don't **argue** very often.

1. *downstairs neighbor*
sing

2. *neighbor's* dog*
bark

3. *upstairs neighbors*
vacuum their apartment

4. *neighbors'* son*
play the drums

* neighbor – neighbor's dog
neighbors – neighbors' son

5. neighbor across the hall
dance

6. neighbors' daughter
listen to loud music

7. next-door neighbors
rearrange their furniture

8. neighbor's cat
cry

9. neighbors' son
lift weights

10.

ON YOUR OWN *Neighbors*

Do you know your neighbors? Are they friendly? Are they helpful?
Do you sometimes have problems with your neighbors?

Talk with other students about your neighbors.

Do You Know Anybody Who Can Help Me?

something	anything
{ somebody }	{ anybody }
{ someone }	{ anyone }

A. There's something wrong with my **washing machine**.

B. I'm sorry. I can't help you. I don't know ANYTHING about **washing machines**.

A. Do you know anybody who can help me?

B. Not really. You should look in the phone book. I'm sure you'll find somebody who can fix it.

1. *refrigerator*

2. *dishwasher*

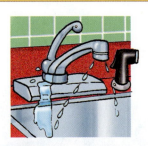

3. *kitchen faucet*

4. *garbage disposal*

5. *computer*

6. *bathtub*

7. *video camera*

8.

Can You Send a Plumber?

A. Armstrong Plumbing Company. Can I help you?

B. Yes. There's something wrong with my kitchen sink. Can you send a plumber to fix it as soon as possible?

A. Where do you live?

B. 156 Grove Street in Centerville.

A. I can send a plumber tomorrow morning. Is that okay?

B. Not really. I'm afraid I won't be home tomorrow morning. I'll be taking my son to the dentist.

A. How about tomorrow afternoon?

B. Tomorrow afternoon? What time?

A. Between one and four.

B. That's fine. Somebody will be here then.

A. What's the name?

B. Helen Bradley.

A. And what's the address again?

B. 156 Grove Street in Centerville.

A. And the phone number?

B. 237-9180.

A. Okay. We'll have someone there tomorrow afternoon.

B. Thank you.

A. _____. Can I help you?

B. Yes. There's something wrong with my _____.
Can you send a _____ to fix it as soon as possible?

A. Where do you live?

B. _____ in _____.

A. I can send a _____ tomorrow morning. Is that okay?

B. Not really. I'm afraid I won't be home tomorrow morning.
I'll be _____ing.

A. How about tomorrow afternoon?

B. Tomorrow afternoon? What time?

A. Between _____ and _____.

B. That's fine. Somebody will be here then.

A. What's the name?

B. _____.

A. And what's the address again?

B. _____ in _____.

A. And the phone number?

B. _____.

A. Okay. We'll have someone there tomorrow afternoon.

B. Thank you.

1. _Ajax Home Electronics Service_
repairperson

2. _Ace Electrical Repair_
electrician

3. _Patty's Plumbing and Heating_
plumber

4. _Larry's Lock Repair_
locksmith

TROUBLE WITH CARS

It might seem hard to believe, but my friends and I are all having trouble with our cars. There's something wrong with all of them!

Charlie is having trouble with his. The brakes don't work. He tried to fix them by himself, but he wasn't able to, since he doesn't know anything about cars. Finally, he took the car to his mechanic. The mechanic charged him a lot of money, and the brakes STILL don't work! Charlie is really annoyed. He's having a lot of trouble with his car, and he can't find anybody who can help him.

Betty is having trouble with hers. It doesn't start in the morning. She tried to fix it by herself, but she wasn't able to, since she doesn't know anything about cars. Finally, she took the car to her mechanic. The mechanic charged her a lot of money, and the car STILL doesn't start in the morning! Betty is really annoyed. She's having a lot of trouble with her car, and she can't find anybody who can help her.

Mark and Nancy are having trouble with theirs. The steering wheel doesn't turn. They tried to fix it by themselves, but they weren't able to, since they don't know anything about cars. Finally, they took the car to their mechanic. The mechanic charged them a lot of money, and the steering wheel STILL doesn't turn! Mark and Nancy are really annoyed. They're having a lot of trouble with their car, and they can't find anybody who can help them.

I'm having trouble with mine, too. The windows don't go up and down. I tried to fix them by myself, but I wasn't able to, since I don't know anything about cars. Finally, I took the car to my mechanic. The mechanic charged me a lot of money, and the windows STILL don't go up and down! I'm really annoyed. I'm having a lot of trouble with my car, and I can't find anybody who can help me.

✔ READING *CHECK-UP*

WHAT'S THE WORD?

1. Charlie tried to fix _____ car by _____.

2. Mark and Nancy's mechanic charged _____ a lot and still didn't fix _____ car.

3. Betty can't find anybody to help _____ fix _____ car.

4. I'm having trouble with _____ car, too. _____ starts in the morning, but the windows are broken.

5. The windows don't go up and down. I tried to fix _____ by _____, but I couldn't.

6. My friends and I can't fix _____ cars by _____, and we're all very angry at _____ mechanics.

LISTENING

WHAT'S THE WORD?

Listen and choose the word you hear.

1. a. him   b. her
2. a. him   b. them
3. a. them   b. him
4. a. yours   b. hers
5. a. yourself b. yourselves
6. a. our   b. her

WHAT ARE THEY TALKING ABOUT?

Listen and choose what the people are talking about.

1. a. stove   b. sink
2. a. dishwasher   b. garbage disposal
3. a. TV   b. camcorder
4. a. headphones   b. cell phone
5. a. windows   b. car

How About You?

Are you "handy"? Do you like to fix things? Tell about something you fixed. What was the problem? How did you fix it? Also, tell about something you COULDN'T fix. What was the problem? What did you do?

How to Say It!

Giving Advice

A. I'm having trouble with my *car*.

B. {
    You should
    You ought to
    I think you should
    I think you ought to
    } *take it to a mechanic.*

Practice conversations with other students. Talk about problems and give advice.

THAT'S WHAT FRIENDS ARE FOR!

Frank has some very nice friends. He sees his friends often. When he needs help, they're always happy to help him. For example, last week Frank moved to a new apartment. He couldn't move everything by himself, and he didn't really have enough money to hire a moving company. His friends came over and helped him move everything. He was very grateful. His friends said, "We're happy to help you, Frank. That's what friends are for!"

Emma has some very special friends. She sees her friends often. When she needs help, they're always happy to help her. For example, last month the faucet broke in Emma's kitchen and flooded her apartment. There was water in every room. She couldn't fix everything herself, and her superintendent didn't help her at all. Her friends came over and helped her fix the faucet and clean up every room in the apartment. She was very grateful. Her friends said, "We're happy to help you, Emma. That's what friends are for!"

It's nice to have friends you can rely on when you need help. Tell about a time when your friends helped you. Tell about a time when you helped a friend.

Listen. Then say it.

Tell him I said "Hello."

I'll be glad to help him.

He can get dressed by himself.

The mechanic charged him a lot of money.

Say it. Then listen.

Tell her I said "Hello."

I'll be glad to help her.

She can make lunch by herself.

The mechanic charged her a lot of money.

SIDE by SIDE JOURNAL

Think about a very good friend. Write about this person in your journal.

GRAMMAR FOCUS

PRONOUN REVIEW

Subject Pronouns	Object Pronouns	Possessive Adjectives	Possessive Pronouns	Reflexive Pronouns
I	me	my	mine	myself
you	you	your	yours	yourself
he	him	his	his	himself
she	her	her	hers	herself
it	it	its	—	itself
we	us	our	ours	ourselves
you	you	your	yours	yourselves
they	them	their	theirs	themselves

SOME/ANY

There's **something** wrong with my washing machine.
I'm sure you'll find **somebody/someone** who can fix it.

I don't know **anything** about washing machines.
Do you know **anybody/anyone** who can help me?

POSSESSIVE OF SINGULAR & PLURAL NOUNS

neighbor – neighbor's dog
neighbors – neighbors' son

Complete the sentences.

1. A. Does your son need any help? I'll be glad to help _____.
   B. No. That's okay. _____ can fix _____ bicycle by _____.

2. A. Is this newspaper _____ or Mr. and Mrs. Lee's?
   B. It isn't mine. I think it's _____.

3. A. Does your daughter need any help? I'll be glad to help _____.
   B. No. That's okay. _____ can do _____ homework by _____.

4. A. How did _____ hurt yourself?
   B. I hurt _____ while I was moving _____ piano.

5. A. How often do you speak to _____ grandparents?
   B. I call _____ every Sunday, and _____ call me every Wednesday.

6. A. Did your parents enjoy _____ at the concert last night?
   B. Yes, _____ did. You should get a ticket for tonight's concert. I'm sure _____ and your wife will enjoy _____.

7. A. Whose cell phone is this? Is _____ yours, your son's, or your wife's?
   B. It isn't _____. My cell phone is larger. It isn't _____ son's. _____ is smaller. It isn't _____ wife's. _____ is newer.

8. A. You look upset. What's the matter?
   B. We're having a problem. There's something wrong with _____ front door. _____ doesn't open. Do you know anybody who can help _____? _____ can't fix our front door by _____.

1 CONVERSATION FOLLOWING UP ON A REQUEST FOR MAINTENANCE

You called a few days ago to request a repair in your apartment, but nobody fixed it. Call again! Practice conversations with your classmates.

A. Hello. This is _____ in apartment _____.

B. Yes. How can I help you?

A. I called a few days ago. My _____ is broken.

B. I'm sorry. Please tell me the problem again.

A. _____

B. Okay. I'll make sure someone checks your _____ today.

A. Thank you very much.

1. dishwasher
It's leaking.

2. stove
Two burners don't light.

3. lock
The key gets stuck.

4. toilet
The water keeps running, and the toilet doesn't flush properly.

5. kitchen sink
The water drips, and the drain is clogged.

6. heat
The apartment doesn't get warm.

THINK, SHARE, & SOLVE What are other common maintenance and repair problems in a rental unit? What should a tenant do if the building manager doesn't fix a problem? Discuss as a class.

2 WRITING A REPAIR REQUEST FORM

You have a problem in your apartment! Fill out the form to request a repair.

APARTMENT MAINTENANCE/REPAIR REQUEST FORM

NAME: _____

ADDRESS: _____

PROBLEM/WORK REQUIRED: _____
_____

Is there a pet in the residence? ___ Yes ___ No
(If Yes, the pet must be secured or the maintenance person will not enter the residence.)

Do you give permission to the maintenance person
to enter the residence if you are not at home?   ___ Yes ___ No

_____   ___/___/___   _____ AM PM (circle)
Tenant's Signature   Date   Time

136a

Read the rental agreement and answer the questions.

Rental Agreement

This agreement is between: _____ Lenora Garcia _____ as LANDLORD and
_____ Frank P. Warner _____ as TENANT.

The LANDLORD leases to the TENANT apartment number __7__ at _____ 15 Russell Street _____
Bryan, Texas 778_02_ for the term of _twelve months_ beginning _April 1, 2011_ and ending on
March 31, 2012.

TERMS AND CONDITIONS OF THIS AGREEMENT:

1. **RENT:** The total rent for the apartment is $_10,500.00_. The monthly rent is $_875.00_ due on or before the _first_ day of each month. If the TENANT does not pay the rent before the _fifteenth_ of the month, the LANDLORD will charge a late fee of 4% of the monthly rent.

2. **UTILITIES AND SERVICES:** The TENANT will pay the following utility and service charges:
Gas, Electricity, Cable TV, Telephone, and Internet.

3. **APPLIANCES:** The apartment is rented with the following appliances: _Refrigerator and Stove_.
The LANDLORD will repair appliances that the LANDLORD owns that need repair due to normal use. The TENANT is responsible for repairing any other appliances.

4. **SECURITY DEPOSIT:** The TENANT will deposit with the LANDLORD a security deposit of $_875.00_.
If the apartment is in good condition when the TENANT moves out, and all rent is paid, the LANDLORD will return the full amount of the security deposit within 30 days.

5. **ENTRY TO APARTMENT:** The LANDLORD has the right to enter the apartment at reasonable times to inspect the apartment or to make repairs if the LANDLORD gives 24-hour notice.

6. **CONDITION OF APARTMENT:** The TENANT agrees to take good care of the apartment. When the agreement ends, the TENANT will return the apartment in good clean condition.

7. **NOISE:** The LANDLORD can end this agreement if other tenants in the building complain about any loud noises (i.e. parties, music, etc.).

---

1. _____ $875 every month.
   A. The security deposit is
   B. The late fee is
   C. The rent is
   D. The utilities are

2. The rental agreement is for _____.
   A. one month
   B. two months
   C. the month of April
   D. one year

3. Frank Warner can move into the apartment on _____.
   A. April 1, 2011
   B. March 31, 2011
   C. March 31, 2012
   D. April 1, 2012

4. The tenant does NOT have to pay the _____.
   A. gas bill
   B. telephone bill
   C. water bill
   D. electric bill

5. The tenant has to _____.
   A. enter the apartment at reasonable times
   B. repair the stove if it doesn't work
   C. complain about loud noises
   D. pay a 4% late fee if the rent is 15 days late

6. According to the agreement, the landlord CANNOT enter the tenant's apartment _____.
   A. to fix things
   B. if he doesn't tell the tenant the day before
   C. when the tenant isn't there
   D. to check the condition of the apartment

Read this tenants' rights notice and answer the questions.

KNOW YOUR RIGHTS!   Advice for tenants from the Franklin County Fair Housing Council

As a tenant, it's important to know your rights. According to state law, tenants have the right to an apartment that is safe and healthy to live in. The heating, plumbing, and electricity must work. The windows, doors, walls, roof, floors, and stairways must be in good condition. The building and the land around it must be clean. The apartment must have a bathroom with a toilet, sink, and bathtub or shower, and a kitchen with a sink. All of these must be in working condition. The apartment must also have windows that open in each room, safe fire or emergency exits, smoke detectors that work, and locks on outside doors and windows.

With these tenant rights, there are also responsibilities—things that you, as a tenant, have to do. You must take good care of your apartment, follow all the rules in your rental agreement or lease, and tell the landlord promptly when there are problems that need repairs. If you do all these things, your landlord has to fix problems that make the apartment unsafe and unhealthy to live in.

If your landlord won't make important repairs, call your city's code enforcement office or health department. You also have the right to pay for the repair and deduct the cost from your rent. For example, if it costs $300 to repair the sink and your rent is $800, you pay the landlord only $500.

Tenants often have questions about security deposits. How much can a landlord charge, and how long can he or she keep the money? According to state law, the security deposit for most apartments can't be more than twice the monthly rent. When the tenant moves out, the landlord must return the security deposit within 21 days if the apartment is in good condition. The landlord can use some or all of the security deposit to clean or repair the apartment, but only if the tenant caused the problem. The landlord has to return any money that he or she doesn't use for cleaning or repairs. If your landlord doesn't return your security deposit or keeps more than you think is right, you can talk to a lawyer and take your landlord to court.

A landlord cannot evict you from your apartment because you complained to your city's code enforcement office, made a repair and deducted it from your rent, or went to court about a housing problem. A landlord can never turn off your heat or electricity or put your things on the street. If a landlord changes the locks on your door, the landlord must give you the new key.

1. A tenant does NOT have to ____.
   A. take good care of the apartment
   B. fix problems that make the apartment unsafe
   C. follow the rules in the lease
   D. tell the landlord when the smoke detectors don't work

2. Call your city's health department if your landlord ____.
   A. won't return your security deposit
   B. changes the locks on your door
   C. complains
   D. won't fix a broken toilet

3. An apartment in Franklin County does NOT have to have ____.
   A. a kitchen with a sink
   B. windows that open
   C. a bathtub and a shower
   D. locks on outside doors

4. If you pay $900 a month rent in Franklin County, your security deposit can't be more than ____.
   A. $900
   B. $1,000
   C. $1,600
   D. $1,800

5. A landlord CANNOT ____.
   A. turn off a tenant's heat and electricity
   B. use a security deposit for repairs
   C. use a security deposit for cleaning
   D. return a security deposit twenty days after a tenant moves out

6. When a family deducts $100 from their $700 rent because they paid for a repair, they pay the landlord ____.
   A. $100
   B. $600
   C. $700
   D. $800

SHARE & COMPARE Do you have a lease or rental agreement? Bring it to class and compare with other students. What tenants' rights and responsibilities are in the agreements? Discuss as a class.

Choose the correct answer.

1. My upstairs neighbors were rearranging _____ until late at night.
   - A. their faucet
   - B. loud music
   - C. their furniture
   - D. the downstairs neighbors

2. If you look in the _____, you'll find somebody who can fix your sink.
   - A. phone
   - B. phone book
   - C. plumber
   - D. plumbing company

3. We were upset. The electrician _____ us a lot of money to fix our light.
   - A. charged
   - B. changed
   - C. gave
   - D. showed

4. When I move to my new apartment, I'm going to _____ a moving company.
   - A. buy
   - B. retire
   - C. fire
   - D. hire

5. We'll be busy all morning. We'll be raking _____.
   - A. cookies
   - B. lunch
   - C. leaves
   - D. the dog

6. I'm having a problem with my _____. Sometimes it doesn't start.
   - A. apartment
   - B. car
   - C. key
   - D. living room window

7. We have to pay our _____ on or before the first day of each month.
   - A. rental agreement
   - B. lease
   - C. security deposit
   - D. rent

8. The landlord has to fix any _____ that needs repair.
   - A. tenant
   - B. gas
   - C. appliance
   - D. agreement

9. I'm going to _____ the cost of the repair from my rent.
   - A. evict
   - B. deduct
   - C. return
   - D. change

10. According to the law, every tenant has the _____ to a safe apartment.
   - A. right
   - B. rule
   - C. responsibility
   - D. condition

SKILLS CHECK ✔

Words:
- ☐ dentist
- ☐ electrician
- ☐ locksmith
- ☐ mechanic
- ☐ plumber
- ☐ repairperson
- ☐ appliance
- ☐ dishwasher
- ☐ faucet
- ☐ garbage disposal
- ☐ heat
- ☐ lock
- ☐ smoke detector
- ☐ stove
- ☐ toilet
- ☐ address book
- ☐ brakes
- ☐ headphones
- ☐ phone book
- ☐ steering wheel
- ☐ video camera/ camcorder

I can ask & answer:
- ☐ Do *you* need any help? I'll be glad to help *you*.
- ☐ Is it mine/his/hers/ours/yours/theirs?
- ☐ Do you know anybody who can help me?
- ☐ Can you send *a plumber* to fix it as soon as possible?
- ☐ What's the name?
- ☐ Where do you live?
- ☐ What's the address?
- ☐ And the phone number?
- ☐ What time?
- ☐ How about *tomorrow afternoon*?

I can give advice:
- ☐ You should/You ought to/I think you should/I think you ought to *call a plumber*.

I can write about:
- ☐ a very good friend

I can:
- ☐ request maintenance and repairs in a rental unit
- ☐ fill out a repair request form
- ☐ interpret a rental agreement
- ☐ describe tenants' rights

SIDE by SIDE Gazette

SIDE by SIDE Gazette

Communities

Some communities are friendly, and some aren't

There are many different kinds of communities around the world. Communities can be urban (in a city), suburban (near a city), or rural (in the countryside, far from a city).

Urban communities usually have many neighborhoods, where people often live close together in apartment buildings or small houses. Streets in these neighborhoods often have lots of people and many stores and businesses. People in urban neighborhoods often walk or take public transportation to get to places.

In suburban communities, people typically live in separate houses. Stores and businesses are not usually nearby, and people often have to drive to get there. Some suburban communities have public transportation, and others don't.

In rural communities, people often live far apart from each other, not in neighborhoods. There isn't usually any public transportation, and people have to drive everywhere.

Whether in urban, suburban, or rural areas, some communities are friendly, and others aren't. For example, in some communities, people know their neighbors, they help each other, and their children play together all the time. In other communities, people keep to themselves and sometimes don't even know their neighbors' names.

In the old days, most people around the world lived in small towns and villages, where they knew their neighbors. These days, more people live in large urban communities. Experts predict that in the future most people will live in "megacities" of more than ten million people. Will there be friendly neighborhoods in these communities of the future? Time will tell.

Describe your community. Is it urban, suburban, or rural? Is it friendly? In your opinion, what will your community be like in the future?

BUILD YOUR VOCABULARY!

Household Repair People

A. Who's at the door?
B. The _____ .

- appliance repairperson
- cable TV installer
- chimneysweep
- exterminator
- house painter
- TV repairperson

FACT FILE

The Ten Largest Cities in the World: 1950 and 2010 (Population in Millions)

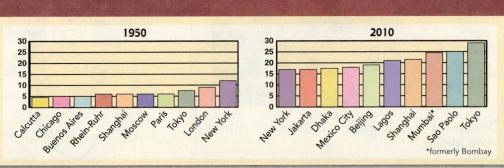

1950

Calcutta, Chicago, Buenos Aires, Rhein-Ruhr, Shanghai, Moscow, Paris, Tokyo, London, New York

2010

New York, Jakarta, Dhaka, Mexico City, Beijing, Lagos, Shanghai, Mumbai*, Sao Paolo, Tokyo

*formerly Bombay

Where Friends Get Together

These friends are meeting in the plaza in the center of Guanajuato, Mexico.

These friends are meeting at a coffee shop in Los Angeles.

These friends are talking in a park in Shanghai.

Where do friends meet in different countries you know?

Global Exchange

JuanR: I'm really looking forward to next weekend. Our family will be celebrating my grandparents' fiftieth wedding anniversary! Everybody in my family will be there—my parents, my brothers and sisters, and all my aunts, uncles, and cousins. We're going to have a big dinner at our home. Then, all the grandchildren will present a play that tells the story of my grandparents' lives together. (I'm going to be my grandfather when he was 20 years old!) We're going to have music and dancing, and we're going to give them a special anniversary present—a book of photographs of our whole family through the years. I'll tell you all about the party in my next message.

Send a message to a keypal. Tell about a family celebration you're looking forward to.

LISTENING

Who Are They Calling?

_c_	① Amy Francis	**a.**	mechanic
___	② Paul Mendoza	**b.**	locksmith
___	③ Jim Carney	**c.**	plumber
___	④ Jennifer Park	**d.**	electrician
___	⑤ Ed Green	**e.**	carpenter

What Are They Saying?

Listening Scripts

Unit 1 – Page 9

Listen and choose the correct answer.

1. What are you going to do tomorrow?
2. What do you do in the summer?
3. When did you clean your apartment?
4. What did you give your parents for their anniversary?
5. Where did you and your friends go yesterday?
6. How often do they send messages to each other?
7. What did he give her?
8. When are you going to make pancakes?

Unit 2 – Page 16

Listen and choose what the people are talking about.

1. A. How much do you want?
   B. Just a little, please.

2. A. Do you want some more?
   B. Okay. But just a few.

3. A. These are delicious!
   B. I'm glad you like them.

4. A. I ate too many.
   B. How many did you eat?

5. A. They're bad for my health.
   B. Really?

6. A. It's very good.
   B. Thank you.

7. A. Would you care for some more?
   B. Yes, but not too much.

8. A. There isn't any.
   B. There isn't?!

Unit 3 – Page 22

Listen and choose what the people are talking about.

1. A. How much does a gallon cost?
   B. Two seventy-nine.

2. A. They're very expensive this week.
   B. You're right.

3. A. How many loaves do we need?
   B. Three.

4. A. Sorry. There aren't any more.
   B. There aren't?!

5. A. I need two pounds.
   B. Two pounds? Okay.

6. A. How much does the large box cost?
   B. Five thirty-nine.

7. A. How many cans do we need?
   B. Three.

8. A. I bought too much.
   B. Really?

Side by Side Gazette – Page 28

Listen and match the products and the prices.

1. Attention, food shoppers! Thank you for shopping at Save-Rite Supermarket! Crispy Cereal is on sale this week. A box of Crispy Cereal is only three dollars and forty-nine cents. Three forty-nine is a very good price for Crispy Cereal. So buy some today!

2. Attention, shoppers! Right now in the bakery section whole wheat bread is on sale. Buy a loaf of whole wheat bread for only two seventy-five. That's right! Just two seventy-five! The bread is hot and fresh. So come to the bakery section and get a loaf now!

3. Thank you for shopping at Sunny Supermarket! We have a special low price on orange juice today. A quart of orange juice is only a dollar seventy-nine. Orange juice is in Aisle 5, next to the milk.

4. Hello, food shoppers! It's 95 degrees today. It's a good day for Sorelli's ice cream! Sorelli's ice cream comes in vanilla, chocolate, and other delicious flavors. And today, a pint of Sorelli's ice cream is only three twenty-five!

5. Welcome to Bartley's Supermarket! We have a special today on bananas. You can buy bananas for only forty cents a pound. Bananas are good for you! So walk over to our fruit section and buy a bunch of bananas today!

Unit 4 – Page 37

WHAT'S THE LINE?

Mrs. Harris (from the story on page 36) is calling Tommy and Julie's school. Listen and choose the correct lines.

1. Good morning. Park Elementary School.
2. Yes, Mrs. Harris. What can I do for you?
3. Oh? What's the matter?
4. That's too bad. Are you going to take them to the doctor?
5. Well, I hope Tommy and Julie feel better soon.

WHAT'S THE WORD?

Listen and choose the word you hear.

1. I might go to school tomorrow.
2. I want to come to work today.
3. Don't walk there!
4. We'll be ready in half an hour.
5. They'll go to school tomorrow.
6. Don't stand there! You might get hit!
7. I call the doctor when I'm sick.
8. Watch your step! There are wet spots on the floor.
9. I'm sick and tired of sailing.

Unit 5 – Page 44

Listen and choose what the people are talking about.

1. A. I like it. It's fast.
   B. It is. It's much faster than my old one.
2. A. Is it comfortable?
   B. Yes. It's more comfortable than my old one.
3. A. I think it should be shorter.
   B. But it's very short now!
4. A. They aren't very polite.
   B. You're right. They should be more polite.
5. A. Is it safe?
   B. Yes. It's much safer than my old one.
6. A. Which one should I buy?
   B. Buy this one. It's more powerful than that one.

Unit 6 – Page 53

Listen to the sentence. Is the person saying something good or something bad about someone else?

1. She's the nicest person I know.
2. He's the laziest student in our class.
3. He's the most boring person I know.
4. She's the most generous person in our family.
5. They're the most honest people I know.
6. He's the rudest person in our apartment building.
7. He's the most dependable person in our office.
8. She's the kindest neighbor on our street.
9. She's the most stubborn person I know.

Side by Side Gazette – Page 60

Listen and match the products.

ANNOUNCER: Are you looking for a special gift for a special person in your life? A birthday gift? An anniversary present? Come to Rings & Things—the best store in town for rings, necklaces, earrings, bracelets, and other fine things. Rings & Things—on Main Street downtown, or at the East Side Mall.

FRIEND 1: That was an excellent dinner!

FRIEND 2: Thank you. I'm glad you liked it.

FRIEND 1: Can I help you wash the dishes?

FRIEND 2: Thanks. But they're already in the dishwasher.

FRIEND 1: Is your dishwasher on?

FRIEND 2: Yes, it is.

FRIEND 1: I can't believe it! Your dishwasher is MUCH quieter than mine.

FRIEND 2: It's new. We got it at the Big Value Store. They sell the quietest dishwashers in town.

ANNOUNCER: That's right. The Big Value Store sells the quietest dishwashers in town. We also have the largest refrigerators, the most powerful washing machines, and the best ovens. And we also have the best prices! So come to the Big Value Store, on Airport Road, open seven days a week.

PERSON WHO CAN'T FALL ASLEEP: Oh, I can't believe it! It's three o'clock in the morning, and I can't fall asleep.

This bed is so uncomfortable! I need a new bed. I need a new bed NOW!

ANNOUNCER: Do you have this problem? Is your bed uncomfortable? Come to Comfort Kingdom for the most comfortable beds you can buy. We also have the most beautiful sofas and the most attractive tables and chairs in the city. And our salespeople are the friendliest and the most helpful in town. So visit Comfort Kingdom today because life is short, and you should be comfortable!

ANNOUNCER: I'm standing here today in front of Electric City so we can talk to a typical customer. Here's a typical customer now. He's leaving the store with a large box. Let's ask him a question. Excuse me, sir. May I ask you a question?

CUSTOMER: Certainly.

ANNOUNCER: What did you buy today?

CUSTOMER: A VCR.

ANNOUNCER: And why did you buy it at Electric City?

CUSTOMER: Because Electric City has the cheapest and the most dependable products in town.

ANNOUNCER: Is this your first time at Electric City?

CUSTOMER: Oh, no! Last year I bought a radio here, and the year before I bought a TV.

ANNOUNCER: And are you happy with those products?

CUSTOMER: Absolutely! The radio is much better than my old one, and the picture on my TV is much bigger and brighter.

ANNOUNCER: So are you a happy customer?

CUSTOMER: Definitely! There's no place like Electric City. It's the best store in town.

ANNOUNCER: Well, there you have it! Another happy Electric City customer. Visit an Electric City store near YOU today!

ANNOUNCER: This is it! It's the biggest sale of the year, and it's this weekend at Recreation Station! That's right. Everything is on sale—sneakers, tennis rackets, footballs, basketballs—everything in the store! It's all on sale at Recreation Station. We're the largest! We're the most convenient! We're the best! And this weekend we're the cheapest! It's the biggest sale of the year, and it's this weekend—only at Recreation Station!

Unit 7 – Page 69

WHAT'S THE WORD?

Listen and choose the word you hear.

1. The clinic is on the right, next to the post office.
2. The library is on the left, across from the park.
3. Walk up Town Road to Main Street.
4. Drive along Fourth Avenue to Station Street.
5. Take the subway to Pond Road.
6. The bus stop is at the corner of Central Avenue and Fifth.
7. Take this bus and get off at Bond Street.

Where are these people? Listen and choose the correct place.

1. A. Do you want to buy this shirt?
   B. Yes, please.
2. A. Please give me an order of chicken.
   B. An order of chicken? Certainly.
3. A. Shh! Please be quiet! People are reading.
   B. Sorry.
4. A. Can I visit my wife?
   B. Yes. She and the baby are in Room 407.
5. A. How much does one head cost?
   B. A dollar fifty-nine.
6. A. Hmm. Where's our car?
   B. I think it's on the third floor.

Unit 8 – Page 79

Listen and choose the best answer to complete the sentence.

1. If I do my homework carelessly, . . .
2. If Sally doesn't feel better soon, . . .
3. If you sit at your computer for a long time, . . .
4. If I stay up late tonight, . . .
5. If you don't speak loudly, . . .
6. If you don't work hard, . . .

Side by Side Gazette – Page 82

Listen to these announcements at different workplaces. Match the workplace and the word you hear.

Attention, all employees! This is Ms. Barnum, the factory supervisor. There were three accidents in our factory last week. Nobody was hurt badly, but I worry about these accidents. Please try to work more carefully. Thank you for your attention.

Attention, all employees! There is a small fire in the building. Please walk quickly to the nearest exit! Don't run! I repeat: There is a small fire in the building. Please walk quickly to the nearest exit!

May I have your attention, please? The president of our company will visit our office tomorrow. Please dress neatly for her visit. Thank you.

Cut! Okay, everybody! That was good, but you're still singing too softly. Please try to sing more loudly. Okay? Let's try that again.

Attention, please! As you know, the weather is very bad this afternoon, and according to the weather forecast, the storm is going to get worse. Therefore, we are going to close the office early today. All employees can leave at three thirty. Get home safely! See you tomorrow.

Unit 9 – Page 91

Listen to the conversations. What happened to these people? Listen and choose the correct answer.

1. A. How did you do that?
   B. I did it while I was shaving.
2. A. When did it happen?
   B. While I was getting off a bus.
3. A. Why do you think it happened?
   B. It was a very hot day.
4. A. The park isn't as safe as it used to be.
   B. You're right.
5. A. What were they doing?
   B. They were playing outside.
6. A. How did it happen?
   B. He dropped the glass.

Unit 10 – Page 97

Listen and choose the correct answer.

1. I couldn't sit down on the bus.
2. Tony wasn't able to paint his house.
3. Jennifer couldn't find her purse last night.
4. They didn't enjoy the food at the restaurant.
5. Why weren't the plumbers able to fix it?
6. Why couldn't you go to work yesterday?

Side by Side Gazette – Page 104

Listen to the messages on Jim's machine. Match the people and their messages.

You have five messages.

Message One, Friday, 2:15 P.M.: Hi, Jim. This is Pete. I just got your message. I'm sorry I won't be able to help you move to your new apartment tomorrow, but I've got to work overtime. 'Bye. [*beep*]

Message Two, Friday, 3:10 P.M.: Hi, Jim. It's Susie. Sorry I won't be able to help you move tomorrow. I've got to visit my grandparents out of town. Good luck! Talk to you soon. [*beep*]

Message Three, Friday, 3:55 P.M.: Jim? Hi. It's Marty! How are you? I'm not so good. I'm having problems with my car. I have to take it to a mechanic, so I'm afraid I won't be able to help you move. Sorry. Give me a call sometime. Okay? Take care. [*beep*]

Message Four, Friday, 5:48 P.M.: Hello, Jim? It's Judy. You know, I really want to help you move, but I've got to stay home all day tomorrow and wait for the plumber. My kitchen sink is broken, and there's water everywhere! Hope your move goes okay. Sorry I can't help. Let's talk soon. [*beep*]

Message Five, Sunday, 9:29 P.M.: Jim? It's Tom. Gee, I'm really sorry I wasn't able to help you move yesterday. I wasn't feeling well, and I had to stay in bed all day. I'm feeling much better now. Call me. Maybe we can get together soon. [*beep*]

Unit 11 – Page 109

Listen and choose the correct word to complete the sentence.

1. A. I had my yearly checkup today.
   B. What did the doctor say?
   A. She said I must eat fewer . . .

2. A. I had my annual checkup today.
   B. What did the doctor say?
   A. He said I must eat less . . .

3. A. How was your medical checkup?
   B. Okay. The doctor said I must drink less . . .

4. A. Did the doctor put you on a diet?
   B. Yes. She said I must eat fewer . . .

5. A. I went to my doctor for an examination today.
   B. Oh. What did the doctor say?
   A. He said I must eat less . . .

6. A. My doctor put me on a diet today.
   B. Really?
   A. Yes. I must eat fewer . . .

Unit 12 – Page 120

Listen to the messages on Bob's machine. Match the messages.

You have eight messages.

Message Number One: "Hello, Robert. This is Aunt Betty. I'm calling to say hello. Call me back. I'll be home all evening. I'll be ironing my clothes. Talk to you soon. 'Bye." [*beep*]

Message Number Two: "Hi, Bob. This is Melanie. I'm making plans for the weekend. Do you want to do something? Call me when you have a chance. I'll be home all day. I'll be studying for a big test. Talk to you later." [*beep*]

Message Number Three: "Bob? This is Alan. What's up? I'm calling to tell you I won't be able to play tennis with you this Saturday. I'll be attending my cousin's wedding in Dallas. See you soon." [*beep*]

Message Number Four: "Hello, Mr. Kendall. This is Ms. Wong from the State Street Bank. I'm calling about your application for a loan. We need some more information. Please call me at 472-9138. You can call this evening. I'll be working until 8 P.M. Thank you." [*beep*]

Message Number Five: "Hi, Bob. This is Rick. Nancy and I want to invite you over to dinner at our new apartment. Call us back. We'll be home all weekend. We'll be repainting the living room. Bye." [*beep*]

Message Number Six: "Hello, Bob. This is Denise. I got your message last week. Sorry I missed you. Call me back. I'll be home this evening. I'll be paying bills. Take care." [*beep*]

Message Number Seven: "Hello. This is a message for Robert Kendall. I'm calling from Dr. Garcia's office. Dr. Garcia won't be able to see you next month. He'll be visiting hospitals in Russia. Please call so we can change your appointment. Thank you, and have a nice day." [*beep*]

Message Number Eight: "Hello, Bobby? This is Mom. Bobby, are you there? Pick up the phone. I guess you aren't there. Dad and I are thinking of you. How are you? Call us, okay? But don't call this afternoon. We'll be exercising at the health club. Well, talk to you soon, Bobby. 'Bye." [*beep*]

Unit 13 – Page 134

WHAT'S THE WORD?

Listen and choose the word you hear.

1. Do you know him well?
2. I'll be glad to help them.
3. Did you see him today?
4. Yours will be ready at five o'clock.
5. Careful! You might hurt yourselves!
6. We're having trouble with her car.

WHAT ARE THEY TALKING ABOUT?

Listen and choose what the people are talking about.

1. I'm going to have to call the plumber.
2. It's broken. We won't be able to wash the dishes.
3. I'm upset. I can't watch my favorite program.
4. It doesn't work. I can't call anybody!
5. My mechanic fixed the brakes.

Side by Side Gazette – Page 138

Listen to the messages and conversations. Match the caller with the repairperson.

1. A. Hello. This is Dan, the Drain Man. I'm not here to take your call. Please leave your name, number, and the time you called. Also, please describe the problem. I'll get back to you as soon as possible. Have a great day!
   B. Hello. This is Amy Francis. My number is 355-3729. It's three o'clock Friday afternoon. My kitchen faucet is broken. I can't turn off the water! Please call back as soon as possible. Thank you.

2. A. Hello. This is Helen's Home Repair. If you break it, we can fix it! Nobody is here right now. Leave a message after the beep, and we'll call you back. Thank you.
   B. Hi. This is Paul Mendoza. My front steps are broken, and I need somebody who can fix them. My phone number is 266-0381. Please call back soon. I'm having a party this weekend, and nobody will be able to get into my house! Thank you.

3. **A.** Hi. This is Kevin's Key Service. Leave a message and I'll call you back. Thanks.

 B. Good morning. My name is Jim Carney. I'm really embarrassed. I just lost my keys while I was jogging, and I can't get into my apartment. I'm calling from my neighbor's apartment across the hall. I live at 44 Wilson Road, Apartment 3B. My neighbor's number is 276-9184. Please call back soon. Thank you.

4. **A.** Gary's Garage. May I help you?

 B. Yes. I think there's something wrong with my steering wheel.

 A. What's the problem?

 B. It's difficult to turn right, and it's VERY difficult to turn left!

 A. Hmm. That's not good. What's your name?

 B. Jennifer Park.

 A. Phone number?

 B. 836-7275.

 A. Can you be here tomorrow morning at eight?

 B. Yes. That's fine. Thank you.

5. **A.** Hello. Rita's Repair Company.

 B. Hi. Is this Rita?

 A. No. This is the answering service. May I help you?

 B. Yes. My doorbell is broken. It won't stop ringing!

 A. I can hear that. Your name, please?

 B. Ed Green.

 A. Address?

 B. 2219 High Street.

 A. And your phone number?

 B. 923-4187.

 A. Will someone be home all day?

 B. Yes. I'll be here.

 A. Okay. Rita will be there before 5 P.M.

 B. Thank you.

Vocabulary List

Numbers indicate the pages on which the words first appear.

Actions and Activities

accept 58c
add 24
agree 47
answer 81
apologize 124a
apply 10c
apply in person 80c
argue 128
arrive 29
ask 53
attach 70c
attend 10c
avoid 92b
baby-sit 96
bake 13
bark 128
bathe 115
become 32
begin 10c
believe 16
bite 83
bloom 32
borrow 115
break 79
break into 83
breathe 92a
broil 114c
buy 8
call 9
call in sick 36
cause 70c
celebrate 10b
change (v) 46
charge 102c
chat online 2
check (v) 124c
choke 92b
chop up 24
clean 5
clean out 115
close (v) 70a
comb 81
come 18c
come home 44
come in 106
come over 100
communicate 8
complain 52
complete (v) 80c
compliment 52
connect 18c
contact 92b
contain 92c
continue 10c
contribute 80e
cook 3
cool (v) 92b
cost 21
cover (v) 92b
crash 101
crash into 83
cross 70b
cry 79
cut 24
decide 23

deduct 136c
deliver 27
depend 38c
deposit (v) 58b
describe 81
dial 92a
disagree 47
disconnect 102c
disturb 102c
do 5
do homework 77
draw 69
dress (v) 74
drink 23
drip 136a
drive 4
drop 83
drop to your knees 92c
drown 35
duck (v) 92c
eat 2
end 29
enjoy 25
enjoy *myself* 96
enter 10c
erase 136b
evacuate 92c
evict 78
examine 106
exchange 58c
express interest 81
faint 83
fall (v) 34
fall asleep 35
feed 126
feel 36
file 75
fill 92c
find 79
finish 10c
fire (v) 43
fix 85
flood 135
flush 136a
fly 99
follow 10c
follow the rules 136c
follow up 136c
forget 7
fry 114c
get back 60
get down 92c
get dressed 126
get home 22
get into 94
get married 29
get off 66
get on 83
get out of 30
get stuck 136a
get to 33
get up 74
give 6
give advice 8
go 8
go back 79
go out 42

go outside 32
go to bed 22
go to college 121
go to school 36
go to work 36
go up and down 133
graduate 10c
grill (v) 114c
grow up 8
hand in 101
hang 102c
happen 70c
have 13
have children 121
hear 79
help (v) 8
hire 43
hold on 120
hook up 99
hope 36
hurry 32
hurt 34
include 102a
insert 58b
inspect 136b
install 80a
invite 38c
iron (v) 115
itch 79
keep 27
keep clear 102c
keep out of reach 92b
keep refrigerated 26b
knit 115
know 6
know how 92a
last (v) 110
laugh 79
lead 106
leak 136a
learn 81
leave 10c
lend 8
lift 95
light (v) 136a
like 2
listen 9
live 8
locate 124c
lock (v) 102c
look 22
look for 102c
look forward to 123
lose 8
lose time 80e
lose weight 111
mail (v) 70a
make 12
make a list 12
make mistakes 77
make *pancakes* 4
make plans 123
make sure 70c
marry 38
measure 106
melt 59
microwave 114c

miss 46
mix in 24
mop 115
move 8
move away 48c
move out 136b
name 29
need 18c
need to 99
offer 38c
open (v) 22
operate 80c
order (v) 25
overdose 92a
oversleep 78
paint (v) 32
pass through 59
pay 10c
pay attention 70c
pay bills 115
perform 92b
pick up 70a
place (v) 124c
place an order 124c
plan 38c
plant (v) 4
pour 114c
pour in 24
practice 85
prepare 10c
present (v) 58c
press 58b
produce (v) 27
promise 97
protect 114c
provide 114c
put 24
put on 34
raise 92b
rake 126
reach 121
read 2
rearrange 115
rebuild 59
receive 58c
recommend 23
register 10a
rely on 135
remember 89
remove 92b
rent (v) 43
repaint 115
repair 102c
repeat 34
request 38b
require 102a
retire 121
return 29
ride 32
rinse 92b
RSVP 38b
rub 113
run 71
rush 22
say 9
secure 92c
see 31
seem 44
select 58b
sell 8
send 8
serve 38c

set up 18c
sew 115
shake hands 81
shave 88
shop 27
shout 91
show 38c
sing 77
sit down 22
skate 5
ski 5
sleep 128
slice (v) 24
slow down 70b
smile 81
solve 95
speak 73
spend 16
spill 83
stand 34
start 10c
stay 38c
stay away 92c
stay home 36
stay in place 92c
stay indoors 32
stay up 78
steal 89
step on 35
sting 92b
stop (v) 70c
store (v) 102c
study 10c
submit 80d
suggest 23
supervise 80c
swallow 92b
tailgate 70c
take 8
take a bath 84
take a break 80b
take a message 120
take a test 85
take care of 90
take it easy 121
take piano lessons 43
take the subway 66
talk 9
taste 17
teach 10c
tell 17
think 6
throw away 114b
touch 34
train (v) 80c
transfer 58b
trip 83
try 44
turn away 92c
turn left 64
turn off 92a
turn on 18c
turn right 64
type 73
understand 80b
use 18c
vacuum 80c
visit 44
vote 42
wait 31
wake up 92a
walk along 63

nearby 70b
neat 48
new 8
nice 41
noisy 49
normal 136b
obnoxious 49
old 40
open 102c
out of this world 23
outdoor 60
overweight 109
patient 49
polite 38c
poor 79
popular 49
positive 35
possible 184b
powerful 39
pregnant 36
pre-school 104
pretty 40
previous 80a
quick 66
quiet 25
ready 30
real 46
reasonable 57
reliable 46
required 80c
responsible 136b
rich 112
ridiculous 45
right 43
romantic 25
rude 49
safe 40
satisfied 44
scary 77
separate 103
serious 112
short 48
shy 82
single 103
sleepy 70c
slippery 70b
sloppy 49
slow 72
small 27
smart 39
soft 39
special 24
spicy 39
sterile 92b
strange 103
strong 92c
stubborn 49
stupid 68
successful 81
superstitious 90
sure 35
sympathetic 44
talented 39
talkative 39
tall 47
tasty 25
terrible 17
ugly 52
uncomfortable 59
understanding 44
unfortunate 86
unfriendly 59

unhealthy 59
unlucky 90
unopened 58c
unsafe 58c
used 42
useful 42
valid 80c
weak 93
wet 90
wide 47
wonderful 15
worried 108
worse 56
worst 56
wrong 68
yearly 108
young 10c

Describing with Adverbs

accurately 73
always 8
awkwardly 75
badly 74
beautifully 80
better 73
carefully 72
carelessly 72
completely 68
confidently 81
directly 81
dishonestly 80
early 74
easily 103
enthusiastically 81
exactly 110
fast 72
firmly 81
gracefully 72
hard 72
honestly 81
impolitely 74
late 74
loud 73
loudly 73
neatly 74
never 8
often 8
on time 101
politely 74
promptly 81
properly 136a
quickly 73
sloppily 74
slowly 7
softly 74
sometimes 129
soon 24
thoroughly 92b
usually 28
well 72

Driving/Cars

car registration 70c
child safety seat 70c
driver 48b
driver's license 80c
driving record 80c
engine 48b
headlights 70c
headroom 48b

horsepower 48b
insurance card 70c
license 70c
passenger 70c
safety seat 70c
seat 48b
seat belt 70b
windshield 70c
windshield wipers 70c

Emergencies

CPR 92b
emergency evacuation
  plan 92c
emergency exit 136c
emergency kit 92c
emergency number 92a
emergency operator 92a
fire 92a
fire exit 136c
fire extinguisher 92a
first aid 92a
first-aid kit 92a
fumes 92b
heart attack 92a
Heimlich maneuver 92b
injury 80c
vapors 92b

Entertainment and the Arts

ballet lesson 99
dancing 138
entertainment 60
jazz 5
movie 10b
music 44
piano lesson 43
radio talk show 46
rock music 5
symphony 96
TV program 58

Events and Occurrences

accident 70c
anniversary 7
birthday 6
blackout 84
car accident 70c
celebration 59
ceremony 38b
concert 96
cooking class 10b
costume party 59
dance 10b
date 25
earthquake 92c
exercise class 10b
holiday weekend 123
hurricane 92c
hurricane watch 92c
pancake breakfast 10b
party 24
piano concert 10b
picnic 43
play 75
prom 95
reception 38b
robbery 86
rock concert 10b

ski trip 10b
swimming class 10b
Thanksgiving 123
trip 10b
vacation 33
wedding 38b
wedding anniversary 25

Family Members

aunt 50
brother 30
children 7
cousin 50
daughter 6
family 5
family members 103
father 4
grandchildren 7
grandfather 51
Grandma 123
grandmother 2
Grandpa 123
grandparent 85
husband 6
mother 32
nephew 51
niece 98
parent 7
relative 123
single-parent family 103
sister 50
son 44
uncle 50
wife 6

Food Containers and Quantities

bag 19
bottle 19
bowl 23
box 19
bunch 19
can 19
cup 23
dish 23
dozen 19
gallon 19
glass 23
half a pound 19
half pound 19
head 19
jar 19
loaf 19
order 23
piece 23
pint 19
pound 19
quart 19
slice 27

Foods

appetizer 25
apple 11
apple cake 110
apple pie 13
bagel 27
baked chicken 25
baked goods 26a
baked potato 26c
baking soda 24
banana 11

beef stew 110
beverage 26a
bread 11
broiled fish 25
brown rice 114c
butter 12
cake 11
candy 6
canned food 42c
carrot 11
cereal 19
cheese 8
cheese sandwich 26c
chef's salad 26c
chicken 11
chicken salad
  sandwich 26c
chicken soup 23
chili 27
chocolate bar 27
chocolate cake 15
chocolate ice cream 23
cocoa beans 27
coffee 12
cookie 12
cream 114c
dairy 26a
diet soda 114c
donut 27
egg 11
egg salad sandwich 26c
fish 11
flavor 28
flour 12
food 17
french fries 13
fried foods 114c
frozen foods 26a
fruit 27
fruitcake 24
grapefruit 108
grapes 11
Greek salad 26c
green beans 26c
hamburger 13
honey 24
hot chocolate 23
hot dog 27
ice cream 12
jam 19
ketchup 11
lemon 11
lemonade 13
lettuce 11
lunch special 26c
margarine 108
mayonnaise 11
meat 11
meatball 13
meatloaf 41
milk 12
muffin 27
mushroom 24
mushroom soup 26c
mustard 11
nut 24
oil 114c
omelet 13
onion 11
orange 8
orange juice 12
pancake 4

149

Cardinal Numbers

1	one	20	twenty
2	two	21	twenty-one
3	three	22	twenty-two
4	four	.	.
5	five		
6	six	29	twenty-nine
7	seven	30	thirty
8	eight	40	forty
9	nine	50	fifty
10	ten	60	sixty
11	eleven	70	seventy
12	twelve	80	eighty
13	thirteen	90	ninety
14	fourteen		
15	fifteen	100	one hundred
16	sixteen	200	two hundred
17	seventeen	300	three hundred
18	eighteen	.	.
19	nineteen		
		900	nine hundred
		1,000	one thousand
		2,000	two thousand
		3,000	three thousand
		.	.
		10,000	ten thousand
		100,000	one hundred thousand
		1,000,000	one million

Ordinal Numbers

1st	first	20th	twentieth
2nd	second	21st	twenty-first
3rd	third	22nd	twenty-second
4th	fourth	.	.
5th	fifth		
6th	sixth	29th	twenty-ninth
7th	seventh	30th	thirtieth
8th	eighth	40th	fortieth
9th	ninth	50th	fiftieth
10th	tenth	60th	sixtieth
11th	eleventh	70th	seventieth
12th	twelfth	80th	eightieth
13th	thirteenth	90th	ninetieth
14th	fourteenth		
15th	fifteenth	100th	one hundredth
16th	sixteenth	1,000th	one thousandth
17th	seventeenth	1,000,000th	one millionth
18th	eighteenth		
19th	nineteenth		

How to Read a Date

June 9, 1941 = "June ninth, nineteen forty-one"

November 16, 2010 = "November sixteenth, two thousand ten" *or*

"November sixteenth, two thousand and ten"

Irregular Verbs: Past Tense

be	was	lead	led
become	became	leave	left
begin	began	lend	lent
bite	bit	lose	lost
break	broke	make	made
build	built	meet	met
buy	bought	put	put
catch	caught	read	read
come	came	ride	rode
cost	cost	run	ran
cut	cut	say	said
do	did	see	saw
drink	drank	sell	sold
drive	drove	send	sent
eat	ate	shake	shook
fall	fell	sing	sang
feed	fed	sit	sat
feel	felt	sleep	slept
find	found	speak	spoke
fly	flew	spend	spent
forget	forgot	stand	stood
get	got	steal	stole
give	gave	swim	swam
go	went	take	took
grow	grew	teach	taught
have	had	tell	told
hear	heard	think	thought
hurt	hurt	understand	understood
keep	kept	wear	wore
know	knew	write	wrote

Skill Index

Grammar Index

Topic Index

Alaska

0 500 Miles
0 500 Km

0 100 Miles
0 100 Km
Hawaii

California
Nevada
Oregon
Washington
Arizona
Utah
Idaho
Wyoming
Montana
New Mexico
Colorado
South Dakota
North Dakota
Texas
Oklahoma
Kansas
Nebraska
Minnesota
Louisiana
Arkansas
Missouri
Iowa
Wisconsin
Mississippi
Illinois
Indiana
Michigan
Alabama
Tennessee
Kentucky
Ohio
Georgia
South Carolina
North Carolina
West Virginia
Virginia
Washington, DC
Pennsylvania
New York
Florida
New Hampshire
Vermont
Delaware
Maryland
New Jersey
Connecticut
Rhode Island
Massachusetts
Maine

Gulf of Mexico

0
0
500 KM
500 Miles

W
S
N
E

ATLANTIC OCEAN

● 156 Map of the United States